The Divine Abundance Portal Activations

The Divine Abundance Portal Activations

One Year of Law of Attraction Meditations

PATRICIA VANCE FORBES

Names, characters, businesses, places, events and incidents are the products of the author. Any resemblance to actual persons, living or dead, or actual places or events is purely coincidental.

Copyright© 2019 by Patricia Vance Forbes
All rights reserved.

This book or any portion thereof may not be reproduced or used in any manner whatsoever without the express written permission of the author or publisher.

Printed in the United States of America

Fort Collins, Colorado

First Printing, 2017

ISBN-13: 978-0-9989757-2-6

Contents

CHAPTER ONE: ENTERING THE DIVINE ABUNDANCE PORTAL 1

    MONTH ONE – DAY ONE 1

    MONTH ONE – DAY TWO 3

    MONTH ONE – DAY THREE 5

    MONTH ONE – DAY FOUR 8

    MONTH ONE – DAY FIVE 11

    MONTH ONE – DAY SIX 13

    MONTH ONE – DAY SEVEN 16

    MONTH ONE – DAY EIGHT 18

    MONTH ONE – DAY NINE 20

    MONTH ONE – DAY TEN 23

    MONTH ONE – DAY ELEVEN 26

CHAPTER TWO: LOVE & MONEY REPROGRAMMING 30

    MONTH TWO – DAY ONE 30

    MONTH TWO – DAY TWO 33

    MONTH TWO – DAY THREE 36

    MONTH TWO – DAY FOUR 39

    MONTH TWO – DAY FIVE 42

    MONTH TWO – DAY SIX 46

    MONTH TWO – DAY SEVEN 50

    MONTH TWO – DAY EIGHT 54

    MONTH TWO – DAY NINE 58

    MONTH TWO – DAY TEN 62

    MONTH TWO – DAY ELEVEN 65

CHAPTER THREE: LEPRECHAUNS & AND POTS OF GOLD 70

    MONTH THREE – DAY ONE 70

MONTH THREE – DAY TWO 75

MONTH THREE – DAY THREE 78

MONTH THREE – DAY FOUR 81

MONTH THREE – DAY FIVE 84

MONTH THREE – DAY SIX 88

MONTH THREE – DAY SEVEN 92

MONTH THREE – DAY EIGHT 95

MONTH THREE – DAY NINE 99

MONTH THREE – DAY TEN 103

MONTH THREE – DAY ELEVEN 106

CHAPTER FOUR: FREEDOM FROM ECONOMIC SLAVERY 111

MONTH FOUR – DAY ONE 111

MONTH FOUR – DAY TWO 114

MONTH FOUR – DAY THREE 116

MONTH FOUR – DAY FOUR 119

MONTH FOUR – DAY FIVE 122

MONTH FOUR – DAY SIX 125

MONTH FOUR – DAY SEVEN 127

MONTH FOUR – DAY EIGHT 130

MONTH FOUR – DAY NINE 133

MONTH FOUR – DAY TEN 137

MONTH FOUR – DAY ELEVEN 140

CHAPTER FIVE: CLEANING & REBIRTH 144

MONTH FIVE – DAY ONE 144

MONTH FIVE – DAY TWO 147

MONTH FIVE – DAY THREE 150

MONTH FIVE – DAY FOUR	153
MONTH FIVE – DAY FIVE	157
MONTH FIVE – DAY SIX	160
MONTH FIVE – DAY SEVEN	163
MONTH FIVE – DAY EIGHT	166
MONTH FIVE – DAY NINE	169
MONTH FIVE – DAY TEN	172
MONTH FIVE – DAY ELEVEN	175
CHAPTER SIX: SUMMER SOLSTICE & USING FUN AS A MANIFESTATION TOOL	**179**
MONTH SIX – DAY ONE	179
MONTH SIX – DAY TWO	183
MONTH SIX – DAY THREE	186
MONTH SIX – DAY FOUR	189
MONTH SIX – DAY FIVE	192
MONTH SIX – DAY SIX	195
MONTH SIX – DAY SEVEN	198
MONTH SIX – DAY EIGHT	201
MONTH SIX – DAY NINE	204
MONTH SIX – DAY TEN	208
MONTH SIX – DAY ELEVEN	211
CHAPTER SEVEN: ELICITING HELP FROM THE FAIRY REALM	**216**
MONTH SEVEN – DAY ONE	216
MONTH SEVEN – DAY TWO	220
MONTH SEVEN – DAY THREE	223
MONTH SEVEN – DAY FOUR	226
MONTH SEVEN – DAY FIVE	229

MONTH SEVEN – DAY SIX ... 232

MONTH SEVEN – DAY SEVEN ... 235

MONTH SEVEN – DAY EIGHT ... 238

MONTH SEVEN – DAY NINE ... 241

MONTH SEVEN – DAY TEN ... 244

MONTH SEVEN – DAY ELEVEN ... 247

CHAPTER EIGHT: HARVEST & REGROUP ... 251

MONTH EIGHT – DAY ONE ... 251

MONTH EIGHT – DAY TWO ... 254

MONTH EIGHT – DAY THREE ... 257

MONTH EIGHT – DAY FOUR ... 260

MONTH EIGHT – DAY FIVE ... 263

MONTH EIGHT – DAY SIX ... 266

MONTH EIGHT – DAY SEVEN ... 269

MONTH EIGHT – DAY EIGHT ... 272

MONTH EIGHT – DAY NINE ... 274

MONTH EIGHT – DAY TEN ... 277

MONTH EIGHT – DAY ELEVEN ... 280

CHAPTER NINE: THE FALL EQUINOX & DIVING INTO THE FLAMES OF TRANSFORMATION ... 284

MONTH NINE – DAY ONE ... 284

MONTH NINE – DAY TWO ... 287

MONTH NINE – DAY THREE ... 290

MONTH NINE – DAY FOUR ... 293

MONTH NINE – DAY FIVE ... 296

MONTH NINE – DAY SIX ... 299

MONTH NINE – DAY SEVEN ... 302

MONTH NINE – DAY EIGHT	305
MONTH NINE – DAY NINE	308
MONTH NINE – DAY TEN	311
MONTH NINE – DAY ELEVEN	314
CHAPTER TEN: PIRATES & VIKINGS	**318**
MONTH TEN – DAY ONE	318
MONTH TEN – DAY TWO	321
MONTH TEN – DAY THREE	323
MONTH TEN – DAY FOUR	326
MONTH TEN – DAY FIVE	329
MONTH TEN – DAY SIX	332
MONTH TEN – DAY SEVEN	335
MONTH TEN - -DAY EIGHT	338
MONTH TEN – DAY NINE	341
MONTH TEN – DAY TEN	345
MONTH TEN – DAY ELEVEN	349
CHAPTER ELEVEN: THANKSGIVING, THE CORNUCOPIA OF ABUNDANCE & GRATITUDE	**353**
MONTH ELEVEN – DAY ONE	353
MONTH ELEVEN – DAY TWO	357
MONTH ELEVEN – DAY THREE	360
MONTH ELEVEN – DAY FOUR	363
MONTH ELEVEN – DAY FIVE	366
MONTH ELEVEN – DAY SIX	370
MONTH ELEVEN – DAY SEVEN	373
MONTH ELEVEN – DAY EIGHT	376
MONTH ELEVEN – DAY NINE	379

MONTH ELEVEN – DAY TEN 383

MONTH ELEVEN – DAY ELEVEN 387

CHAPTER TWELVE: WINTER INTROSPECTION & WHITE BUFFALO CALF WOMAN 391

MONTH TWELVE – DAY ONE 391

MONTH TWELVE – DAY TWO 394

MONTH TWELVE – DAY THREE 397

MONTH TWELVE – DAY FOUR 400

MONTH TWELVE – DAY FIVE 403

MONTH TWELVE – DAY SIX 406

MONTH TWELVE – DAY SEVEN 410

MONTH TWELVE – DAY EIGHT 413

MONTH TWELVE – DAY NINE 416

MONTH TWELVE – DAY TEN 419

MONTH TWELVE – DAY ELEVEN 423

INTRODUCTION & HOW TO READ THIS BOOK

In this series of these monthly, 11-day journeys through the Divine Abundance Portals, we take on many adventures and lessons to help open and clear what I see as deactivated or blocked codes. The emotional aspect of some of the journeys will bring codes forward into awareness so they can be realigned or turned on. When these codes don't work, we cannot manifest what we want. It is like having a short in an electrical appliance. Current can't get through.

I have been asked what these codes look like. To me, they are various sacred geometries or Angelic writings that aren't complete or have been damaged like a broken rung on a ladder. When we travel through these journeys, these codes show up ready for you to realign or heal themselves. Once activated into your whole being, you can easily create what you want with ease.

That doesn't mean that you don't have to work a little, but it is often less traumatic and emotional without the Victim part of you being activated. This shuts down the whole code. Once you finish reading these Divine Abundance Portal Activations they will have been activated. Thus, even if they get snagged momentarily, they are easy to reactivate.

To get the full effect of the Divine Abundance Portal Activations it is to your benefit to complete all 12 chapters in 11-day increments. Once you finish reading the chapters in consecutive days, take the rest of the month off to let the changes integrate. Your progress may feel gradual, even frustratingly slow at times. However, by the time you have reworked your codes throughout the year, there will be an undeniable change in your abundance consciousness.

With Truth, Love, and Gratitude

Pat, The Cosmic Cowgirl

CHAPTER ONE: ENTERING THE DIVINE ABUNDANCE PORTAL

MONTH ONE – DAY ONE

As I begin this meditation energy session, I align my vibration with the collective of anyone and everyone who comes into contact with these experiences and the Creator.

I look into the Divine Portal of Abundance, and it is dark with swirling energies. I realize all of you involved in this event have a collective mess of stuff that is going to get cleared throughout our year-long journey.

I suppose you can hang onto it if you really want to, but you are here for a reason. One we have all been brought together for because we have matching weird stuff working in our collective consciousness to keep our dark blockages active. So, I advise you to let it go as we do this work together.

Off we go! My Dragon breathes a huge flame of light into the dark, illuminating the path. My saddle bags of tools bulge with the energy of what is to be done next.

Swords fly into my hands. I start cutting away the numerous hands of Time Stealers. They represent procrastination, non-working rules, boxes we tried to fit into, and age-old programs of who we are and what we do here. Some are old beliefs— job rules, family patterns, and generations of habits. I get glimpses of many of these. So many different realities to keep us from Abundance of health, wealth, youth, time, and whatever else you have tried to achieve.

Once this is cleared, the Portal begins to light up. An opening is now visible for us to dive into. The tunnel turns a beautiful golden white, spinning with twists and turns. We fly past dark doors that call to some. We seal them, and the keys are burned. I am under the impression these are related to addictions – another Time Stealer.

It is going to take a bit of calibration within one's self to assimilate the beginning of these changes.

See you tomorrow!

MONTH ONE – DAY TWO

The tunnel is lit in a yellowish glow, and there are shadows within the folds of the spinning vortex. We slow our flight a little to investigate these folds. They look like the fold in a rug where dirt and debris are collected to be hidden from the immediate view of our own consciousness. I get closer to examine them better. They are of a dark, sticky, gooey substance. I don't want to touch this very old collection of energy. No need to define it or label it. It isn't supposed to be here for the new vibrations we are going to create.

I call in one of my spiritual Teams who help me in my work. This one is what I call the Cleanup Crew. They have the most powerful vacuums available. All the dark goo is pulled into impenetrable containers. The Cleanup Crew then removes the containers to an area where they will be emptied and cleaned without damaging the environment of the Galaxy.

Now I see there is greenery, and healthy enzymes are being implanted in the tunnel's folds. When we participate in cleaning up the Divine Abundance Portal, it also cleans out our own Manifesting Abundance systems.

I can now see the fluidity of the Divine Abundance Portal's entry. There is a clearing for a deeper ride in. I remind my Dragon Avatar and my Spiritual Teams that we are all on a quest for all forms of Abundance. I am reminded that, as we are within, we are without.

We fly along very peacefully until we come into a darker area. There are many memories in this area about wars. The aromas of death, fear, blood, and gunpowder are sickening. This must be cleared.

These fears are held inside many of you. So much violence is seen on our media that it is in the consciousness of the group. We carry it in our inherited family memories, and it is embedded in the Planet's consciousness.

We say a prayer for those that have been lost, for those left behind, and those who have no recognition of what this Planet has endured. Now the Portal can be cleared, and we can travel a little further inside.

The water on the Earth and your body contains the energy of these traumas and is being cleaned, purified, and activated, because water is a powerful carrier of frequency. We are each a water body, and we inhabit a water Planet.

I notice Universal codes from the Divine Creator that are being dropped into this group to assist in the clearing. These bring us out of woeful Victim energy like, "Oh, poor me," "What if …," "I just got fired!" "How are we going to pay for any of our needs?" The new codes help to heal and clear all those "Oh, poor me" energies dwelling within and without.

I feel the Divine Abundance Portal starting to come alive with a newness created by Activated Codes of Abundance. Many types of Abundance are being downloaded into this Portal.

This is quite the healing Journey. Take the rest of the day to bathe in the codes and allow them to activate within your system. Breathe in the newness of each moment. Allow yourself to be readied for the rest of the journey, as it has only just begun!

See you tomorrow

MONTH ONE – DAY THREE

I hope all of you feel better today. I'm going to help you find an Avatar of your own to ride and serve you through the Divine Abundance Portal. An Avatar is anything you envision. Some of you already have spirit animals, and these may or may not be your Avatars. Whatever appears is meant for this journey. Accept it, and mount it with gratitude.

First, since yesterday was a huge clearing, I will do some balancing of your own field. Take a moment to breathe. I noticed some of you experienced a physical release of the old programing codes we encountered. This is very good. However, it caused some of you to go back to the beginning of the Portal wondering if this will be worth the ride. I assure you, it is safe, and the rewards will be wonderful. Take a deep breath and prepare for a new adventure.

Mount up! Everyone is now entering the Portal. There are a few of you taking your time to see what is ahead before you decide to participate completely. It's okay. You don't need anything like Dramamine. We are all together now as we dive into the spinning funnel of the Portal.

The opening has stayed clean and shiny like sunlight. As we go a little deeper it isn't as bright. You will notice head lamps on your forehead. You ride your Avatar gracefully.

This new, unexplored area is covered in a dark gray, foggy substance. My Dragon breathes the Fire of Clearing and Illumination to lift the veil. I ask the Creator for each of you to have your own healing Teams. You are now surrounded with your own specific Angels, Guides, Totems, and/or Extra-Terrestrials who normally work with you, even if you're not aware of it.

I see relatives who have passed come forward to remind you to clear yourself of the energy of Lack, going all the way back to when they lived on this Planet. There are energies of struggle, greed, temptation, death, starvation, sorrow, and fear for self and those they were responsible for. I see them coming out of the mist directly to you.

They are here, in Love and Respect, to ensure that you can now participate in clearing this energy they carried with them and passed on to you. It can now be cleared from your heritage.

We follow the energy of each ancestor back to the period during which they lived. We recognize the turmoil of their situation and ask it to be cleared in a manner where your DNA no longer resonates with these lower vibrations of Lack, Fear, and Sadness. This clearing will be available to living blood relatives who are ready to receive it. Allow yourself to breathe the release through all your cells, and experience the DNA shift as the emotional trauma leaves each generation that receives the healing. Just breathe and allow the shift within.

As you do this clearing, the mist lifts a little more. You may experience a little sadness or grief, but know it is just the release and shifting of energy making room for you to be able to Receive. Take your time with this, and let it be as complete as possible. If you forget you have an Avatar of some sort, it will be taken care of by the nearby Teams, and it will be available when you are ready. There is nothing to worry about.

Notice how you now feel a little lighter? Your personal vibrational frequency is changing. You may notice you can see colors differently. The sky may be more vibrant now as well. Pay attention to the little changes.

You may want to experience this again as many times as you feel is necessary. Take the time to notice what is different without regenerating the past. You are awesome.

See you tomorrow!

MONTH ONE – DAY FOUR

Today, as we continue our journey through this Divine Abundance Portal, I notice music being played like in old black-and-white films. I can see the violin, the stage with velvet curtains, the conductor, and cushioned chairs. You are sitting in the front row along with very few people in the auditorium. It feels like you're sort of auditioning for a position in the next phase of life. Not knowing how to move forward, you're stuck in an energy loop.

I notice many of you taking a break, sitting on spiraling ledges which are like steps. You chat with others in the group and ignore the person auditioning. You have feelings of being invisible and a lack of respect for others and self, along with fear of who's turn is next. Yet, you have a flirty attitude along with beer and cigarettes as props. Everyone wears clothing from the 30s, 40s, and 50s. There is still a feeling of recovering from war and much pretense about who you are to yourself and to the world. This is a very strange energy loop.

I have asked the Divine what we are to do with this and why is it showing up now. I am told there is an energy still resonating within the group related to all war and a depressed economy.

We are moving in and out of this depression, money, and jobs. There is also want and readiness to have a little fun.

Some of us remain stuck in "What Was" energy with fear of moving into the Now. It's an energy of knowing what it's like to be where you are while also being afraid of what it would be like if it were different, not able to recognize that it might be better than ever.

Please imagine or physically do this exercise. Stand with your back straight, focus on your bare feet on the ground, pull the energy of the Divine up through your body, all the way to the top and out of your head. Feel the flow. Bring the energy of the Creator down through the top of your head to create an electromagnetic field that runs through the center of yourself. Notice the intensity. Let it increase to the point of being able to really feel it.

Ask the energy to balance and harmonize with that of the Divine Abundance Portal. You may notice how it expands from the center out to encompass your entire being and clear out the old black-and-white energy. The Cleanup Crew is here to contain and dispose of it.

Next, you need to step into a shower stall and let all the colors in the Universe flow through every cell of your being. Ask for the Rainbow Shower to clear the programs and emotions still creating a lower vibration within you. Allow vibrations of fear, lack, and procrastination to be deleted and washed down the drain. Notice how easy it is to let go of the traumatic energy you have been resonating. As you do this, your DNA changes to match what you are to become.

I now see you in color with a variety of updated music. As you stand in this Portal generating this level of energy, feel it clearing out of the Portal. See it light up. Now, let's walk a while in this energy and feel how the Portal is becoming brighter. It too is starting to pulsate in alignment with your vibration. Your own individual Divine Abundance Portal is coming to life as you participate in the larger Universal Divine Abundance Portal.

As we come to a nice, flattened out area we can take a break and allow ourselves to process what we have just cleared. Remember, your Angels, Guides, ET helpers, and other types of Teams are with you as you go through this very personal shift. Take your time, remember to breathe, notice what is different without bringing What Was back into your being or your focus.

Bless and clear your water and drink a lot of it today. As you bless your water and your food, ask that it match the vibration your body needs, and allow it to be absorbed as needed.

See you tomorrow!

MONTH ONE – DAY FIVE

You may be having a great experience, or you might be having a rough time emotionally. What we are doing is clearing old programs which, in turn, clear and heal old DNA patterns so you can vibrate at a purer level. This cleaner vibration is stronger and capable of holding the same clarity without being pulled into other drama that drags you off your path and whatever you are working toward. This kind of deep DNA-level change can feel intense, scary, or uncomfortable at first. Make sure to be gentle with yourself and allow time to get used to the new vibration.

Today, we are going to mount up on our wonderful Avatars. Mine, of course, being the Iridescent Purple Dragon. Let's line up side-by-side in this Portal where we will all move ahead at an equal pace for the moment.

We'll start by walking or flying slowly forward into the depths of this swirling energy. The first thing we come to is a huge, complete, Portal-sized rainbow waterfall. It has come to the attention of our guides that you need a boost to make clearing easier, gentler. Allow yourself to feel new colors flowing to fill each cell and the spaces in-between. Let your body's liquids also take in the Rainbow of Newness.

Breathe in this rainbow of colored energy. Let it permeate every single bit of you. Give yourself a moment to integrate this.

Now we are ready to move to the next level of the Divine Abundance Portal. Put your backpacks on and mount your Avatars. Take the place you want in your travel group. You can lead, hang in the middle, head off to the side, or hold back to see what happens. You can always change your position at any time.

The area we are entering is a green pasture type of swirl with obstacle courses. The one you go into is based entirely on you and your capability to work with your Avatar and/or guide. This is to loosen up your imagination. It's a way of examining yourself to see how you handle these types of challenges.

I see some in your group having to go through the center of a spinning barrel hanging from a rope. It expands to fit the size you need. Next, we head on down the field of tall, dense grass.

Can your Avatar fly if you ask it? Just because it has legs and no wings doesn't mean that it can't fly. Just think it. Ask it. Do it. Stay steady as the Portal itself changes. As you change, it changes. Keep clearing the fear, and don't freak out. Ask what this is all about, and why you are doing this. Stay in fun-mode. The more laughter you have, the more money falls into your backpack. When it is full to overflowing, it drains into your bank account.

You're flying over the tall, tangled grass. See how easy this is? Feel the light wind on your face and in your hair. Remember how a dog looks when his head is hanging out of the car window? It feels like that—enjoy it. No Fear. You are protected. Your Team is with you always.

Enjoy this space, as we're nearing the halfway mark of our first Divine Abundance Portal Activation. You are getting stronger and surer of yourself. Experience your day with Love and Gratitude, visualizing money falling into your back pack.

See you tomorrow!

MONTH ONE – DAY SIX

We passed the halfway mark! I can feel the shifts and learning you're experiencing. You might be tired, angry, afraid, and having vivid dreams. That's all okay at this stage. Remember, these are enormous changes you're making, and it can take a lot of energy.

Learning to be in control of your Avatar equals being in control of yourself and your life. You're learning to stand in your own power, developing confidence. Recognizing your worthiness to have Abundance is a huge change in your entire makeup. You probably aren't finished processing what we've done yet, which is why we take breaks between 11-day sessions.

You signed up for this because you were ready to do the work. Don't forget that you can go back to any of these practices any time when you need a review or need to reboot yourself to the New You. You've Got This!

We are now ready for a new experience. Let's get started with the knowledge that you are in the ever-changing, whirling, spinning Divine Abundance Portal. You are at the top of the largest water slide you have ever seen. Your Avatar will meet you at the bottom. Your Team is always with you for protection and whatever else you need. You are never alone.

You have your own event to navigate today, there is no follow the leader. As you start off it isn't too steep, but it doesn't take long before there is a huge drop. You are going faster and faster, your heart is racing, you are not sure if you should close your eyes and scream. You can hardly breathe.

There is so much water spraying up, you aren't sure when or if you should breathe. You are going so fast you can't see what is around you. You can't see or feel your support system, but a part of you knows it is there. You don't know if there is ever an end to it. Is there a bottom? Will you drop into a void to be eaten up by the Universe?

Now, consciously slow it down. Slow the entire scene down to where you can see the structure you are on. Can you see it in 3D? Notice how you can see in all directions at the same time? Can you see if it's a rickety or firm structure? How wet are you, really? Can you see the Portal's walls, ceiling, and floor? What color is it? Can you see the wrinkles in it?

Consciously calm the panic. Notice that your breath slows, your heart rate slows, and your fear subsides. If it doesn't, take a deep breath and slow it down even further. Visualize the entire experience in slow motion. Turn it all down. You may need to see a knob with the word Experience on it, turn it to the left. Remember, you are in control of your own experience. Now, slow it down a little more.

WOW! There is nothing to fear. You did it. Notice the bottom of the tube. Where did the water go? It is now like a pit full of balls kids like. You can now land in this soft pile of Abundance balls. Notice how these balls are transparent. Inside them is more than money. It is programmable Energy.

The balls contain the Abundance needed in the moment. When you look at them and feel fear, pick one up that is calming. If you need to feel love and supported, pick one up filled with Love. If you need to make a car payment, pick one that says Car Payment. They are what you need in this world of ever-changing, Abundance-filled Energy.

Fill your backpack with these as many times as required. Remember, it flows into where your needs can be met, whether that be your heart or bank account. Most of the time you don't even have to think about where it is needed, as Energy always knows. It is Conscious. You may want to take one of these balls and throw it into the bath or hot tub and let yourself just float for a bit.

That was quite a workout! Take care of yourself, bless what you eat to match the vibration your body needs. Bless your water, too, and drink lots of it to detox the adrenaline we created.

You may want to do this experience all over again—it takes a lot of practice to control yourself on this level. If you can control yourself, you are the Master of your Life.

See you tomorrow!

MONTH ONE – DAY SEVEN

This is an exciting time! You are learning to be the Master of yourself. Be patient, it takes practice. All those balls of Abundance you collected are more than enough to last you forever. Do you feel like you have enough, or do you still have an inner fear of not enough with thoughts like, "What will happen tomorrow?", "What happens when I run out of these?", and "How do I make them be real money?" These are the big questions.

Let's dive further into this Divine Abundance Portal and see what appears today. I am activating my Guides, Teams, Angels, and all of yours. Notice what you feel. Remember how the Law of Attraction works. What you focus on is what will attract to you.

Energy goes where it is acknowledged. If it's negative, you get low vibrational victim stuff. If it's positive, you get happy. A happy You equals happy people around you because you are in an easy state of receiving.

As we journey deeper into the spinning Vortex I see a level of a dark veil. This is not from ancestors. It is from life experiences in this lifetime. You stop as you come closer to this veil. Take a moment to notice how it feels. It may feel differently to you than it does to another. I notice some hesitation as well as some curiosity.

Stand up and align yourself. Remember, bare feet on the ground, energy running up the body and out, then down from the Creator and out the feet. Take a few breaths, and do it for yourself. I will help if needed to connect you to your Guides and Teams.

As you breathe in the refreshing energy notice the geometric writing around you. These are codes that will help you cross this veil. Reach out and take as many or as few as you would like to start with. Ask them where they need to be placed – within or on your body. Once you have placed them, ask them to activate! Notice how these codes provide even more clearing and alignment with who you are.

There is a key and a door beyond the veil. When you are ready, reach out, take the key, and step through the veil. If you can't find the key, or the door won't open, you're simply not ready to receive. If you need more codes to assist in more changes, reach out and get them. Remember to activate them. Take your time, you will not be left behind. Breathe. These codes are benevolent, they are here to assist you in an easy transition to being able to receive.

Now that you are through the door, feel golden sunlight on your skin. It is refreshing and regenerating. Let yourself receive it as deep into your body as you can. Let it penetrate your core, warming and awakening your being. The sun carries more activation codes of receiving. Ask them to turn on and activate within you. They will assist in manifesting the Divine Abundance you've been requesting. If you feel like it, you may lie on the green, lush grass or sit under a nice tree while you rest and let the codes realign your DNA into a receiving mode.

See you tomorrow!

MONTH ONE – DAY EIGHT

Are you beginning to see a shift in your finances, or have you received more Abundance opportunities, such as discounted or free items? How are you at receiving them? Do you graciously say thank you, or do you disbelieve it to the point that you push it away? I see that we still have some work to do.

Grab your Avatar. Today, you are going to be experiencing some new ways of working with a partner. Mount up. Make sure you are in charge and that flying attire and gear are with you.

As we go deeper into this portal, we are going to ride between some ginormous canyons. The walls on each side are incredibly steep. They are beautifully colored with a trickle of water running down in some places and waterfalls in others, there is a small stream below.

Reach out with your fingers and feel the temperature of the water. Take out your water bottle and fill it from one of these streams or falls as you ride by. Taste it. Notice the purity of its taste.

Watch your balance. Sometimes the space between the earthen walls is very wide while other areas you can barely fit through. Stay calm and aware at all times. The down drafts can be a little surprising. Be prepared. Hang on.

Notice your emotions. Is this easy for you? Are you having fun? Or, am I bringing you to the edge of your ability to remain centered? Take a moment to breathe. As you calm, your Avatar will also calm.

Pay attention to the details around you. Is there a rock jutting out from the side? Are there caves to explore later? Is anyone or anything else flying along with you? Is your Avatar being guided by your mind, legs, hands, or is it just doing its own thing? How are you feeling? Is it getting easier? Relax and enjoy the experience. All of life is an experience.

We are now coming into an opening where you can once again see the sides of the Portal. Notice how it is narrowing. What color is the sky around you? What is the texture as you move through the air? Is it easy to breathe?

As we come more into the center of the Portal we notice an area of soft grass below. Prepare yourself for a smooth landing. Take a moment and get your legs back under you.

We just had an amazing experience of noticing how you handle yourself in various situations. Be very proud of yourself – you made it without getting hurt. It took me a while to learn everything about this type of riding and flying through the spiritual realm. You are learning to be One with situations presented to you. A calm Oneness.

You may want to take a few minutes to sit in the grass or a large warm rock where you can visualize your dreams flowing into your backpack, which is the funnel into the Creativity. It may funnel money into your bank account or directly to pay a specific bill, or to a manifestation fund for your next project. Take a few breaths as you let your visualization manifest. Remember to drink and bless your water.

See you tomorrow!

MONTH ONE – DAY NINE

I can feel that today is going to be an amazing adventure in renewing our Divine Abundance Blueprint within this Divine Abundance Portal. Even as you read this, I am energetically checking in with you, and I get the feeling there is bit of quicksand beneath your feet.

Something is holding you back. Is it that we are getting closer to being finished with this first part of our journey and there is still more renewing to be completed in such a short time? Are you holding on to the old ways of doing things in your life? Perhaps that is it. Well, time is a wastin', so let's get moving on this journey!

Today, I do feel a new path before us to follow. It looks like a dirt path. I am told we are to walk, at least to start out. Do you have the equipment you need – a walking stick, water bottle, compass, maybe some food? Do you remember how to create what you need in the moment you need it? That way you don't have to carry so much. I am taking a walking stick, water, and my backpack to fill with money if I find some. My Dragon will be flying above to help scout the way before we get there. You may choose to invite your Avatar as well.

It appears to be a mining journey today. We are coming upon some mountainside caves. Pick the one you think will have in it what you wish for. As I look them over I see many precious items. However, what is precious to me may be silly to you.

I see a cave of beautiful clothes and shoes that, if you touch them, they automatically become the size and color you need them to be. My grandkids would love this! Perhaps, if not for you, then for someone else you know who is in need.

I notice one cave is full of gold, but not in a form that is easy to just pick up. You must pick it out of veins in the cave walls. There is a cave filled with sweets and one brimming with organic fruits and vegetables. How much of this can you carry with you, or do you even need to?

More caves are replete with silver, copper, and crystals. Healing stones are already cut to be easily used. The orbs and balls we found in the ball pit are piled up in their own cave. Where else would they have come from? I also see a cave of flying, coded symbols. Wow, such a magical place!

Take your time as you examine each cave. What is it that you want now or later? What is each one telling you? Perhaps, "Take me, Take me!" Or, do they simply have stuff to look at and/or enjoy in the moment as you eat you fill now? Do you need to fill your backpack and then funnel it into another place? Do you need anything to help you move into the You that you are becoming as we move forward another day? Maybe, for you, this is all just a distraction.

My Dragon reminds me it's time to get moving on down the trail as the light fades. We need to make it a little further down this Portal, perhaps nearer to the trees and that stream. I notice the sides narrow more and more each day as the Portal spins around us. Once we get our camp set up you can empty out your backpack and see what your treasures are. You could find a special place to do this on your own or invite a special person who you want to share this with.

As I walk around and chat with those who read this, I ask how you fared at the caves. I see some surprised reactions. Most backpacks are nearly empty. The items that were put into them started disappearing. This is quite unexpected!

The question is, did you put in enough to funnel into areas you intended the products to go to, or did you only think of the moment? What a dilemma this is! How does it represent what is going on in your life? How can you bring it back or make the changes needed to be ready to receive it?

Take a moment to sit quietly on your rock, blanket, or chair. Create the most comfortable space. Now balance yourself. Take a breath and ask the Creator or the Universe, "What happened? Why did I not receive more?" Listen to your answer, it may be a feeling, or it may be words. If you have more questions, ask them now and take a moment to listen. Remember to bless your water and food throughout the day.

See you tomorrow!

MONTH ONE – DAY TEN

Today is going to be a great day! As I look around at how the Portal is shifting more frequently, it reminds me of how I created this community. You are all here based on a certain desire or need and are collectively looking for a way to obtain it. Sort of interesting. It doesn't feel like you're needy, greedy types who fall into the victimhood that many gravitate to. Those people don't tend to take journeys like this. They simply say, "Do this for me, get this for me, fix me so I can have whatever I want." No, you are ready to move to the next level.

As you can see, the path begins to thin due to the narrowing of the portal. The spinning seems to be faster, also due to being in a tighter area. As I look around, I ask our Teams what is needed next before sending you out into the world during your break between sessions.

What do you need to help you bring abundance into your world? More clearing? I'm not fond of this word. It reminds me of being in a humid, hot jungle whacking away with a machete at things blocking the path. It's hard, physical work doing it that way. When we spend so much exertion, mentally and physically, we experience exhaustion. Interesting the 'ex' in each word.

There is neither time nor energy left to move forward. We just keep looping around, like on a hamster wheel.

For forward movement, a different path must be taken. To take a different path requires trusting yourself and your Guides, Teams, or Avatar to support you, even carry you part of the way. Know that they are available to assist you in what you ask for.

Before we step out of this Portal and take a break to assimilate these DNA-level changes, I would like you to do a little exercise with your Avatar.

Mount up. Think a command to go forward, turn left, then right, roll to the left or right, dive almost to the bottom, then climb back up nearly to the ceiling of the Portal, then back down, and now hover. Do you see what your thoughts can do! I feel a little resistance in the idea you are in charge of how the world around you reacts and behaves. It feels sort of like when I would get on my horse and she would start bucking, not wanting to participate in what I had planned. Some of what I noticed wasn't just from your Avatar, it was also from you.

In order to be a You that is secure in all abundance, you may have to find new ways of participating in your life. No more couch potatoes who hide in video games. No more watching someone else participate in games (football, movies, etc.). This is your life, live it. Not in a selfish way, but with boundaries.

To have an Abundant life you must participate in it. There are choices to be made moment by moment, even if it's opening your eyes to get out of bed.

It feels like we need to find another Rainbow waterfall. I know exactly where one is located, follow me. We have to find the perfect waterfall that gives you what you need right now. One that not only flows with abundance, but also washes away any procrastination and fills you back up with Love and Gratitude. I see it just around this bend. You may want to ride your Avatar into it and let the flow also assist it in being in the same Dimension as you.

It really helps with the alignment of communication between the two of you. When you feel the flow and are ready, come on out and just be. Prepare yourself for the last session of the month.

See you tomorrow for our last ride in the Portal!

MONTH ONE – DAY ELEVEN

I am amazed how heavy my heart is knowing this is our last day of this first session of the Divine Abundance Portal experience. I also know we will have a fantastic adventure today as we make our final journey within this part of the Divine Abundance Portal. It feels like it is ready to let go of us. We have processed and received many tools and much information during these amazing 11 days.

Let's come together in a group of all who have participated and will participate in this Divine Activation. Put your hands in the center to touch, then reach to the sky with a final "Let's Ride!" cheer. Remember, you do not have to do this alone. You're doing this not only with myself as your guide but also with every other person who has participated in these Activations whether past, present, or future. Collectively we seek to create more Abundance in every way for ourselves and everyone on the Planet.

Hop on your Avatar and feel how strong your bond has become. How did you ever go about your day without your Avatar? As we begin gaining altitude, the energy from our group spreads throughout the Portal. It is so beautiful to watch and feel it wash through the entire area.

Take a moment to scan your memory banks of the area to see if you left anything behind. Is there any specific area you want to return to at this moment? If so, it will only take a moment of thought and you are right there at the spot. If there is something you want to take with you, now would be the time to get it. I think I would like a few more of those balls that can be turned into whatever I may need to use for today's journey. They can be found either in one of the caves or at the bottom of the waterslide. I think the cave is closer. It can all happen in the blink of an eye.

Now, I want to take a quick ride through one of the Rainbow waterfalls with the intention of staying clear in receiving and holding onto the created Abundance. Oh, we didn't cover that one, did we?

How do we hold on to the Abundance we receive? Of course, we must pay for the usage of items on this Planet. How do we not let it slip through our conscious awareness to have it disappear moments later? As I ask this question I see various geometries appear: a spinning pyramid, a circle, a connecting line of light, and some interesting forms of writing.

I see a line of light where money travels each month to us, then the bank, then the bills. These seem to be stationary glowing lines since they're used on a regular basis. The spinning geometries allow the money to be siphoned off with thoughts like, "Oh, I want a special coffee, or a snack, or some new technology that just came on the market." I am sure there are others in your spinning, siphoning world.

How aware were we that we really didn't need any of the extras that sort of jumped into our field today or yesterday? How do we stay consciously aware, so we don't fuel the money siphons?

As I ask the question, I am shown a well-hidden area in the Divine Abundance Portal that we just flew past a few days ago. We need to take time to go back there and receive this piece of information. It only takes a moment to get there. I see quite a few options we can use.

One looks like a tar-like substance which is sticky on the outside that can be dumped over our heads. Another is like a suit of armor— thick, heavy, and clunky. A third is a spray on sticky substance that's shiny, dries clear, and is sticky on the inside.

I will go with the one that is sticky on the inside. It feels like it's what I need to hold my money with so it doesn't get grabbed up by things that don't create a better Me. I am consciously aware of what I can enjoy and utilize on a regular basis, whereas things like fast food and drinks are gone just as quick as I hand over my money.

I put the spray substance on, and it doesn't feel weird on my skin. I think it's just what I need for when I leave the Portal. You get to choose what works best for you. I hear a calling for us to hurry on down the wave of the spinning interaction of the Portal.

Now we are back, just in time, as the Portal spins even faster and more chaotic. It pushes us to the end. It is narrow and dark down there. Take your Avatar with you if you want to, take a breath, and allow the Portal to sort of spit you out.

This is a very strange feeling. Take stock of yourself and notice how you start to interact in the real world with all your new tools. This has been a most enjoyable journey with all of you.

It is most important that you do not continue the activations immediately following an 11-day session. These are very, very powerful and intense. I don't want you to crack from too much change all at once. We are doing 11 days per month for a reason: to give your body, mind, and spirit time to calibrate, adjust, assimilate, and integrate this very powerful work. Over the next few weeks you'll see changes. Notice them. Feel into them. Write them down.

See you next month!

See you soon with Truth, Love, and Gratitude

Pat, The Cosmic Cowgirl

Journal the Changes in Your Abundance Levels

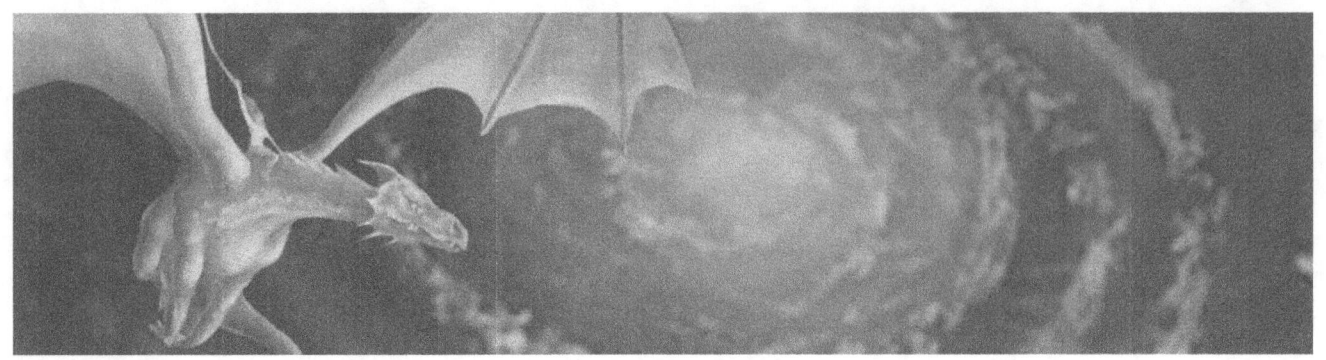

CHAPTER TWO: LOVE & MONEY REPROGRAMMING

MONTH TWO – DAY ONE

I tapped into the group energy and asked for all we do to be done with ease and benefit everyone involved as we ride through this Divine Portal for the Magic of Love and Money. I include this energy as we shift into the power of who we are now and who we are to be after this 11-day journey to transform in ease with Love and Gratitude.

I find it quite interesting as I fly over this Portal that it's in the shape of a heart. I also see you lining up to begin this adventure with me and our collective Teams. There is a golden rope across the opening as we wait for everyone to arrive. Today, it looks like we're going to be journeying like we are in an old-fashioned Tunnel of Love at an amusement park. We get to ride in our individual heart-shaped boats which float in the water yet have wheels underneath on a metal track. Fasten the safety bar across your lap or not.

The interior of each boat is made of various colors per what we want to experience as a group. I notice some are purple with white and red ornamentations, some are sunshine yellow with green vines and leaves for decoration, and some are traditional pink with white and red variations. Pick the one you will be most comfortable in. I am starting out in one that is various shades of purple and white. The colors may change as we move along. Ready?

We are moving through the water slowly, and it is getting darker. Carnival music starts playing. This Tunnel of Love looks to be fun but strange as we ride without a partner to lean on. The music suddenly changes to old-fashioned love songs. I found a dial in the front of my boat where I can change the music to what I want it to be.

Look for yours. Reach out and change it to your liking. I found some soft yoga music, but I also feel like switching between rock n' roll and country. It only lets me select a few different artists to keep the theme of Love, but not necessarily the romantic love.

It gets darker, yet there is soft lighting. The track starts to make a ratcheting sound as it gets steeper. We climb, but the music is still soft and comforting. As you go past, notice how some things hang down, like rings of various types, heart shapes, and various geometric shapes such as multidimensional triangles and dodecahedrons. All are unbelievable colors.

Reach out for ones that you are drawn to. Put them on your head as halos or crowns, on your arms as bracelets, or lay them on your heart or abdominal area. Perhaps one of them feels like it needs to be on a knee or ankle. Just take what you are drawn to and put it where you feel they are called to land. Notice how they meld into the area where you place them. They also replicate into however many you want or need.

WOW! How do you feel about that? Too many? Too fast? Take a moment to breathe. You can also stop your boat if you need a little more time. Notice how the area feels. How do you feel? Is there less pain, drama? Are you happier, lighter?

Oh, the music and lighting changed again. Now that we are at the top of hill it levels out and becomes brighter. Let's get ready to leave the boats and step onto a dock. It is a little wobbly, but there are helpers to assist in climbing out. Notice your surroundings. Is it tropical, mountainous, desert, or like Disneyland?

The helpers present a welcoming gift bag to you as you are escorted to your individual cabins. This is where you open your gift bag. Each is specific to your wants and needs. Find a comfortable place to go through this gift bag. Some contain food, supplements, flowers, money, a bubble to wrap yourself in, or whatever you need for your time before the next journey begins.

Let yourself shift with the items you put on yourself while in the boat. Utilize all the items in your gift bag as tomorrow will be another experience.

See you tomorrow!

MONTH TWO – DAY TWO

I hope today finds you rested and fully integrated with the shapes, colors and music you were given yesterday as well as the gift bag supplied with exactly what you needed. It is so great to get downloaded with such fantastic help on the first day.

I remember why this event was created. This Divine Portal of Money and Love, or was it Love and Money, or the Love of Money, or maybe the Power of Money and the Power of Love. As we go through our day to day, year after year lives, we create various ideas about both, and we probably experienced the power of both along with the power that others have used and abused. This creates a variety of emotions along this type of a journey. Let's see what adventure comes our way to clear up some of this.

Today, as we gather outside of our cabins, notice how you are dressed. I feel like we need some hiking clothes to start with. If you need to run back inside to get changed, do it quickly and bring a backpack filled with what you may need.

While you were readying yourselves, I quickly asked my Dragon to be available at the ready and to round up some rideable Avatars for you, just in case we need them later in the adventure. I also did a quick check on my own backpack, hiking shoes, and a few things that might be fun. Take a quick look at yourselves to see if you are adventure-ready. Are you feeling a little uneasy about the bugs, snakes, spiders, scorpions, or other strange critters we might come across? Are you fit enough? New adventures bring up new excitements.

I have some special shoes for each of you. Try them on and tie the laces securely. These are very expensive because they are magical. Chose the color you want for the moment and they will become that shade. They will be comfortable all day, and even the most vicious snake will not be able to bite through them. They also have other properties you will discover as we move throughout the day. Let's go!

The trail starts off easy. Notice, as we put each foot down, the dense foliage moves out of the way. The path is steep but is easy to maneuver with these magical, extremely expensive hiking shoes. If you see some plant or stone that you are really drawn to, put it in your backpack. It will be yours to be treasured when you get back to your cabin.

We rapidly gain altitude, but you keep walking as if the day has just begun. The magical, extremely expensive hiking shoes seem to emit an energy that keeps you energized and aware of everything around you.

Take time to consider the colors of the leaves, the flowering plants, the sounds of the birds, the texture of the pebbles under your feet. How long have we been hiking? Moments, or hours? It also seems like we are gliding up the path as if we are being pulled along with ease. Our group laughs and races to each new item to investigate and to see who can climb onto the biggest rock first. Is it the shoes, the company, or the experience of a little freedom?

As we turn this last corner there is a stream to cross. It roars up to the bottom of a log being used as the bridge. No need to worry – your very expensive magical shoes will not let you slip and fall into the raging stream.

Can you hear it roaring? Feel the water as it splashes and pulls at you as you walk across. This is a great accomplishment. Many have lost their lives in this stream when the water is this high.

You are doing amazingly well. No Fear! Feel your heart swell with satisfaction that you are accomplishing this. Nothing like a magical pair of new shoes to do the trick for you.

Wow! We made it to the top of the mountain. The path has ended, but we have a whole new exciting adventure available for us. My Dragon found each of you a very special Avatar to ride down the mountain. I want you to pick out the one you feel the most comfortable with or that you are just drawn to. Take a moment to connect with the Avatar you seem to align with the best. Feel its skin, fur, feathers, or scales. Make sure riding equipment like a bridle, saddle, or loop of leather to hold onto fits your needs. Each of you will need to find your own way.

Notice how skittish your Avatar is. It notices something isn't quite real or true about you. Take off your magical, very expensive hiking shoes. Is this easy for you to do, or is there a hesitation? Observe how you feel about this. It is your journey, but you can't get on any Avatar with these shoes. You need to be your true self. The Avatars can only connect with the real You. This connection can't be made with that type of magic. You will learn how to make your own magic in Truth, Love, and Gratitude as we move through this journey.

Take your time. As you take off the hiking shoes, they disintegrate. You don't need them anymore. Actually, were they magical, or did the idea of them being so, help you make it over the log or to the top of the mountain with so much energy? The Power is in You!

Mount up! Give yourself a moment to align with this new form of travel. Let's give the command to head back to the cabins. It has been quite an eventful day. Once you get into your cabin empty your backpack and notice what you put into it. Take the time to examine each item and what it means to you.

See you tomorrow!

MONTH TWO – DAY THREE

I am so glad to see all of you again today. You look amazingly well. How are you with the Avatars you rode yesterday? If it doesn't fit you, there will be an opportunity to choose a different one. Just close your eyes for a moment (read this through, then close your eyes). Feel within yourself the type of animal or beast you would like to be able to ride through our journeys.

Let yourself feel what it would be like to fly with the animal upon its back. Is it a creature that has varying lengths of legs that can take you across any terrain? Can it fly or take enormous leaps? Take a moment to wonder what it smells like. Is it male or female? Does it matter? Really recognize the reason you are choosing this One.

Open your eyes – and there it is! The Avatar you dreamed of having, even the exact color and temperament. I realize the term Avatar in this realm is probably different for those of you that play certain games. My Teams told me to use the word to give the idea of having a magical assistant of some sort that isn't human. Instead, perhaps it's a counterpart of who you really are.

Now we are ready to journey into the Portal. Yes, today is the day we will venture in to not come back the same, nor the same way, when we reach the other side. Take along the things you may need, and remember, you will be gaining tools as we go deeper into the Portal. Food and water will be provided. Remember a backpack or saddlebags.

As we prepare to enter the Portal with your Avatar take notice of a veil of Golden Light you will be going through. This veil keeps the darkness out of the Portal. It does a great job of detecting Greed, Envy, Hate, Anger, Jealousy, and Victim and the level it is being carried by our group. It can remove the active layers of these human elements which normally take a lot of therapy to remove.

Let's get on our way and see what happens. Remember to connect with your Avatar before you get on. It just makes the ride go easier.

We start by circling the outer rim. This gives you a great look at the whole Heart-Shaped Portal. Wow, it's beautiful! It seems to have a pulse, as if it were beating like a living heart. As we get ready to enter, can you feel the Golden Veil waiting for you? How do you feel about going through? I feel an excitement of flushing out some of the of the old, clinging-on, Earth emotional programs. Here we go. Wow! It isn't wet, just sort of like a light breeze blowing through every cell. I feel lighter and happier.

This Portal is starting out with a lot of foliage, trees of unusual varieties, vines and moss hanging out of what seems to be the sky – the energy of the vortex holds them in place. As they brush against your head, hair, skin, face, fingers, and feet they leave a vibration that is individual to you alone. It's as if they are filling in the blanks created from the cleansing powers of the Veil. To me, it seems like potholes are being filled with the opposite frequency of what was once there. It looks and feels like the Creator's Golden Healing Goo which generates a firmer foundation to move into an initial healing of loving yourself. It feels great. After all, how can you love someone else or expect to be loved if you aren't whole?

I also notice the variety of birds flying around. They are of such beautiful and unusual colors with sounds I have never heard a critter make before. Some sound like crystal bowls being played. Is that what you hear? Perhaps it's the sound I need, so that is what I am hearing. Remember, this is all individual to you and your journey through the Divine Portal of Money and Love.

We are coming upon a place to land and make camp. It is a flat ridge on the right, near the waterfall. Do you see it? Mentally command your Avatar to land in that area. This is where you will get to assimilate the changes within.

There are beings there to take care of your camping needs and those of your Avatar. You get to take time for yourself and prepare for the rest of the journey.

See you tomorrow.

MONTH TWO – DAY FOUR

Good Morning! This is going to be a brilliant day! The light is magnificent in here. It seems everything is a bit more sparkly than the day before. The dew on the plants, the molecules in the air, even the huge waterfall just over the ledge glows.

Have you looked over it to see how far down it is? I did, and I couldn't see the bottom. No worries, I'm sure there is one down there somewhere. Let's find out. Ready … Set … Jump!

I can't believe I just did that! I have always been so afraid of heights, and I just jumped without seeing where I was going. What is happening? Okay, I'm okay, I can do this. This free falling is like flying and doing somersaults & back flips with so much ease! It's taking so long to reach the bottom that I can look at the plants and rocks jutting out from the sides as I fall past. I actually have time to think about more than … I don't know how to swim! But I'm not really scared.

I hear the water at the bottom gently transition from falling water to flowing. This is quite unusual. I expected a huge crashing with water spraying upwards, pressure all around, and being sucked into the depths.

I expected not being able to breathe, or the bigger panic of not being able to swim. And how long would I be held in this swirling vortex? Oh, my fears of the unknown can get the better of me.

Now, as I enter the water, I feel the soothing, refreshing, healing properties of the liquid's molecules. I'm floating in it. It's moving around and through me at the same time. I feel an inner calm, a rare moment for me. It gives me clarity and peace. As I absorb and clear more cells, I notice specific number sequencing and DNA coding taking place within me. I also notice everyone in the group changing. Wrinkles disappear, laughter becomes more authentic. Not simply "being nice to the person next to me" type of laughter, but real belly laughs!

This is amazing. I love seeing the willingness to associate with each other now and be helpful as the moments arise. This is an amazing group of people beginning to connect as a tribe would.

After lounging on the plush grass on the bank my clothes are finally dry. I'm looking at the steep mountain with a feeling of not really wanting to climb back up. The plants are abundant where rocky outcroppings give room for them. It looks like quite a challenge, even for the best rock climber.

I am not sure about the connection to your Avatar, but let's see if we can summon them. Sit in a circle with me, close your eyes, and think of your Avatar. Feel the exhilaration of riding on the back of your amazing companion. In your mind, call it to you. Even if you didn't give it a name, focus on what it feels like when you are together. Send the Love from your heart to activate the bond where your thoughts can override anything else your Avatars are doing. Tell them to come ... Now! ... with a gentle and loving command.

My Dragon is here! I now see others arrive and greet you as they prepare for some fun. Take your time and move slowly with your newly-revived body. Notice how your balance has changed. Do you stand taller? Remember when you were in your 20s or younger? Let yourself recalibrate to that body awareness. Now, as you get on your Avatar, you can feel yourself communicating easier. You know what is going to happen before it happens. At this point, your Avatar has a sparkly resonance, too. Let's take a little time to explore the area individually then meet back on the ledge for camp within a few hours.

Take your time to learn more about your surroundings and how you handle them. Just notice what is different and new, including how you think and feel about yourself and those around you here and at work or at home. In general, your attitude.

See you tomorrow!

MONTH TWO – DAY FIVE

I'm glad to see you made it back to camp last night without any incidents. However, I was told about a few little snafus. For example, one person nearly fell off their Avatar due to a misunderstanding. You must be specific in your communication with them. If your mind wanders all over the place, and you think you want to go left and then go right or higher or lower, or faster or slower, your Avatar will get confused and may decide to leave you on the ground, even though they are not near the ground. Just as all in the game of living.

Mixed messages may not get you what you want or where you want to go. It can really cause problems with business and loved ones. Hopefully, we can get some of it cleared up in the reprogramming of our DNA and thought processes before we finish this Portal experience. This Divine Portal of Money and Love is a process to clear out the old to make room and receive the new.

Since yesterday was such a major clearing in the water, I think we all deserve more fun today. Maybe that was fun for you, but I found I had a few fear issues to get resolved. I was going to tell you to select a new Avatar because you have difficulty communicating with the first one you chose. Yet, my Teams told me NOT to give that option right now.

Trust your first choice. You made it for a reason. I am supposed to help you with the one you have. So, I want all of you to ready yourselves for a full day of riding/flying. Bring your backpacks in case we come across something truly awesome you may want to keep.

Let's take it slow with a few deep breaths, release your frustration and fear. Let it just slide down your arms, out your fingertips, and shake it off. Wriggle your back and your backside a little. Relax. Walk over to your Avatar with the singular thought of having a great day. I am putting the riding gear on you. This is going to be amazing.

Send a feeling of Love and Gratitude to your Avatar. Run your hands over its neck, down the legs. A few gentle pats with some whispers of awesomeness always helps them to calm down so you can connect. Don't forget to breathe! Keep your attention on only your Avatar. Isn't it getting easier?

I think I may have pushed some of you too fast in this direction without enough beginning steps. I should have provided a few more options in the process of picking an Avatar. Some of you really picked huge beasts. I was just so excited to explore this Portal. Sorry!

Now that you have properly readied yourself and your Avatar for a wonderful journey, let's go! Give the mental or whispered command to slowly lift off and follow ME on my Dragon. Let's just take it easy for a while as we gain altitude and move further into the Portal.

Ease your breathing, even though the scenery is beautiful, and we are getting up there in height. Follow me in taking a nice easy dive. I mean, what is easier than diving straight down on a flying beast? Oh, it's so much fun! Climb back up to the top where we can get a closer look at the plants that grow from the ceiling. Some of them have clustered fruit like grapes hanging down. Except they're of various colors and shapes. Let's see what they really are.

As we get closer I realize they aren't fruit after all. They're Balls of Manifestations. Tell your Avatar to hover as you find some you may want to pick. Some you may want to eat as they have nutrients like nothing else you have ever encountered. In this environment, you may need them.

You probably haven't noticed, but the air you breathe is a little different from what you are used to. I feel like I need some of the red, orange, and purple manifestation balls at this moment. Pay attention to what your body cries out for, and find the ones which feed that need.

I see some have essences of the type of Love you need. You may put some on your heart and let them meld into yourself, or smash them into the top of your head where they can run down into your hair then disappear as they are absorbed into your brain and emotional body. Of course, you may put some into your pack for later.

I discovered some have money in the middle of them as well as opportunities for earning money. Pick a few, and put them into your pack. When we find our new camp, you can figure out how to get to the treasures.

As the light changes, I feel the pull for us to move to a lower altitude and start looking for our new camp site. It's hard to leave such an abundantly different area but we must. I feel all of you are doing so much better with your flying skills! I also notice you're getting tired. It has been a workout learning how to balance and work with these amazing beasts!

I view where our camp has been set up. Can you see the tents just over that ridge, in the valley surrounded by the purple trees? Yes, purple trees! What an easy way to pick out our site from someone else's. Think the command to slow down, and land at that site as you see in your mind's eye. Let your Avatar take its head in that direction as it may require a little more time to maneuver himself into a landing position.

My Dragon needs a lot of room away from the tents. Once on the ground, have one of the caretakers teach you how to attend to your Avatars' needs. This is another way of showing Love and Appreciation to this wonderful new partner. Give your Avatar a great big hug before going to your own tent.

Take a moment before going to bed to see if you can open the items you picked that have various treasures in them.

See you tomorrow!

MONTH TWO – DAY SIX

I hope you rested well under the energy of the purple blossoming forest. I love the smell of these amethyst-colored blossoms, and, wow, how they create some very busy dreams for me!

I see the expressions on your faces today. You must have had some great dreams last night. Or was it the findings from the treasures you picked yesterday? I'm curious as to how you got them open. Or did you? For those that couldn't see their treasures, the key is to meditate into a vibration of Love. Even the vibration of Love of Money works, because it's still Love. You can give it another try when we return to camp.

Today, we're exploring some deep underground caves. I can already tell this is going to be a challenge for me as I easily get claustrophobic. My guides tell me not to worry I'll do my best to trust them. Get changed into some spelunking clothing. Remember the backpacks. The gear you need will be ready for us when we arrive.

Let's start with an Avatar ride as it will save us a lot of time. We'll head down the center of the Portal until we see the great underground tunnel entrance. Give your Avatar the telepathic command to locate these underground caves.

No sooner had I thought about the location, my Dragon knew exactly where to find it. Yours will, too. I'll meet you there.

We are waiting for a few of the tribe to land. Be patient, there is plenty of time. What do you think we'll find in these caves? I think it's an amazing surprise.

Everyone get your gear on. Check the battery in your helmet light. Gloves? Knee pads? Oh, the entrance starts out rather small. We have to crawl. If you have some problems crawling in your physical life, don't worry, your body will remember how to do it here. Mind your thoughts.

This area is interesting depending on your thoughts. Do you see spiders, scorpions, snakes, webs to crawl through? Is it dusty and dry? Wet and slimy? What you think appears. I let go of the creepy crawly things and their surface habitats. This isn't Earth. It is what you create it to be.

I see a larger area up ahead. Yes, opens enough where we can all stand and do some more exploring. This is a great place to do a little stretching and deep breathing. The air in here is good for you. It seems to have a special sparkle to it, a sort of healing resonance. Take some time to get your bearings and feel your feet under you. Walk around and see what is in this room. It is much bigger than I first thought.

I see specific cutouts on the walls where items may have been placed at one time. I also see some paintings. They're very abstract and have specific meanings to each one of us. The more I tune into them the more brilliant they become.

Colors have a resonance, a vibrational frequency. Sometimes they can be heard as sounds or they absorb into your body to create various shifts in your cells. These seem to be about Happiness.

Happy is a Loving feeling. Happy is also about Money. For example, I am Happy when I can easily pay all my bills every month. I am especially Happy when I have money left over at the end of each month to put into savings for something special at another time.

Maybe a vacation, a house, a down payment on a car, or some special thing I haven't even thought of yet, but may show up later. Happy is being with those that you Love and those that Love you.

Can you hear the tone coming off these paintings? They seem to have come into resonance for this tribe. They're sending a vibration throughout the entire cave, so a circle is being created in the room's center. It's glowing and getting larger. As it expands, it encompasses the entire room.

Specific stones materialize in each of the wall cutouts. It's as if a snapshot of each of you was sent out to the cave and it sent back these stones. Take the ones that call out to you, then return to the center of the room. Take your time to really tune into which one is yours. Yes, there is really one for everyone. Listen to your soul – it will help guide you to the one that is best for your needs.

As we gather into the center with our very powerful stones, I see a beam of light rising to the top of the room. The ceiling is opening. The floor seems to have become an elevator. We are being lifted to the top. Take a moment to walk away from the group with your stone and tune into it.

For those that don't know how to do this ... Sit quietly and hold the stone in your lap, toward your abdomen/center area, your heart, or maybe your head. Hold it where you feel comfortable. If it's too big, ask it to shrink down enough for the moment. You can let it expand to its natural size once you get back to camp or physical home.

Just hold your stone. Breathe. Greet it either verbally or telepathically. You may or may not feel or hear its message right away. You may get a specific message especially if you ask a question. There is no limit on what you may ask. It could be for Fun, Love, Money, or Life in general. You may get a message in your head or a vibrational shift in your cells. It's individual to you and your experience. The message may also be waiting for you at a later moment.

It's time to call your Avatar to come to you. Notice how easy it is getting to do this and how fast it responds to you now. You are developing great skills! Take a moment to show your appreciation. Did you bring a treat as your trainer probably mentioned?

Check your pack. Give your Avatar a special hug or rub its neck and ears – if you can find its ears! These little things really do matter to a loved one.

Check-in your equipment with the people that gave it to you. You're such a wonderful responsible group and don't need to carry all the extra stuff back to the camp. Of course, you don't want to forget your stone. It should fit into your pack. If not, command it to shrink enough in size and weight for you to handle it easily.

We're now ready to mount up and head back to camp. As always, a quick reminder that once we are there, take care of your Avatar first, then take care of yourself. In your tent take more time to tune into your stone and the tone that the paintings emitted. If you shrank your stone, you may need to expand it to tune in to it. It's as you command. These frequencies may also help in opening items you picked the day before. Give it a try.

See you tomorrow!

MONTH TWO – DAY SEVEN

This is going to be another great day in our exploration down the Portal of Divine Love and Money. As we have progressed in various events and clearings each day, I would like you to examine where you were in your life just a few days ago, how you felt about yourself and those around you, and how you felt about receiving money. Not just something like I love money, I need money, but how you feel in your heart about your money situation and what you can do about it if need be. Take a few notes about what is different, if anything

Today, let's see how far into the Portal we can get. If you have anything strewn about your tent, get it packed so the attendees can move it for you. You will not need anything in particular today. Just be comfortable. Get your Avatar ready to travel too. Remember, you are responsible for your loved ones, and since you picked this one, he is most certainly family by now. Keep the trust in this being at all times, as today you may really need it.

Let's get mounted up. We will circle the camp as a quick farewell to the purple forest and head on down the center of this Portal. Today, it seems to be spinning a little more than I remember. It could be turbulence in the atmosphere up ahead.

Do a check in with your Avatar so they are ready with their balance as you should be. We need to go lower. At this altitude, I can see a river below that we can probably make better time using. Let's see if there's a way to move down the river. There is a dock. Perhaps there will be equipment we can all fit on.

I never expected this! This is something highly unusual even for me! There is no raft, nor motorized boat. Instead, there are these large balls you can get into and float down the river. I think this may be hugely fun. Do you want to put your Avatar in one with you, have him fly above, or into his own bubble, tethered to yours? Not with a tangible tether, but with an energetic one. This could be a challenge for even the best rafter or one that knows how to ride the waves of the rapids in a river or the waves in the oceans. The vote is … Let's do it! After all, this is an adventure of a lifetime!

I will tell you how I am experiencing this, but your experience may be quite different. I notice that these balls are not exactly the plastic as I thought they were. They are alive and communicate with me and the water. If there is fear within me – for example, if I see a huge set of rapids in front of me and start to set myself for the bumpy ride, or perhaps I sense falling in and being dragged down the river gasping for air – the bubble and the water work together to calm me. They clear my inner fears, balance the adrenals and cortisol in my body. Sometimes I forget how wonderful water is at this job. The bubble and liquid also help me to stay upright if that is my choice. Then, the ride becomes smooth, gliding over the rapids.

As I adjust to this communication availability, I find myself relaxing enough to have some fun. I take a moment to lie down and let the water energy from my surroundings flow through me and help me relax. I also find myself sending a message through the water to all of you to relax and enjoy the ride. Let yourself clear the old programs around the creation of the world as you would like it to be. It be very helpful in your every day to day life.

I now see that we are going to go over a waterfall the size of Niagara Falls! It is, however, very sparkly and vibrant with the energy of the flowing downward rush where it crashes into the rocks and river below. I am so thankful that I had the fear clearing earlier!

This so fun! I am calm enough to see all that is around me. The colors, the BIRDS! I have never seen so many different types of birds. They also communicate with us. Can you hear them? Can you understand what they say? I can feel the energy of Love and Gratitude sharing the space with them. They are excited to see us as they have never encountered such a strange group of beings either.

They want to know about us. How much about you and who and what you are will you share? It's sort of like walking into a new job or giving a presentation to a different group of clients. How comfortable are you with laying yourself on the table to be examined? What part of You will you let them see? What part will you keep hidden, and why? It could mean the difference in life or death in the business world. How will you trust them to not puncture your ball if they see a part of You that doesn't resonate with their belief system or their lifestyle? Just take note of how you feel.

WOW! Hitting the bottom of that waterfall was really fun. I did get sucked down into its depths for a little while. Way down under the surface I came into contact with some new beings. I am not sure what to call them. They are like us but breathe underwater. They are beautiful, in body and soul. They seem to be very curious about me and why I'm in their world for the moment.

One decided to merge through the bubble's outer layer and come inside with me to see what it was like. The bubble didn't leak! This being could also breathe the air I was breathing. He communicated telepathically.

I learned that his Tribe helped with the water's eco system and was very excited to have all our interesting emotional energy to help their eco system move to another level of their lives. Our energy, intermingling with theirs, created waves of newness in their environment. They reached a point of needing a catalyst – which is what we are– to help them move to another level of their work and development. I am thankful for their help as they were thankful for encountering us.

I am now on the surface of the river again, moving rather fast as the beautiful plants fly past me while they reach out to graze the energy of my ball. I look around and find all of you catching up rapidly!

I see some of you still have your Avatars cuddled up in your balls while some are in their own bubble following you.

I hear flying overhead. My Dragon is above looking for the place where we'll land. We are in constant communication. I also notice you are learning to do the same with your new companions. Some of you are still having communication trouble in differentiating between a command with Love and a command out of ego. It is a challenge as one comes from a program of power based on control and the other is a power of and with Love. For many, this is an inherited program and is changeable. Of course, that is your choice.

I now see our landing zone. I wondered how we were going to gather all our fast-floating balls at one point where we can get out of them comfortably and safe. It seems to be a giant net that gives a command to the balls to gently stop here and line up at a dock that floats on or slightly above the river.

There are extremely nice, helpful people that know how to help your Avatars out of the bubbles. Once out of the bubbles they seem to dissolve and meld into the water. We are escorted to a meeting room where refreshments are available, and you can discuss your experiences with the Tribe you are now a part of. You also have individual cabins ready for you with all your items as you need them. Take your time to decompress from this long journey.

See you tomorrow!

MONTH TWO – DAY EIGHT

I hope each of you rested well and were able to integrate the revelations that came up yesterday. If not, you have now come across quite a few experiences of clearing. You can always go back and review a day that may be of help to you. I also want to note that, when I use the word HE in reference to your Avatar, it is to mean He and or She. It just seems to come out as He.

Today, we are going to do a little experiment. First, get your Avatar ready for an adventure. Is it clean and well fed? When you are ready, I would like all of you get into a circle with your Avatar on your right. Make the circle plenty big so there is no nervousness among the group. I want you to step forward, leave your Avatar, and walk to the person's Avatar that is across from you.

Greet this Avatar with Love and Respect. If you have a treat, give it to him even if it isn't suited for this type of beast. Take a little time to pet his neck, face, back, legs, and notice how you feel. Are you a little nervous? Is the Avatar a little nervous? Does he let you connect? Do you hear or feel your Avatar trying to connect with you to find out what to do with this stranger around him?

Do not get on this strange Avatar, even if he seems to be fine with it. Just make some connections with your heart. Does this beast allow you in at all? Or is it a one-person beast? There are some species in reality that mate for life. Once they find that 'soul' mate – that is it. Are you that type of person too? How does this relate to how you connect with this other person's Avatar, and how it is connecting to you?

Walk back across the circle to your Avatar. Pay close attention to the greeting you get and how you greet him. Is he the jealous sort? Are you? Does he even care, or did he become attached to the other person? What does he do when he smells the other Avatar's scent on you?

Make sure you do all that is necessary to let your Avatar know that you are totally connected! The hugs around the neck, extra treats, and soothing whispers – reconnect at the heart. Now, take a moment and examine your energetic field. Ask it to clear. You may want to brush yourself down from head to toe down the front, as much as you can across your back, from your head to across each shoulder, and down the arms and out the fingers.

Now do this to your Avatar. Cover as much of his body as you can with the intention to clear off other attachments of any type. Breathe. Take a moment to clear your head and heart. Notice how well the two of you can connect on a much clearer level. You might ask yourself if you have some clearing of this nature that needs done in the real world. Then do it.

You are probably wondering why I took you on this journey of experiment. It's about trust and how you handle yourself in these situations with friends, work associates, and companions. What you do with your Avatar in the 'cheating' roll and 'make-up' roll is related to how you may be in the normal world. How much clearing and deprogramming needs to be done around this?

My Team laughs and tells me we need to take another adventure into the High Country. Mount up. Let's check to see if everyone can get on their Avatar as there was a lot of shifting in everyone's vibrations after that experiment.

Remember, it is about the Heart connection and Trust. Create that telepathy communication again. Okay, now we can take off.

We are going to the right. Set the intention with your Avatar to follow mine even if we get out of sight. That way, I won't be concerned if we run into some crazy situation. We are going up into the cliffs near the top of the Portal's ... what may be called a ceiling.

The cliffs appear to be green from here, but as I get closer I find that only part of them is green. There is such a mixture of yellow blossoms and blue leaves, the energy is similar to green.

We are nearly to the landing site. Find a flat place with plenty of room. Allow your Avatar to roam free with a command that, when you call, he will come immediately.

The first thing is to find those yellow flowers and pick a handful. Bring them back to the camp I am creating. I'm building a fire and creating two large pans. One has water, the other is just getting hot. Once you have your large handful of only the yellow flowers, no stems or leaves, bring them to me.

I ask each one of you, "Do you want to consume them crunchy or as a tea?" Drop them either into the hot pan or the boiling water. I will cook them all at the same time. Both actually smell really good, but you can only have it one way. To consume both would be too much for anyone.

After you take your bowl of crunchy or tea-infused flowers, hold it in your hands a moment. Raise it to your belly and your heart. Tell it to be exactly what you need for the moment. Ask it to be the frequency that will assist you in being exactly who you are. I will give you a few minutes to consume it. Once you are finished, find a quiet place to lie down. Notice how you feel. You may fall asleep for a few minutes or go into a deep meditative state. Do you dream or just melt into a nice nap?

As you wake up, take out the pad and pencil in your pack and write down the message you received. If you didn't receive one this moment, it may come to you as we go about the journey back to the main camp. Take a little time to walk around and explore the area. You may do this alone or with a partner. Notice if you see the plants in the same way as you did an hour ago. Is the sky a different color, or does it just seem more vibrant? Do the clouds stand out to you more than they did? Just notice what is different and how you feel about it.

We are now ready to head back to the base camp. Call your Avatar to you. If he doesn't come immediately, go into your heart and feel him. Find his heart, and place a call to him from there. You may discover that he looks and feels a little more vibrant now too. He may also notice a difference in you, so take a moment to reconnect. This is a way of respecting each other as you move through this journey together. Only get back on when you are both ready.

The command has already been given to follow me back to the camp. You won't get lost. As we arrive, remember to take care of the partner first, then yourself. If you need debriefing, there are people to talk to. Sometimes, when you are at the point of being so tired mentally and physically that you can hardly move, I realize it is hard to take care of a partner.

Your cabin is already set for when you get there. Food, drink, bath ... What you need is what you get. When you get a moment, look at the message you wrote down. Take some time to think about it.

See you tomorrow!

MONTH TWO – DAY NINE

I realize that I have been pushing you pretty hard with clearings and learning the skills it takes to not just gain abundance but to keep and take care of it once in your possession. Also, how to work with your Loved ones to make the best of your relationships – be it with a partner, a family member, a friend, and yourself.

Today, we are going to be making a deeper journey into the Portal. We have only a few more days together and a lot of territory to cover. Let's start by leading your Avatar down this secret path I found while you slept. It is true, I don't sleep much. There is just too much to explore and learn.

You may lead your Avatar with a physical tether or an energetic one, so they will be there when you need them. They probably won't walk this path with you, but just be nearby. Yes, we could fly over this path much faster, but, for some reason, the One directing this journey tells me that we will walk for a while. Follow me.

We are looking over the top rim of a canyon. As we walk around the ledge, I find the trail to lead us down. Looking over the edge a trail cannot be seen, but it is here! Follow me as we start the descent.

This is not just a little walk on a park trail – it is incredibly narrow and steep. I am checking, and we don't need to tie off anywhere. We will be fine.

A few levels down, I find myself going through a bubble type of veil. It is as if it's raining bubbles of all sizes. It is a Bubble Waterfall! They glisten as the sun shines on them. There are so many, and I can't tell where they come from. Now I see they're being shot out of a giant bubble blower on a ledge a little bit above us. There is a mist around them just like a regular waterfall. There must be a reason for this besides just being bubbles.

As I touch one it doesn't exactly pop to leave a slimy mess on my finger, it is more of a merging into my body. As I walk into the bubble waterfall, I feel them merge into areas of my body where I have old traumatic injuries. Each one gives me a feeling of being lighter, as if the burden of the trauma is being removed. This feels nice and gentle, and the result is so easy. Now it's your turn. I will wait on the trail on the other side. Take your time, because this is your opportunity to get some help with your physical body as well.

I see that part of the trail has washed out. We are going to have to help each other through this area. Now is the time to tie off to one another. I will go ahead and see where I can tie the other end of the rope. I am not much of a mountain climber with this type of equipment, so we will learn about it together.

Okay, I got the other end of the rope tied to two very large trees. Now. as we walk across this area of the trail, there are sections where you must jump or there's a very steep journey down if you miss. Each of you must be aware of what the person in front of and behind you is doing. If someone falls you must be prepared to hold tight to the mountain so you don't get pulled on down with them.

Let out a call to everyone else to hold up as you help that person climb back up, onto the trail. You will be fine. I know how capable you are. I will also sprinkle some magic onto this rope and your feet. This will help you hold onto the trail as well as your teammates.

I am so proud of you! You only had a few small slipping moments. No big disasters. You are getting so good at adventures! That magical rope is amazing I will cut it in-between each of you now so you all have a piece of it to keep. It will be helpful to you in your next move down the trail.

I scouted up ahead and discovered a big problem. I am sure that we can come up with a solution. We have reached a point where, if we turn back to climb out, it would take about two days, plus, we'd have to overcome the obstacles again. Not to scare you, but up ahead the trail has been removed as it slid down the mountain during the latest storm. The rest of it isn't visible at all. This has created a huge challenge for you.

I can only see one solution. As you come to the ledge where the trail is gone I want you to call to your Avatar, then jump off the ledge where your Avatar will come up under you to catch you. I know that sounds extremely dangerous, and it is. I won't lie to you, it makes my stomach quiver a bit. I also know that you have overcome so many obstacles within your fear zone that you can also do this one. I have a little bit of the magic dust left to sprinkle on you to help connect with your Avatar.

Who wants to go first? Since there are no volunteers, I pick you! I will help you if its' needed. I will start by sprinkling some of the magic dust on your heart. Now, go into your heart where you can feel the connection to your Avatar. Once the connection is made, tell him – show him the situation in your mind. Show him how the trail is gone, you need to jump, and he has to be right under you, so you can land on his back or in his talons. I feel you are now ready for this. No time to hesitate.

Ready ... Set ... Go! I knew you could do it! This is great! You are so brave! Look at all the fear you have released! Just fly around the ravine for a while as I help the others get onto their Avatars, then I will get onto my amazing Purple Dragon. We have so much Love in our hearts for each other that I know that he won't let me down.

I watched all of you being so patient by holding focused energy for each person in the group as they made the jump out into nothing and trusted their Avatars would be there to catch them.

My heart swelled with so much Love and Gratitude for all of you. It's not easy to come into an adventure with people you don't know. You are amazing!

We will head back to a new camp not too far down the Portal from here. It was being set up for us during our hike. Even though you may be tired, take the time needed to care for your Avatar first.

You will have a new cabin with exactly what you need tonight. You will also find a special drink. You might call it a Love Potion for only your needs. Take notes for yourself to review later.

See you tomorrow!

MONTH TWO – DAY TEN

I hope you recovered from yesterday's harrowing experience. Wow! So much to process. You were so brave to jump off a ledge into nothingness and trust your communication skills so your Avatar was there for you. Plus, the activations. Lots to recalibrate within your systems.

We are near the end of this Portal. I can see a different glow from what we saw a few days ago. And there is a new sparkle in the air. I feel it calling to us, can you?

The Avatars are restless. They know there is a change coming. You have worked so hard to create the bond. Question is, can your Avatar be with you as you go back to the real world, or will it be left in the Divine Portal? Of course, you can take your Avatar with you and bring it back for next month's ride. Why not have both as an option. This doesn't have to be decided right now. There is still fun to be had on this journey, and it looks like a storm is brewing over at the other end of the Portal. We better get moving.

I see you got the telepathic memo! We are now in the sky, bright and early, with backpacks filled with what we may need later. Let's try the left side of this swirling, beautiful vortex of energy. The air feels calmer and easier to just be in on that side.

Oh, my, we can glide the air waves! Feel the waves lift us up into the pink layer without any effort? Now it pulls us into the dark yellow layer. I didn't expect it to feel this nice. The colors contain individual vibrations and wavelengths as we navigate the changes. It's like moving through a rainbow. Not the bow part – more the straight line of powerful waves. Oh, I spoke too soon. Some are spinning. I'm glad I don't get nauseated under these conditions.

This is more fun than an amusement park! Each color we slide into creates a different feeling, a different vibrational clearing deep within our entire body, soul, spirit, and emotional aspect. It can be relaxing and invigorating all at the same time.

I see the end of it. Strange how it just stops like an invisible wall that holds it within its boundary. However, I can go right through. I feel sparkly clean, like taking my vehicle to a car wash, and, as I pull out where the dryers blow so hard, they suddenly stop. Wow! What fun!

Ready for the next step in our journey? I feel like the left-wall of the Portal still calls us. Let's see what it's all about. I see cliff walls of all different colors; Deep chocolate brown, licorice black, cherry red, grape purple, sunshine yellow, and orangey orange. Oh, and emerald green. It's like there are signs on them telling me their names.

What are we supposed to do over here? I hear from my Teams ... just taste them. Really? I thought they were dirt, like Earth cliffs are dirt or rock. As I fly by, I'm not sure about landing, I suddenly have a long tasting spoon in my hand. I reach out with it to taste the dark brown color. Wow! It does taste like the best chocolate ever created. Not too sugary or too bitter.

I think I'll try the cherry red. It seems super sweet without a hint of sugar. Like dark red cherries. I feel my intestines wake up and feel happy. They react to the true flavors, or the product, or the enzymatic reaction of their healing powers. I also find them to be very satisfying.

Did you take a moment to taste them? I wonder what emerald green is all about. I reach out my long-handled spoon expecting a lime flavor of some sort, but no. A real emerald is placed in the spoon. I am told to put it in my pack for a later time.

As we go beyond the vortex-like turning point of this area, it feels like a very sacred place. Let's land and investigate it further. I see a cabin where we can take a break. Fresh water from a spring flows for us to drink from and fill our water containers. Its smoothness is an indicator to me that it has been blessed with Love and Gratitude. There is a pool where we can soak in this healing water. I saw swimsuits in the cabin. It will only take a moment to change. I will meet you in the pool.

This is amazing. It feels like I'm being carried and supported in so much Love. The vibration of Love within these waters is being infused within the Body, Mind, Spirit, and Soul on a level I never thought possible. As I look at you, I can see the same thing happening.

Remember to breathe. As you inhale, your cells take in the frequency of Love. I notice how you're starting to resonate with the water, becoming one with it. You're becoming more fluid. I can hardly believe my eyes. You are so sparkly, yet fluid. I too am doing the same. I notice my aches and pains from yesterday's journey are gone. My worries are gone as well. I am one with the moment. I think I could stay here forever!

Oh, I hear my Dragon calling, reminding me we still need to make it to the new camp, and it's getting late. Okay, okay, I will climb out of the pool with the knowledge of this feeling and go back to it at a moment of thought. When I get back to reality I can also take myself back to this moment with just a thought. This is a great tool to use as I head back to the world of physical working and my Body, Mind, Spirit, and Soul need a boost of Love.

I see you're feeling better, too. As we glide over the tops of the trees, I can sense they know we will soon be leaving this Portal, but not yet! I see our camp from here. Race you to it!

See you tomorrow for our last ride in the Portal!

MONTH TWO – DAY ELEVEN

Today is difficult. I'm sad it's my last day with you in this Divine Portal of Love and Abundance. I see so many changes within you that have happened since we began just a few short days ago. I am also excited we get to have this one last day as we finish up our activations for this Portal.

Before we take off for our adventures make certain you have all the things you want to take. Any bubbles with hidden treasures inside? How about special stones, plants, or other items you collected along the way? A quick reminder – you have these activations at your service. You may go back and redo any of them as many times as you feel like you need to. Of course, the activations will continue working when you're ready to move to another level.

The one thing I wonder about is … Will you take your Avatar with you? Or, will you leave it in the Divine Portals ready for another adventure or when you re-read any of the daily activation adventures? Either way, just spend a little special time with your Avatar as the opportunity presents itself. Well, time's a wastin'!

Today, we will head straight down the middle of the Divine Portal. It looks like storms are raging on the sides, and we don't need to be a part of that intensity. I nearly said insanity.

Sometimes that type of energy feels like insanity to me. A few gentle showers are one thing, but this looks to be much more intense. There is still much to explore in the center of this spinning, narrowing vortex. I ask the Team that works with me what the plan is for today.

I just saw us bounce down the center. The bounces were quite large as if there was no gravity. Let's see what it feels like. WOW! This is fun. Even my Dragon likes the feel of it and is laughing only the way one can laugh.

Hang on; this experience is a little surprising at moments. There is no controlling the direction of the bouncing. I keep hearing a song from some cartoony thing I saw on Facebook about bounding! It feels like being in a program of clearing and realigning from much of the shifting we have completed while in this Portal. Also, it's to remind us not to go back to the old ways once we complete this journey.

Yes, it's possible to draw your old self back to you and undo or erase all that you have shifted out of. So, make sure you notice the difference and select new choices if opportunities present themselves. Just for now, stay in this moment and enjoy the enormous bounces along the Portal's center. I see where we'll end up. Just a few more miles of his fun. Take the time to feel the energy of the amazing plants which grow here. You will not see anything like them anywhere else.

As we come to the Center of all Centers there is calmness within as excitement rushes through us. We have found a way to be centered amid chaos. There is a conference room available, and I have found a tool box prepared ahead of time. Take a moment to refresh yourself. Fill your water bottle with this Heart-blessed liquid, and then join me. It's okay to bring your Avatar in with you as all this pertains to You as a whole.

As you take your seat, I find myself on stage watching the room fill with several groups that have been traveling this Portal. I'm told this is the exit debriefing room. I only know what we have experienced together, but not necessarily the adventures of other groups.

I conduct the debriefing as I am told. First, my Dragon gives a huge roar and breathes a cool, fiery flame overhead. It opens a doorway in the ceiling where I can access the information tool needed to use with you and the rest of the group. As I reach up into this doorway I am given a handful of various coded symbols and told to spread them out into the area above your heads. Next, I take out my amazing Dragon Wand and notice how the symbols start spinning and shining. They make a high-pitched tone but don't hurt our ears. They are of a frequency pleasant to the ear and brain.

As I wave my wand, the symbols start moving over to each person and their Avatar. Once they reach a certain tone and speed of spin, the symbols get bigger and bigger and surround each pair. Then, the energy merges into each person, providing you with the last set of activations needed to exit this Beautiful, Divine Portal of Love and Money. To assimilate this frequency, some of you may fall into a deep meditative state while others may not get the fullness of the activation until bedtime.

The meeting is over. You get a little time to visit with some of the others to get a feel of how their experience has been here, or it may just be a way of prolonging the departure. You may also take a little walk with your Avatar outside and converse on if they are going with you, staying here for another person, or going to the Portal Sanctuary for Avatars where it is available for you at a later journey.

It's time to either mount up or get on the transportation device you originally arrived on. The Portal is moving and spinning faster and faster as the end prepares to close. I have loved the time I had being with you these past 11 days. We will be connected for a very long time through the memories of mind and heart. I wish you a great journey on your way back to your place on Earth.

I have another room to enter before I leave where I will be given the Sacred key to the next Portal!

See you next month!

See you soon with Truth, Love, and Gratitude

Pat, The Cosmic Cowgirl

Journal Your Love and Gratitude Levels

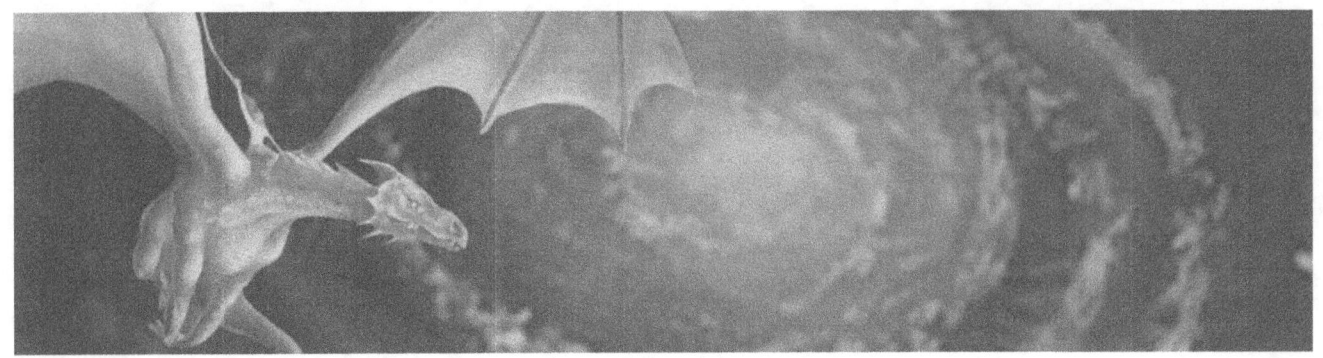

CHAPTER THREE: LEPRECHAUNS & AND POTS OF GOLD

MONTH THREE – DAY ONE

Oh, my! This month is so full of various excitement that I have gotten glimpses of this Portal for several days. The Irish in me must be breaking through a bit. There have been glimmers of the wee folk for several days just waiting to take us on this journey.

To begin with, we have been presented with a huge four-leaf clover we can all fit on to ride into this Portal. It's like a giant magic carpet as it carries all of us with such ease. As we fly over the mountains and valleys a multitude of green shades vibrate at a level of intensity you can't help but notice. They reach out to welcome us into this land of Magic. The excitement penetrates through every pore of my skin.

We land within the entrance of this Magical Portal. Everything sparkles! We have plenty of help as we step from our magical flying device. As we enter this Kingdom I am told we will be given a device that looks like a beautiful flower. They are all the same color – sort of a golden white. Inside its center are something like earbuds to fit only your ears.

They are translating devices. It's sometimes difficult to understand various accents languages, and certain meanings of theirs. I see these devices can either fit into your pocket or be stuck on your shoulder with its roots wrapping into your clothing to hold them in place. They also untangle themselves for transfer when you need to change clothes or put on a jacket.

Please take care of this device, as it is a living being in your care for this journey. Make sure you take it with you every day, even if you don't need it or think you'll need it. It's checked out to you, and you will be asked for it on the last day.

Now, pick the one you want. There are variations of color within this one shade, but they are of the same plant orientation due to their function.

You are also given a treat. Take a very small nibble of it. Remember, I said small, because we'll need to become smaller to function within this Portal. We don't want to step on any of the Wee Peoples, and this Portal changes sizes and shapes as we enter various rooms. I think we are going deep into the Earth where the Fairy peoples and the Elemental Kingdom reside.

Don't eat this treat yet! Put it into your pack for now.

I am given instructions as to the orientation of the rules here. To start with, always be cautious of where you step, and stay on the path unless otherwise instructed. Also, if something comes whizzing past your ear, please don't swat it away. It's probably one of the residents of this Portal, and each living being within this environment is important to the workings that go on here. It's a very delicate environment. We will be able to see the inhabitants more clearly as our vibrations adjust between us and the Portal inhabitants.

We are being directed to a room. Not an indoor room, rather, a place where we're surrounded by trees in a circular pattern that gives us some privacy. It is so vibrant within this circle. Love and Gratitude are shared with us being here. We are given food and water and a chance to get to know each other before we begin our amazing Portal trek.

Are you ready? I see everyone has been issued a pick and a rope. Some have been given shovels. I heard one of you ask if there are beings that can help carry much of this equipment, like a llama or burro. I've been told not yet – everyone must carry their own.

That's okay, as these tools aren't very heavy, and if you speak to them, they can shrink down to a size which fits into your pack. This frees your hands for other needs.

Put in your translating ear buds and the device on your shoulder. Now we are ready to head down the narrow winding path. Use your discernment as to what you believe. I know the Wee Ones are very good at spinning the tales somewhat. They love a bit of trickery. I'm sure they have great information as we begin, but be careful of turning left when you know in your gut you need to turn right. Use that sort of discernment for now.

I am really enjoying the various foliage. The colors and species are much more than I could have ever imagined. I hoped to see lots of Foxglove. Their flowers look like they could be Fairy Hats. There are so many more plants with flowers that seem to have a type of living quality I've never seen before. They don't seem to stay planted in one place. They move around as if they aren't plants at all. Must be why we're told to stay on the path.

The trail ends with nowhere to go. It's too narrow to even turn around. What do you hear? I'm hearing we need to take out the treat we were told to put into our packs and nibble on just a corner of it. Oh, this is a very strange feeling. I shrunk! So, did you, along with our clothes and equipment! Wow! And I thought I was short before.

I see a different path we are to follow, and it goes into a cave. Our journey into the Earth has really begun! Time to take out our picks and shovels. Let's get to work and see if we can find a way through.

Wow! The stones in this cave are vibrationally powerful. Just standing here is a clearing treat. I get the impression we're not to take any of these with us right now. Just pick away an opening, and if precious stones are in the way, please set them aside to make an outer lining for a new trail. What? You didn't know you had to work on this journey? The Information Center told me we need to do this a little once in a while.

I can now see light breaking through. A few more stones to shift so we can easily get through again if needed. The cave has opened into a beautiful valley. It seems we're on a ledge with a steep trail going down the hill. Pull out your ropes and tie off to each other. We don't want to lose anyone with a misstep.

I'm so impressed with how good at knot tying each of you are and how you care for one another. For all of you to work together this way isn't common for those who don't know each other. However, some of you are not here for the first time, and that helps a lot.

It's very steep in some areas, so you will need to help each other up and over a few of the boulders. Remember, you are still in a shrunken state. I have not yet heard how we are going to get back to our normal size, have you?

I see a camp set up for us near a lake at the bottom of this mountain. We can make it there by nightfall. As we get into the area closer to camp, I'm told in my ear buds to turn right. We will go this direction and see what we find. There is a little stream ahead where it'll be good to soak our feet and wash off some of this cave dust.

The sun is starting to set, so we must hurry. Leave your clothing on as you go into the water. I feel it's our key to getting back to a better size for our environment in this valley. The water isn't the color we're familiar with on our normal mountain hikes. This is a stream which seems to constantly change for some reason. I also notice it's a different color and scent for each of us. So very individual!

I will test it out by putting my foot in. Oh, I can't just do that. I am getting pulled in completely – all the way under! Ah, this is so soothing, and I can feel myself growing. Not all the way back to my normal size. Yet better for the size of the plants around me. How does it feel for you?

Now, as we walk out of this stream, we are sparkly/shiny. Either there is gold, mica, or Fools' Gold in that water! Or maybe some other sparkly mineral native to only here. I can feel it soak into my skin, soothing and healing my tired body. At this point I don't care if it is gold or not, it's what I need at this moment.

I hear the dinner bell. We're being called to the camp before darkness sets in. There has been a huge feast prepared for us! I also see dome-shaped tents for each of us with skylights, so we can look above as we take our time to prepare for sleep. I wonder what their sky looks like?

See you tomorrow!

MONTH THREE – DAY TWO

Welcome to a new, exciting day! How much sleep did you get? I, for one, was so enthralled with the nighttime activity I saw through my tent's skylight that I had a hard time getting my brain to shut off so I could sleep. Honestly, I didn't see many stars, but I did view a lot of Portal life we didn't see during the day. I wondered what lived here besides the plants. Now I know about some of it.

Today, I would like each of us to put on our translation devices and take a few hours to wander through the area. Find a trail and just investigate. Are there really Fairies? Or Leprechauns? Is there really a pot of gold at the end of a rainbow in this land? Watch the sky for rainbows. If you find one, follow it and see if you find the pot of gold! Of course, use your translation/communication device to call us to come see, but only if you want to find the answer to this riddle.

Now that we've spent some time doing our own investigations, gather a few things you may need in your pack as we will be hiking for a short time. Bring a tablet and pencil – not sure why yet. I'm never sure why I'm told to tell you certain things until they happen. Oh, also don't forget the shrinking treat. Careful not to nibble on or lick your fingers after handling it.

Okay, I'm tired of waiting around for that rainbow to appear. Let's go find one. I was shown where the stables are. I would much rather ride than walk through these trails.

I see animals which are not the normal horses I thought we were going to get. We are in a Fairy Land Portal. So, these are Horse-Flies! Yes, they look like a cross between a horse and a common horsefly, like those I've swatted where I am from in Colorado. They are also color-shifting. Cool!

I see the one I want. Take time to pick the exact one which fits your personality. Have the trainer give you a few tips on riding and working with these new lovely beings. Mine told me to just lick a corner of my treat to help me be a size my Horse-Fly can handle for the ride. It wears off about dark, so to be sure to be back here by then.

This is wonderful! I'm up high enough to see many new things and, yes, I do see a rainbow a short distance away. Let's go see what a rainbow in this land is made of. As we get closer, it is even more sparkly that I thought. I'm actually close enough to touch it. It has a mass and density connected to its coloring system, so it makes a tone for each color and its varying shades. My ride doesn't seem to like being too close to it, and it's overreacting. Yep, I am now sliding down one side of it. Hopefully, my ride is waiting at the bottom of wherever this ends.

This really is quite fun. Each color interacts with me and shifts my clarity of what I thought was and wasn't real. It's like the rainbow changes color as I touch it according to what it is that I need. It gives me experience of understanding how color and money are related. This is something I really hadn't thought about before. Since it showed up, it must be important to pay attention to. I will just breathe and allow this to happen.

I now reached the point where I can see the bottom of this rainbow. There's definition at the bottom. It looks as if it continues into the ground. There's a little man sitting on top of a pot of gold. He's so cute with his golden pipe as he waits for me to get there. He really does look a lot like the pictures I have seen of storybook Leprechauns!

I land on my rear, right in front of him, and am so stunned about him being real. I am still reeling from the experience of shifting so much of the programs I was carrying while riding the rainbow slide I didn't know what to do.

He puts his hand on his hip and tells me I'm getting closer to being able to handle the energy of the pot of gold. Then, with a quick blink of an eye, he disappears along with all that gold. It took me a while to gather myself up after being plopped on the ground and seeing everything disappear right before my eyes, including with a little man on top of it. And the recalibration from the Rainbow Ride … I think I need to take a few notes about all of this tonight as I sit in my quiet tent.

I whistle for my Horse-Fly, and he actually comes to me! I am ready to head back to our base camp before I grow too much to ride this sweet creature.

Take your time and I will meet with you later.

See you tomorrow!

MONTH THREE – DAY THREE

Good Day! Of course, it is! We are in the Divine Portal of Manifestation where we get to learn the best of the Magicalness of everything within. The Fairies, the Elementals, the plants, the rocks… Everything here is a part of our learning experience. They are here to teach us, and we are here to learn and experience the manifestation abilities firsthand.

I hope you are well rested and recalibrated from the experience presented to you yesterday! I finally slept and awoke with a new outlook at my learning down here. As you can see, I am dressed in a multitude of colors like the rainbow and pot of gold showed me to shift my programming around. Not to say your programming is anything like mine, but WOW! You probably won't find me wearing khaki again for a while. I learned it doesn't suit my vibrations, even if it is practical for hiking.

I have been directed to the north side of this Portal today. Have you noticed how the spin of this place makes it sort of hard to truly know what is north? I think it's that way! I perform a self-check to see if I forgot something important since these new colors are so much fun. I could easily rely on them to be all I need. Oh, yes, I must remember the translation device. It's now anchored in place and blends in very well.

This is a great direction to walk. The other Portals made space for my Dragon Avatar. I think I can try giving him a little of the shrinking treat to get it to be with me.

Wow! Just the thought of my wanting and needing my Avatar with me is all it took. It had the ability to shrink itself to fit into this world! I'm certain if you want an Avatar of your own, all you have to do is ask with your heart.

I am so excited to see how good all of you are at this. Each of you picked different beings for your Avatars that have some amazing abilities. This is so wonderful. Now we can fly through this Portal much easier and faster. I wondered if we would make it to the other side at the rate we moved.

It's time to take our first journey in this Portal with our wonderful Avatars. They feel like they can be of so much help in finding our Manifesting Abundance capabilities. After all, you just manifested them being here! We can travel to the north end of this Portal with ease.

As we fly in this direction it gets colder and the wind gets stronger. I can see some caves a bit further where we can take a break. There is some snow on the ground, but I think we'll be fine inside a cave as the storm blows over.

As we land and go into the cave, there is already a campfire going to warm us up with a huge pile of wood ready to keep it going. I also notice a pot of warm broth ready for us and a lot of food for our Avatars. Since I am one of those who question things -- which one in our group manifested this? You are really powerful! Thinking north means cold and snow. Not wanting to freeze or starve we were given a cave with a fire and food. You are very good at this. Notice how the thought of what north means created all of this!

I notice a shelf of things to add to the broth. They look to be food-worthy and very magical for manifesting. Take a moment to go inside yourself and notice what it is you may need to shift to help your manifesting ability. Pick one of the things on the shelf and drop it into the pot of broth. As each of us does this, how does it make you feel? Can you feel the entire room shift with an added item? I will give it a big stir with the intention of activation for each of us individually, not collectively, as we each have our own needs and don't need to go into a quantum entanglement with each other when it comes to the manifesting abundance.

It looks like it's time to for us to dip some of this tasty refreshment into our own cups. As you sip, how do you feel? Relaxed, energized, tingly, on fire, cold, or is some other form of alchemy going on inside of you? This is the cave of Abundance Manifestation. You will be changed forever! To complete the reaction, you may want to rest for a little bit for some recalibration time. It feels like we all need a little soul nap.

I feel so much better after that. My Avatar is ready to go, and the sun is shining again. The snow has melted, and the wind has stopped. It's incredibly wonderful to smell the fresh air and know the weather can change with just a thought.

I step outside of the cave and see some berries of various colors growing on the bushes nearby. We need to pick a few and put them into our packs to eat later as a late-night snack. You will know which ones you need by how they call to you or maybe how you see their sparkle. You'll know which ones are needed, not wanted. I hear you should not even lick its sticky juice off your fingers. Wait until you are alone in your tent as it is your own to experience alone. Hmmm, I wonder what that means?

Let's mount up and head back to camp before nightfall. I see new stables were built for our Avatars while we were gone. Of course, they were! It's as if this Universe of the Divine Portal of Manifestation meets our needs before we even speak them.

I have been told it can be this way on Earth, too. We just have to create it to be that way. Perhaps the berries we eat tonight are a part of helping us create that ability. I am excited to get to my tent to try them. I hope they taste good.

See you tomorrow!

MONTH THREE – DAY FOUR

Good to see you again! How was your experience with those berries? I must say that I was quite surprised! Each one was a different flavor, even though they came from the same plant. Plus, with each new flavor came the vision of a new type of Magical Being dancing in my tent! I am not sure of what to call most of them, except that they were full of Love and Happiness to share their time with me. I feel like we created a new friendship that I can call on at any time with just a thought of asking for them, which I intend to do in the future as they have some amazing stories to share.

I wonder what waits for us on today's Divine Journey! Yes, we are all here, and I see that you have already retrieved your Avatar. You must have enjoyed being able to cover greater distances easier too. Plus, it is so much fun to fly with them!

South it is! My Dragon is also ready for a new adventure. He actually has flying goggles on. I don't believe I have ever seen those on him before. I wonder what he knows that I don't. Maybe they are just fun to wear.

Let's get moving ... So much to explore in this place. We are heading south – at least I think it's south. We will be moving to a higher altitude than we did yesterday. The air is so much clearer here, and we can see better. As I look down over my Dragon's shoulder, I see other flying beings. From what I can gather, our flying is like being in a road system. Our layer goes in one direction and another goes the other way. I didn't expect to see so much air traffic. I hear that it (don't know what 'it' is at this moment), is due to the energy being spread throughout the Portal. I converse with the Beings and am assured that we are not interfering in their life by us being here. I hear WE are the entertainment and the Portal is being shifted into another level of movement due to us being the catalyst.

We are at an altitude – or level – away from the center of the Portal where we have covered a lot of distance incredibly fast. This area seems to be shaped like a whirling tunnel or like the center of a tornado, but in the ground. I am reminded that this Portal is connected to Pot of Gold energy, Manifestation, and Spring! We are most certainly moving like we are within a spring, but I think it is the wrong kind.

My mind is feeling a little strange with this – which is a great reminder that we receive what we think about. So, to manifest abundance, we may want to decide what type of abundance we want. Is it Love, Peace, Perfect Health, or Money as in that Pot of Gold? Actually,

I just realized what one of the blocks is about receiving the Pot of Gold! How do you spend or use a Pot of Gold? It won't work at gas station pumps or credit card sliders at the grocery store. What does one do with a Pot of Gold? I think if I walked into a bank with one, a lot of chaos and suspicion would occur. Police would arrive with a lot of questions. WOW! That is a huge block.

What if the Pot of Gold is just a metaphor for a never-ending supply of funds in your bank account? By stating it that way, I notice a definite change in breathing patterns. That is so much easier to accept. So, are we looking for a Leprechaun that has cash or a debit card in his hand at the end of the rainbow?

Just by thinking about this brought a rainbow into the horizon. Let's see what this one is made of and if there is a debit card-holding Leprechaun sitting under it somewhere. Oh, my Dragon loves this rainbow. He so much easier to be on than that Horse-Fly, even though the Horse-Fly was a magnificent experience for me.

Notice how much different this rainbow feels. Is it because it is from the south, or maybe because we have been doing some shifting the past few days with these fun experiences? I feel a better affinity to it. I'm not sure how to describe it exactly. Maybe it has more of a silky smoothness to its vibration. Actually, that doesn't even come close to how nice it feels. It isn't too rough to be around. The air currents are also calmer.

Oh, but it is sucking my Dragon and me into its morphic field. I tell myself and my Dragon to just relax into the flow, don't fight it – it's quite nice. I feel us floating along through all the sparkly, shiny, pearlescent … I can't even describe the colors. But I do feel them as they seem to flow into each cell of my body, removing bits of debris as they fill each one with exactly what it needs. Then, a new color moves into that cell, blending with the last one and creating an electrifying effect. I am staying alert as I watch and feel all of this happen to and around me, including my Dragon.

We are nearing the bottom where I can see the ground and some Leprechaun footprints. I guess I just missed him. Maybe next time. Oh, he does have a sense of humor though. He left a treasure chest with coins that are golden foil-covered chocolate treat with a note.

DO NOT EAT YET. OPEN AND EAT IN YOUR TENT

I guess it is time to go back to the base camp. Sweet Dreams.

See you tomorrow!

MONTH THREE – DAY FIVE

Are you ready for a fantastic day? We will be moving deeper into this Divine Portal of Manifestation today. The camp staff will move all our belongings to the next place where we will stay the night. If there is anything you think you may need right now, get it and don't forget the translation plant. Have you learned how to feed or maintain it properly? You might want to ask it if it needs anything occasionally, as everything in here is alive.

Now that we are gathered in this large open space, take a good look at each other and yourself. Remember what you and this group looked like a few days ago? Notice the changes! WOW! You look so much more aware! Your eyes are so alive with wonderment, ready to enjoy the challenges of the day. This is just so exciting to see, and we are not quite to the halfway point yet. Take a look at your Avatar! Did you ever think you could work with a beast of this caliber? Manifestation levels are increasing dramatically within you!

Just a little heads up, in case we get separated up there. We are going quite high, and then the plan is to head straight down the middle most of the way, unless we see something we must explore. Then, who knows what will happen! Got your gear? Mount up!

You are such a seasoned rider already! It's so fun that we can travel like this. We are going right up near the top to catch the easier air currents. You were supplied this morning with a high-powered telescope that is attached to your riding gear. If you notice something incredible for us to explore, let me know. The device on your shoulder has a way to send as well as receive information. Just think it and it will be communicated to me. Telepathy is a part of the network here.

Have you noticed how this place smells? I noticed that each level of altitude we climb through has a different scent that activates a distinct part of the brain. Sort of like a street name has a certain vibration. None of them are offensive to me as some strange smells are, I would like to explore some of these later. I am finding it wonderful to be in an environment that is openly utilizing and enhancing our abilities. If you aren't intuitive on some level, you may get hurt in this arena. Of course, you are intuitive, otherwise you would have never signed up for this journey to work with me.

There is a lot of information stored in the fabric of this place. Just notice what is around you as we go zipping down the center of it. Oh, I hear ... SLOW DOWN! OK. Who said that? What is going on? It is one of ours pointing to a distant, now not-so-distant, funny, strange, different-looking clump of trees. We're surrounded. Maybe we can create a distraction of sorts? I have no idea why just yet. I just got the okay for us to land over in that area.

Take a group with you to that clearing up ahead and help them rest their Avatars, and if I am hearing correctly, you get a little more time to take a break as there is a team arriving right now to make sure it is secure for you. My thoughts are, *secure from what?* I will see what I can find out. You are welcome to come with me if you want.

As I walk closer to the clump of trees, I hear someone or something crying as if they are lost or hurt. We get close enough to see the situation, and it is a baby Dragon that has fallen into an area it can't get out of. Its mother is very upset. The people that live here are too small to help. Well, we arrived just in time, didn't we?

We are used to working with larger beasts. Talk to your Avatar about what you can do to help. I have my Dragon translate for me to this Dragon. The mother is giving us permission to step into the area, carefully, so that she can sense us. If you don't feel safe doing this, that is okay. Just stand back and watch.

She is purifying those who are here and urging them to help with a blue flame. I am surprised how this feels. It is a little cool, yet I can feel it burning out the debris of fear and panic at my core level. Is it affecting you the same way? I feel like I can stand taller and am stronger. I can communicate telepathically easier as well.

We are now ready to work as a team with each other and our Avatars. I can see that this little Dragon has gotten himself into an area where he is covered with rocks and trees. We are quite capable of removing these so that its Mother can move the baby out of the area.

This requires you being on your Avatar, guiding it to work with the other Avatars, using its feet with talons, or its beak to drag what it can grab to lift the trees one by one. For some of you, get out a rope and wrap it around the rocks to pull them out of the way. Some of you seem to have mastered the art of levitation! I am impressed beyond what my heart can contain. Ready, let's get this baby out of there!

Great Job! Well Done! Thank you so much for being able to save this baby! Mother Dragon wants to thank us. We need to move in front of her with our Avatars, for they are also to receive this gift of thanks. She gives us a gift of renewal with her fiery breath. It doesn't burn. Instead, its red-orange flames are sort of like the birth of a Phoenix from what I can see.

Don't be afraid, just let the flames move through every aspect of you and let yourself receive what you need from it – the same for your Avatar. We have just received the most valuable gift possible from this amazing being. Take your time to let yourself recalibrate to the new You. We can now get back on our Newly-Blessed Avatars. Notice the level of communication between the two of you. It is as if we are now aligned on a whole new level.

It's getting late, and we need to return to the campsite before dark. I just saw a way to do this quickly and easily. Focus your intention on the campsite's vibrations and all your belongings. It is a great way to find where the site is. Now with your intention, let us be there ... Now! We did it! We did a time warp to the camp.

Take exceptionally good care of yourself tonight and enjoy the new You!

See you tomorrow!

MONTH THREE – DAY SIX

Welcome to this new day! How did you feel after the amazing Thanks given by the very appreciative Mother Dragon? That was a whole new type of healing and clearing for most of us.

I understand if you are still doing some recalibrating today. Be gentle with yourself. Take it slow and easy. Let yourself continue to clear and recalibrate to the new You. If you are experiencing some emotional release, don't shut it back inside of you. Let yourself complete the clearing. It is all part of finding the You that will help bring this Planet into the reality of what it needs to be. Remember, it isn't what you Do to help the Earth with its changes as much as it is the vibrations and resonations with what needs to be and where we are going. The Divine Portals are just a way to help each of us with our vibrational resonance.

Let's start out today with a little hike just to get our heads clear and ready for a new adventure. The day before seems to still be running through your energy fields. Yes, it is going to really help you be able to manifest. After all, you were doing more than you could have ever dreamed possible with that rescue.

To be able to become One with your Avatar and work in unison with the entire team with the speed and accuracy needed and given was phenomenal! I am so happy to currently be a part of this group. You are AMAZING!

I see a picnic lunch has been prepared for us near a lake going that way. With the spinning in here, I am not sure what direction to tell you we are going, just follow the translating device, it will get us there. As we walk along this trail, take time to relax with it. Let your feet glide along the path without having to think. Simply know you are on the path. This gives you more freedom to look around and notice other things.

While I don't have to think about staying on the path, I notice the plants are different here than at the other camp area. There is even a different glow to them. Yes, they are many shades of green, but they have a different vibrational aura of intelligence. I am being told that, because we can venture this far into the Portal, one must also be of a vibrational intelligence to be happy here. Simply be able to breathe in this environment. I am very happy here. How about you?

Have you noticed the type of insects, bugs or other beings around you? Maybe I am still being affected by the Dragon's 'Thank You' Fire, but I think it feels sort of like what Alice in Wonderland felt like walking around in her adventure. Maybe it's because I think I can hear the plants talk to me. The crawling and flying insects are talking very loud.

Of course, they would be talking if they were the Fairies or small people that live here, but this is different. It is like I can understand them without the translation device helping me. Are you noticing anything like this, or is it just me? Yes, of course the little people are also chatting to us with very important messages. Have you taken the time to listen to what they have to share with you? Perhaps that is what we are to do today since there are so many of them in our space right now.

We have arrived at the picnic area with some very appetizing foods laid out for us on the tables. Take your time to find what your stomach and body are ready for. Prepare your plate. Find a place to eat quietly and be at peace to prepare yourself to listen to the messages you are to receive.

Once you have finished eating and are plenty hydrated, take some time away from everyone and call the Beings who have a message specifically for you. This is a very sacred opportunity, and you may want to take notes. Once you have spent time with the beings, listen to their specific message, and are ready to move on, meet back at this picnic area.

I see you were able to do some interchanging of information and energy with a variety of peoples that live here. I guess I call them peoples because I don't have another way of identifying them. They are mostly bipedal and walk upright. There are some that do fly but are still of a similar build. There are so many different peoples that I would need a dictionary of identification with photos just to keep them straight. Everyone is in such a Heart Space, it's easy to be in that level of communication, and that is all that matters.

If you would like to share any of your information, I would love to hear all about it. I actually feel most of the information was downloaded to you, so it may take a few days to process. I'm also highly aware that everything you receive here is in direct relation to you being able to manifest with your intention being clearer than ever. You also understand that everything has a consciousness, including Abundance.

Since we are in the Divine Portal of Manifesting, this is what your learning is centered around. This manifesting includes the Energy of Money. I feel you were given understanding of the Consciousness of Money – where everything is Energy. And, if you can Manifest saving a baby Dragon while becoming One with your Avatar and working in unison with the other rescuers, you can Manifest anything! It's now time for you to believe in Yourself enough, the truth of that statement, and how it applies to you. The ultimate level of consciousness is Faith and Trust in yourself and the Divine.

I am sure you have noticed we are not interacting with our Avatars today. They also need time to recalibrate after the blessing and clearing from the Mother Dragon. We will now make our way back to the campsite and prepare for being in our tents with the skylight top.

You may want to simply watch the sky all night or meditate with the information you received, or both. Be at peace within yourself to recalibrate much easier and faster.

See you tomorrow!

MONTH THREE – DAY SEVEN

Are you ready for an amazing day? I woke up well rested and feeling like the recalibrations over the last few days are finally moving me into a better, more aware and alert space. In other words, my brain is working better, at least for the moment.

We have not had a chance to explore this area yet, so we will utilize our Avatars' abilities to move from place to place today. Since the spinning in this Portal is a little hard for me to determine what direction we are going, we will go to the left and take it slow moving up in altitude. Remember when I mentioned I would like to know more about the various levels in the altitude assignments of direction and how traveling is managed here? Well, I think it's a good day to see if that's possible. Of course, what was I thinking! Anything is Possible!

Let's start out going left at about tree top height. Oh, there is a traffic person saying we can't do that. We must move at another angle toward the left. Okay, I think we are safe now. What do you notice? I feel a whole new vibration here. It smells like lemons. Very nice and refreshing. I also feel my brain and heart being triggered with this. I am not sure what it is bringing up, but some sort of processing is going on. Probably clearing some family history trauma. Now I feel a little better. We will stay this course just a bit longer.

I see how we can sort of make lane changes – well, altitude changes. It's sort of a stop light where an elevator involved. I guess it will work. Let's try it.

Now we can go up to the next level, and it turns about fifteen degrees to the right. Oh, this is a unique energy. A little faster-paced traffic, and a lot noisier. At the next light I see a misty veil to go through. It is very pearlescent with a tonality of pinkish purple. It's on the map that just showed up for us. And it says we're to go through it.

I guess I was wrong about it being a veil. It's more of a torsion field of colors with one direction of energy being purple and the other a pale pink. It's like being held in this electromagnetic field of going one direction shifting into another, and then back again, over and over. How do we get out of this?

Of course, once the question is asked the answer is given. The energy just opened for us to ride out into another much higher level of traffic. Yes, the energy here is calmer and resonates with me and hopefully the rest of you. It is so nice to just glide across the Portal being able to see what else is going on around below us.

I forgot to look up above. Did you see that? I think we are supposed to follow That. I am not sure what it is, but we are going much faster as it must be communicating with our Avatars about keeping up. I see the cave we are headed for. Let's land near it and leave our Avatars out here. Oh, I guess that wasn't a part of the plan, as mine is not listening right now.

We are going through a huge waterfall flowing over the cave. The water didn't feel like water. I was all set for being soaked, but it didn't happen. It was more of a purifying energy. As if we need to be purified anymore. Actually, I do feel better. I didn't realize that I had a few aches and pains from all this riding and detoxing from all the recalibrations that have taken place.

This cave is huge! My Dragon found a place to land and let me off, so I can walk into it deeper. I see a little Leprechaun sitting on a large throne-like chair at the end of the room with more Pots of Gold lined and piled up all around than I could ever dream of. He motions for us to come forward. He's really a nice person. He has refreshments for everyone. Now, he is ready to get down to what we are here about. -- Divine Manifestation of Abundance. He has some amazing words of wisdom for us.

As our consciousness shifts, our perspective, ideas, and belief systems about Money change. There is a Morphic Field of Money. What I think is meant by that is there is a resonance of what we believe Money to be and our relationship to it. We get attached to a belief system which can also be a Morphic Field of Money. We attach ourselves to the one that resonates to our beliefs.

For example, if we believe we don't deserve money, we are probably attached to the Morphic Field of No Money stored within it. Another example could be a belief of having more money than I could ever spend, and that Morphic Field would be overflowing with Gold, Silver, Coins and Paper currency. There is also a Morphic Field of Money with no agenda connected. I had never thought about that before. It's a Morphic Field of Money the exact amount exists, or a little more than needed. Which one do you resonate with?

The King Leprechaun mentions that, as we go through each of the mists, waterfalls and other activations, we come into a closer point of being able to handle one of the Pots of Gold, if that is what we want. He also dangles a never-ending debit card in front of us. Which one do you want? At the moment, we don't get either. We still have some work to do. He said he will meet with us in our dream time to help get us ready for the choice we will get to make.

Great information! I also see it is rush hour outside. Let's use our consciousness to think of the camp. Make certain you are with your Avatar as this is going to happen quickly. The workers are coming near us with feathers. I guess we need to be brushed down to calm our nerves. Plus, brushing down your Avatar can be quite healing for it and you. Ah, much better.

Now take a moment to align with your Avatar. Next, just think of the camp that we are to be going back to. I mean really think of it, see yourself and your Avatar there. Yes, that is all it took. We made it back in record time!

See you tomorrow!

MONTH THREE – DAY EIGHT

I am ready for a new day. Ready to find out what else is needed to align with the Divine Portal of Money Manifestation, especially in relationship to the Leprechaun's descriptions of alignment levels. I think the best one for me would be to have that never-ending debit card, or bank account, or cash in my pocket. The chaos and stress involved with having actual Gold Coins to cash in before they can be used isn't my idea of the best way to live and spread financial support to those here on the Planet. It may have been the currency of a different lifetime, but not for me right now. Of course, I would not turn them down. There is something about holding a gold coin or nugget in your hand and knowing it's worth something.

I wonder, what is the best way for aligning with this new Consciousness Energy or Vibration of Money? One of the ways that feels right to me is to have fun. Of course, everyone has a different definition of fun. Fun is an energy of no worries and no fear. It's the ability to flow within the moment of whatever life presents and be happy. Of course, laughter is a huge part in this frequency shift. Not just a little *he-he* type chuckle, but huge belly laughs. I know that I don't engage enough in that type of laughter.

We only have a few more days in this portal to experience the amazing beings and energy here. We'll start by walking down that path today. Make sure you have your translation device secured on you somewhere. Your Avatar may follow along or fly above us in case we need them later.

I noticed we have a few more beings with us today. They are very busy around my feet and flying around my head. They just sparkle with so much joy and laughter. It's all about the joy of being able to accept who you are today on this Planet, no matter what! I have one small being holding my hand as we walk. I can feel the energy transference between us through our hands. If I even think about stumbling over a twig or rock, I notice a higher vibration being sent into my hand.

I hadn't realized how much a little shift in thought can create a lowering or raising of one's vibration ever so slightly, it is still a shift in one direction or another. The energy going into my hand from theirs is like the energy from those flying around my head. It is the frequency of Love. It has a scent to it, too.

Let your ability to notice the spiritual scent open, even if it is ever so slightly. You may think you smell a specific thing in the physical, but that item could not possibly smell like what you're picking up. Then, you start to notice the difference. I find that a spiritual scent also triggers a response in my physical body. Sometimes it is a tingle on my skin or a trickle of sweat on my brow when something really needs to be noticed.

I now see where we are being led to. It looks like a pavilion of various insect species. We are being instructed to be careful of how we enter this containment. We don't want to let the inhabitants out, or others in. We are also asked to watch closely where we step or sit. Yes, it is to experience the beings of this Portal, but to also help you learn to enhance the self-control of your frequencies. I just realized a better way of understanding this. Now I know what we are doing in here. This is not what you would expect to experience at the Butterfly Pavilion! Each of us will experience our greatest challenges.

The first thing that came to me is a snake. Everyone knows that I'm not the best at being around snakes or spiders. The snake triggers a feeling in me that is very hard to control. It slides across my feet, and I know that I must hold still, I must not panic or move away. It can sense everything I think and feel on an overloaded system right now.

I am shaking, my nose quivers, it's hard to swallow, and it's all I can do to simply be right here in the moment. Yes, to me, this is fear on a level I didn't know I had. This is a primal fear.

The wonderful small beings are holding my hand and sending me energy to experience a calmer me in this situation. I had no idea I would react like this. It was such a deep-centered emotion hidden within me. How are you doing in this situation?

We are now moving into a deeper level of mastery of this. I am better at letting the snake be on my feet, but now they want me to hold it. This is very intense. Yes, I have been told it's not poisonous. My mind knows it will not hurt me, but my other senses doesn't care – it is a snake!

I remember being told as a child to be careful and watch out for snakes as we had both poisonous and nonpoisonous ones around the house. I was on guard of them, but I think this goes deeper than just my childhood experiences. Not only are these beings holding my hands and sending energy, but now they're touching my back and shoulders.

It helps me calm down within myself. I am now calm enough to sense and hear the snake sending its message to me. I will have to journal this back at camp.

This was a great lesson for me. I had thought I had mastered fear. I guess I did only in certain areas. This one was a great awareness. How did you do with this experience?

Take time to journal about this. Remember, you can go back in your mind, in a meditation, to experience this again to clear even more of your inner fears. I would advise you to do this again in your tent while you are still in this environment. It will only take a thought to call these wonderful beings to help you through the balancing.

There may be more than one thing to work on. These fears can block the abundance flow of the Manifestation Energy of Money. Take time to do this as often as possible.

See you tomorrow!

MONTH THREE – DAY NINE

Interesting information in yesterday's experiences. How did you do with it? Did you get to experience a clearing in one or more of your primal fears? I'm still not completely finished with it, as there are many more things coming to the surface besides the snake and its many meanings.

Such as the snake being a symbol of transmutation. I am using the snake as an example, because there are a lot of people with the fear of snakes. The alchemy of how a snake sheds its skin is the life, death, and rebirth cycle. It is the alchemy of creation. Each day we recreate ourselves as we get out of bed, go through our routines, and go back to sleep to start all over again the next day. We create a little differently throughout some days, but the basics are the same to be rebirthed the next day. The transmutation is when we rebirth ourselves to be different. That would be starting each day with a different vibration than the one before.

What happens when we get sick? Instead of beginning a day with a new higher vibration, we begin the day with a lower one which could be caused by an emotional trauma decreasing your vibration to that of the illness.

To get well and stay well we must be in a constant state of increasing our vibration. We are either in a state of regeneration or one of decay.

The Divine Portals we are journeying through, give us the opportunity to make some great changes as we encounter the basic rebirth of each day. It is up to us to allow the changes within to happen. Of course, this is a choice. Do you wake up at a higher vibration of Happy, ready to move into the new day with Joy, Laughter. Is the Manifestation of Abundance frequency turned on or not? Is the Abundance in the realm of Love, Gratitude, doing what you Love to do with those you Love, or Money? Or is it an Abundance of sadness, anger, depression?

As we make these conscious choices it brings us closer to being able to hold the various frequencies of Abundance. One of the changes we are in the process of making as we go through this Portal of Transformation is shifting the frequency of Money itself.

There are many teachings around our Planet on how Money is good, or Money is evil. Also, if you earn money you are evil. Another big one is the belief that those with gifts of what we are working with here are not supposed to charge for our services. My belief is that God gave us these gifts to assist us in our mortal workings.

For example, a 'Gifted' Doctor may be the best at surgery because she can foresee the possibilities of how the procedure will go for a certain patient, or foresee how to create a better way of helping a patient. Perhaps knowing what illness a person has, then running tests to make sure she is correct. She proves this with lab results. She was given directions for which tests to schedule via her gifts, her higher power, her knowledge. No one hesitates to pay this person for the manifestation of her gifts.

What about the lawyer who knows just how to pick a jury, or what to tell this jury so they exactly understand the information required to make the best decision? There are gifted musicians, lawyers, teachers, artists, and carpenters ... So many gifted people, that we could go on and on. But a person that uses his/her gifts, instead of a degree, is in many cultures deemed wrong to charge for their gifts.

Most people keep their abilities hidden due to some Fear. When we do that, we deny what God gave us to better ourselves, to protect ourselves, and to make life better on this Planet.

Bottom line is, Money is neither good nor evil. Money is a medium of exchange in and of itself, having no power other than what you give it.

Clearing your primal fears includes the clearing of being treated as if you are not good enough to make money, or have a lot of it because you are a healer, or you use your various gifts to earn a living and have to keep them hidden.

The old pictures of healers or spiritual people are seen dressed in rags, walking everywhere, instead of utilizing a mode of transportation of the best quality, to get them to a client who needs them. This indicates to me that there is a program of consciousness, or a Morphic Field, of those who use their Gifts or Spirituality that are being taken advantage of. They're not paid their worth or burned at the stake.

Let's take a short ride as we process this information and see what happens. Everyone on their Avatar? As we head down the Portal, the air currents flow one way, down and to the right. As we head back up, the air current flow pushes against us. As we feel and think Happy, Positive, moving forward thoughts. we go with the flow. When we think unhappy, negative thoughts – fear, anger, or other lower vibrational feelings, we are going against the flow. Notice how that feels. We are going to experiment with that.

While on your Avatar, you come up against a huge monster. Do you notice what automatically happens? Do you end up being turned around and going the opposite direction, or do you continue your journey past the monster as if it wasn't there? Just notice, no judgement.

Another one might be while on your Avatar in this Portal. Remember a huge situation which came about one time when you were young. You brought home a report card from school with bad grades. Or, you thought a friend was lying about you. What direction are you going in this Portal? Now, recall a memory of when you came home from school and had perfect grades, or a person you admired gave you some extra attention or included in you in a big event. Now, which direction are you going?

When you have mastered this lesson to a degree of satisfaction, notice how you feel. Then, head back to camp and either meditate on it or journal about this experience.

See you tomorrow!

MONTH THREE – DAY TEN

Yesterday was very educational on what we are doing here and in all the Portals throughout the year. This has been quite a learning event for many of us, myself-included, in our emotions, what we deal with, how it controls us, our vibrational resonance, and how it influences our ability to attract the Abundance of Money. How long did you work at the exercise given yesterday? It is one you may want to practice daily until you can be clearer in your emotional reactions and how they control you.

We have a lot of area to cover today. Let's get on our Avatars and go directly to the center of this Portal to see what shows up for us. Yes, make sure you have your translation device on you as this is uncharted territory we may be going over.

The sky is beautiful, a slight breeze keeps us alert, and the view is amazing. Which altitude do we want to travel in? I think we don't want to be too high as there is so much to see, but we do want to be out of the air traffic. We are in luck, as not too many are going deeper into this Portal today. I say let our Avatars pick the speed we go for a while and see what shows up.

Wow! This is so much fun. Along with going super-fast to start with, we had to ride a few freedom spins and crazy dives. Now that's out his system we can settle down to a nice medium speed. One that lets us see the many deep canyons and valleys along the way.

I have a whole new picture of what the Leprechauns, Fairy folk, and Elementals are really like. I have noticed a few small villages, mostly hidden in the trees and rock formations.

We are making great time. Let's take a few minutes for a break down at that stream. Maybe we can soak our feet and let our Avatars rest a little before we continue to the next camp. Yes, this stream feels great. It feels like it is purifying my entire body just by putting my feet in. Oh, my, I spoke too soon. It is now pulling me into its swirling pond. I guess I will be getting wet after all. Okay for just a little bit. The swirling water is clearing every cell of my body, including my hair. I'm starting to feel so much lighter.

Now it is like a hand within the water lifted me up onto the bank. How nice! I will just take a few minutes to dry. Something is making a sound I've never heard before. I see it is a Unicorn! I heard they were in this Portal, but not usually seen. It's amazing how the translation device helps me understand what it wants. We are to follow it, not too far.

It was only to an open meadow, beautifully surrounded by trees very close together, creating a perfect circle. In the middle is a tall backed, golden chair. A lady with very long golden hair sits in it. We are motioned to enter the circle and given a very difficult choice. We each can have either a Pot of Gold to take with us right now back to our tent to learn about it and decide if we are ready to have it for keeps, or we can have a special activation by the Unicorn's horn. I am glad this is an individual choice. We each get to choose for ourselves without judgement from anyone else. This is really a tough one.

Pot of Gold for the night to see if we can figure 'It' out ... What is it? This could be quite a riddle, or it could just be figuring out if you personally are ready for it. Can you hold the vibration of this type or amount of money to keep it, or will it disappear once your vibration changes?

I know I'm pretty good at holding my vibration, but after going through some of these experiences, I realize I still have some work to do within myself. At this time in this journey, I feel like I need the activations of the Unicorn. I have no idea what they are about, but I just feel I need them. Perhaps they are to help shift my frequency to hold onto or work with the Pot of Gold. Those taking the activations go to one side of this circle. Those getting the Pot of Gold go to the other side. Pay attention to the instructions given. Take notes if needed.

As for me, with the Unicorn, I experience a bold yet refreshing energy from its horn right to my heart. It is so strong that I feel as if I could be levitated for a moment. Then I come back into a normalcy of being able to function again. How are you experiencing it? I guess we will see what the lasting effects will be as we journey on.

How are those of you doing that chose the Pot of Gold? It looks so shiny and amazing. I am very happy for you and can't wait to hear what you receive from it, or do you get to keep it? How are you going to carry it back to camp? I hadn't thought of that. Maybe your pack can double as a saddle bag.

It's time to get back on our Avatars and continue down the Portal to the new camp. It is near the exit point, our destination for tomorrow. We will easily get there to enjoy some time with the space. Or, of course, you may just go to your tent to integrate either the Pot of Gold information or recalibrate from the Unicorn activation.

See you tomorrow for our last ride in the Portal!

MONTH THREE – DAY ELEVEN

Well, I guess we all know what today is. I can't believe how fast the days for this journey flew by. Remember, you can go back to any of this information at any time to redo, reintegrate, or just experience any of these again. Each time you do, it will help you come into a higher level of resonance with your goal.

For this last day together in the Divine Money Portal, let's take a look at the direction we are going. Can you see how tiny the end of the Portal is? Remember how wide it was where we entered? We have been moving through a live, spinning Portal. We still have a while to go before we reach the exit. We will do that in just a little bit.

First, I would love to know if you still have the Pot of Gold you picked yesterday. Did you learn anything from it? Did you get to experience each coin, one at a time? Don't forget to pack them and all your belongings. Yes, you may take your Avatar with you if you want and continue to have him as a part of your normal life on the Earth. Of course, you may also leave him with the keepers at the end of the tunnel where he will be well taken care of until you decide you want him with you always or for the adventure we take next month. I think that is all the housekeeping information.

Let's get on that amazing Avatar you have become so attuned to. Don't forget the translation device as we will be turning it in before we exit.

I think we can start in a zig zag pattern as we learn what is at this part of the tunnel. We don't have to exit until nightfall, so take your time and notice what you can all around you. Let's start with the ride going to the left. If we go at an angle, it will be a longer distance and we can see more. We will be flying about house height. Good, everyone is here at the same time.

We have the workings of a gymnastics team below us, just in case we lose our ability to stay on our Avatar – you know how they can be sometimes when they get excited with some crazy flying moves. Also, as you can see, tree height isn't the same in here as it is in the flat terrain on the Earth. In here, we are in a circular, winding Portal, sort of like being inside of a tornado, but big enough that you don't notice it too much, only when it decides to move within itself; which is right about now.

Did you feel that shift? The first thought I had wasn't the best to share, but I will. It's like being inside of a stomach as it just moves everything around a bit for better digestion or circulation. I know weird -- creepy weird.

Don't worry, we aren't being digested. It's just energy shifts we are creating while being in here. As above, so below. Remember that saying? Well, in here it is all about energy. As we, or anyone, or anything for that matter, shifts, all is affected. It is the same above ground, we are just so busy with our everyday lives that we become desensitized and don't always notice it.

Back to our journey. Did you look up? Notice the sky! Breathtakingly beautiful! That 'cloud' is quite different from anything I have ever seen before. Rain! But not rain. It is bubbles falling from the sky. They are beautiful and all different sizes and colors. I wonder what they are all about. Let's just hover in this space for a while and see what happens.

I notice that, as each bubble touches me, it doesn't pop. It just melts into me. I notice my frequency change, as well as my entire being. Even my clothing changes. It is becoming a purer color. Yes, even my Avatar is enjoying this change. It feels so lightening. How are you being affected? Take the time to notice and feel. Just breathe in the change you wish you to be and create.

Time to turn and zig zag back across to the other side. Did you see the villagers waving to us? Flying this low gives a whole different view of what this place is. What are they sending to us? Waves of Love and Gratitude is what I feel. I am going to miss this place. Are you ready to make the last turn? It will take us to the exit point of this Portal.

I am amazed how this place turns into portions of how we think of things. Someone must have been thinking about the exit on an airport when this area was created, as we have a large flat place to land and leave our Avatars or have them put into a stall of sorts they fit into. Oh, yes, remember how they can shrink themselves? They may even fit into your backpack if you want them to go with you. There is also a place here for them stay and be well taken care of. Your choice. Don't you just love choices? On to the next checkout area.

This is where we check-in our translating device. I forgot to tell you that you can always create a copy of if needed by thinking of it and remembering how you used it and how it felt. Just think and feel it being exactly where and how you played with it, and a hologram of it will appear for you. That is just one of the ways you can take the magic of this place with you.

One thing you really can't take is the treat that causes you to shrink. If you have any leftover, you can leave here on the table. Or, if you leave with it, it will disappear and take itself right back to this Portal. It is one of the magical items that are only for this location.

It is always hard to say goodbye, perhaps it is best to say … Until we meet again. Perhaps in the next month's new Divine Portal.

Just thought of one more thing. When you get back, look in your backpack and see if you can find the imprint or hologram of the Pot of Gold. Take time to feel it and remember it as you move into your new level of your Money Manifestation.

Let it help you hold the frequency the Leprechaun referred to. Maybe carry one of the coins in your pocket.

See you next month!

See you soon with Truth, Love, and Gratitude

Pat, The Cosmic Cowgirl

PATRICIA VANCE FORBES

Journal Your Feelings About Money and Gratitude

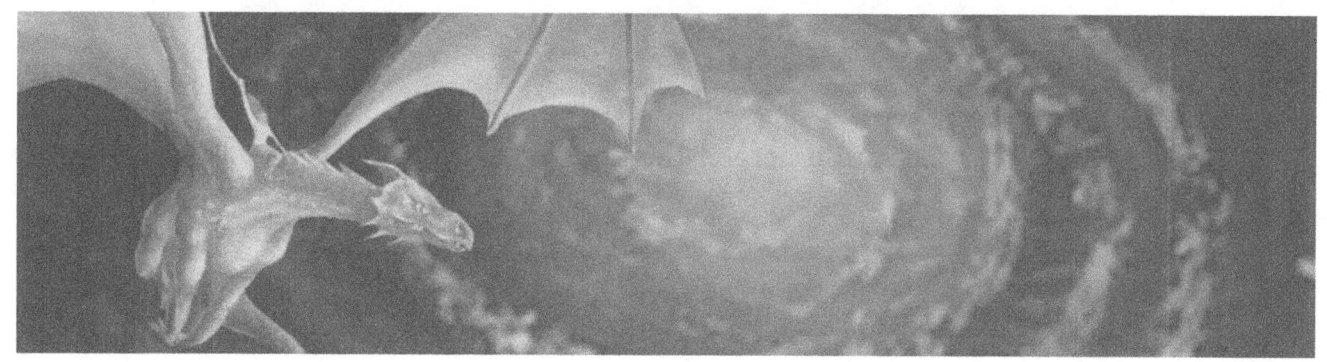

CHAPTER FOUR: FREEDOM FROM ECONOMIC SLAVERY

MONTH FOUR – DAY ONE

Welcome to this Divine Abundance Portal. As you know, I have never been near a pyramid, nor have I really done much studying of them. But this month, the Portal wanted to take us through an experience where we will help clear old energy blocks within the tombs and pyramids around the Planet. I feel a touch of somberness as we begin, as this is some important work we are to do this time. Of course, that doesn't mean we can't have some fun.

From a distance, this Portal does look like a black swirling tornado headed toward Egypt. I ask, "Why do we start there?" I am told it's because this is where this Dark Belief System that was pulled into the Morphic Field of Slavery, was the strongest.

In my work, I generally go to the core of the problem to start with if it is the best way to begin the process of healing the situation dealt to me at the moment. This time, I am told this is a great place to start. So, it is what it is.

We are beginning at the door of the Great Pyramid. I ask which door, as I see several. I am told it is not the one most people, like tourists, enter. It is an underground door. I feel the Portal pull us into it before the thought can even be expressed in my brain. It seems to be a long way down. It feels like we are spinning through the tunnels within underground chambers, gathering up old patterns of light and information.

WOW! This could be a ride at an amusement park! These patterns of light and information seem to shift rapidly right before my eyes. I wish it were that easy to do 'spring cleaning' at my house! I see this as flashing. One moment, it is a dark, dreary pattern, the next there is a spark like lightning, and within the flash it is changed to light. This is an amazing way to clear old, dark energy.

I see how it was in ancient times. We seem to be slowing down enough to look around and see some of the great items in each of these rooms. Even though much has been removed in the present, we can experience the reality and essence of each item and person that was in here in ancient times like they are here in the present. Pause and take a deep breath and relax your mind, heart, and, yes, your stomach. Sometimes the swirling of the Portal causes my stomach to feel a little out of sorts.

Now, notice the size of each room and what is written on the walls. What does it say to you as we go through some of the rooms and halls? Take notice of the beings as they walk past you and what they carry. Be careful not to bump into them. They look to be carrying some fragile, vital items. I wonder what they are for. I get that maybe I will find out later.

What I notice is that the information is reverent. Where there is a passage that feels a little glitchy, I notice how the Portal swirls over it, and soon is light and free. Some areas seem to be trying to tell me that what happened has been mistranslated and we are to carry the Truth.

I am being told most people have no idea what the pyramids were created for. Those who have excavated found some truths, but it's not time to come out yet.

The Morphic Field created around these pyramids is incredibly strong in Slavery–Victim energy. It shouldn't be, as the creation of the pyramid wasn't meant for that. This Morphic Field has been created by our storytelling system. It has been broadcast at least once a year for many years in the telling of the story where Moses frees the slaves. This has created a huge Morphic Field of Religion with a lot of energy related to victims, being poor, and slavery.

It isn't a normal Victim–Slave energy as we understand it, with a person ruling over another. This is deeper within, as if the DNA has been changed in the linage of those people to the point of them being mostly comfortable in a slavery situation. There is a Fear energy involved here, too. I am not sure of our job with it just yet.

Did you notice how we have made a slight, yet steady climb while moving down the hallways? If there is a room that draws you in, take time to go inside. You will not be left behind. If you really want to know how this one was built, just ask it. It will reveal its secrets to you as you ask in truth of wanting to know.

I find a table in the center of this pyramid with food and water for us. We are to stay here and rest as the stability of the pyramid and ground around it is shifting with the energy we carry. I guess it is time for us to have some relaxation here and allow the shifting to take place around us. If you notice some shifting inside you, take time to breathe and allow it to happen. This will prepare you for the journey that is yet to come.

See you tomorrow!

MONTH FOUR – DAY TWO

As I relaxed and took time to allow ourselves to recalibrate with this shift, I realized the energy went a long way back in time on this Planet. The Slavery-Victim energy didn't have much to do with Religious beliefs. It is related to power and control from some ancient civilizations that were once here.

We do have some strange energies to navigate through on this journey. I will do my best to not use names of Kings, Queens, Pharaohs, and others that may trigger adverse or overly amazing energies within us. This cannot be worked within the Energy of Judgement. Whether positive or negative, it is still judgement.

I see we are again going to be riding this Portal wave as if it is a Magic Carpet. It can move through walls of time and space at the same time. Right now, as we begin to go through a wall to enter another chamber, I find us transported back in time to an era of … I won't say the name. Let's call it the era of the bird-headed, tall being. Some of this energy feels lovely, but some is difficult to allow near me. We were only to see this being for a moment. I notice that, if he sees you, additional information will be given to you in this journey.

We are being zipped away to another chamber. We are right in the center. Around us on the walls are some writings in an interesting language. It is similar to something I have seen before.

It looks to be quite ancient, yet there is some Angelic intermingled with it. Oh yes, I have seen this on one of the ships I was on as a child. Very interesting energy that happened here at one time.

As we walk around the outer walls of this center area of the pyramid, I feel an energy building. It is as if each step we take creates an energy of higher vibrations which rush through each stone in the structure. I also feel each stone vibrate back one tone, then a different one as it changes. Then another tone. And another tone. Each one different with each step. I can feel it resonate throughout the entire area where we are also being affected. It is going deep into some underground area and back up.

I feel waves of energy now going into the center of the Earth and back up to this point under our feet with each step, creating a percussion type of shift from the center of the Earth to the tip of the pyramid. It feels like, if we were outside, we could see a beacon of light blinking on and off with each step.

I can feel it reverberate up through my whole body now. We are shifting this entire area of ... I have no idea ... but it feels like the right thing to be doing. As we suddenly stop, a beam of light shoots up through the center and out of the top. It is a pure cleaning light resonating throughout the entire structure.

Our Magic Carpet Portal ride sweeps us into an area where we can walk outside to see for ourselves. I now see all the pyramids in our area glowing and beaming a light to the Universe. The ground vibrates higher as we walk around and take it all in. Our work here is done here for the moment. We will see what tomorrow will bring.

See you tomorrow!

MONTH FOUR – DAY THREE

WOW! That was quite an experience. Together we are really a powerful team, being able to create such a change in just two little sessions. I can feel the energy begin to increase in vibration and clarity moment by moment. The ground is settling down as is the intensity of the light around us. I feel we can now begin a new journey.

I am being told it is time for each of you to create a being for transportation. It's easy to think of them as an Avatar of sorts. Mine is a Purple Dragon. He does change colors from time to time, but maintains a glow within the purples. He can be oh-so-loving and sweet yet do what a Dragon can do – breathe fire and protect me as the need arises, and, of course, fly! Pick your own according to your needs and likes. Flying may be a good asset. Also, being able to change sizes at a moment's notice helps, as we will be maneuvering through some various sized areas. Don't limit yourself as to what magical capabilities you may want or need.

Are we ready? The tornado-like Portal is ramping up again for us to ride within. We may take our Avatar with us or, if you prefer, an Angel. that is okay, too. I sense we really need to hang on for this one. The Portal is taking us to the top of the giant pyramid then right down the center of it, on into the center of the Earth.

I have heard of this place, but never ventured here. I see cities and various inhabitants that are sort of human looking. They seem to be very advanced and welcome us. We have been asked to take some time and fly around to acquaint ourselves with the area.

It is beautiful. I had wondered how a place in the center of the Earth could have sunlight. I still don't quite understand it, but it feels very much like our above ground sun. The ground has lush crops growing everywhere. The plants have fruit similar to what I recognize but not exactly. It feels like they're purer and more nutrient-laden than we have had before.

The animals around seem to be working with the people who live here. Not exactly as pets, but more like partners in doing the harvesting and other caretaking needs. There is an energy of Love coming from them to one another and to the land. I think this is to show us how we are to learn to live and help people on the Earth move into the direction of their evolution.

I know we aren't anywhere near there yet, but it is time to plant the seeds. It doesn't mean we have to garden if you don't want to, just that it is available for those who like to do that. I see that they have they also have incredible technologies beyond our current abilities. Keep planting the seeds!

They are waving to us as we are being pulled up to the top of one area through a doorway. Our Divine Portal is opening the way for us to go to the next area we are to participate in. It is a small opening, so we will be shrinking to fit through, and there isn't anything we have to do – it just happens.

The cave we entered contains pure crystalline structures that seem to cover a bandwidth of types and frequencies. There are the darker, what we call the earthy crystals continuing in a variety of types and colors as we get closer to the exit. I also look at how the tunnel is lit up. I don't see any torches or lights of any type. It must come from the knowledge of what we present before us. If we need to see where we are going, the light will be there.

I now see a light ahead and a huge cave opening up for us. Yes, we are in the mountains of Peru! This cave seems to be lined with Amethyst crystals. I remember this cave, it is very familiar to me. I am certain that it has many small rooms where we can rest and prepare ourselves for the next journey.

Some of the rooms have healing tables in them made of crystal. Some of the rooms were used to prepare the bodies of those that have passed on for disposal of the shell. It is a very sacred place for us to experience.

See you tomorrow!

MONTH FOUR – DAY FOUR

I had forgotten how wonderful it is to sleep on a crystal healing table. I feel so much better now, and it appears that my Dragon does too. He slept right inside the doorway of the room I was in, so he got a lot of healing done whether he needed it or not. I hope you had a great recovery time as well. Not just from this journey, but from the many you have traveled.

Today, as I look out this cave, I see other pyramids. They are not as well known worldwide, but they are all around us. Some are hidden in the growth of the forest and mountains. I will ask the Divine Portal to take us to the one that we are to explore on this day.

Oh, this one is quite different from any others I can remember experiencing either through a book or in dream time. Carvings cover the outer side blocks and are somewhat reflective of the Tribes that lived here throughout the time period. It doesn't appear as ancient as I thought it to be. As we get closer,

I hear that we are to enter through the secret passage on the northeast corner. I don't see an opening, but let's wait and see what happens.

I feel a tingling in my toes and fingers. The doorway opens between two blocks that looked to be completely non-movable. Great camouflage for a secret entrance. Now we get to find out what is really in here!

Oh, it is much older than I expected. The outside carvings must not have been done by those who created this structure. The halls are large enough for us to walk into. I am experiencing some creepy dampness in this room on the left. Instead of entering it, I think I can just send some light in there to help clear the darkness.

I still need to remind myself not to judge with words like creepy, dark, freaky, evil. Someday I will remember. It is all just patterns of light and information. Well, I think I can say that the patterns of light and information in that room were of a vibration that would not be helpful right now.

As we continue down this specific hallway, there are writings on the wall. I first spelled the word 'righting's', which is their purpose. There is a vibration created within them that clears and cleans those who walk past so they can complete their mission. Ours is to do some spring cleaning by clearing out the old Slave-Victim unrighteous power that is creating patterns held within these walls. What I notice is the same energy is within many of these ancient structures we will visit. As we clear ourselves of these patterns we also clear all that is around us in our daily lives.

I am so thankful we have our Avatars with us to help in this mission. They have been chosen wisely as they are so very protective of our own energy changes and the Planet's. They are so magical. It looks like they dilute then delete these old patterns, so we don't have to take them into ourselves to create changes carried over from our ancestors. It is some crazy alchemy method that is easy, fast, and complete. We are setting the pattern of intention within this pyramid to continue the clearing on anyone that walks these halls from all Dimensions.

\

This is going to be interesting to watch as I see soldiers and slaves of many eras pass through here as we stand in this space. I think we will do more exploring tomorrow after a lot of this type of clearing is done. We don't have to do it. We can watch what our intentions can create.

I see us sitting on the bleachers with ringside seats. Pass the popcorn!

See you tomorrow!

MONTH FOUR – DAY FIVE

That was entertaining! I had never seen some of those types of beings before. I heard of them, but never saw them, even in the crazy world I live in. I'm so thankful we were able to start the ball rolling for them to get cleared and be able to move on. Now, check yourself and see how much of your matching programs were cleared. This is the easiest way to go through some of our deep, ancestral clearing. If it needs to be more specific you may have to ask your Teams to help.

We can go on and have some fun exploring this pyramid. Lots of halls and rooms with so many artifacts. This is the way I love to study history. Uh, Oh, we just came upon a dead end in this hall. How can that be? we must be only in the middle of this pyramid. Let's just tune-in and see what we are to do now.

The floor just opened into a spiral slide! This is very nice. It seems to be hewn out of stone then polished to the highest level of slickness for this purpose. Do you think the beings that lived here actually had fun like this?

Wow! It is a long way down here. I see there are writings we are interacting with again as we slide past them.

Okay, there's the bottom, but what is happening? It is a sort of vortex lifting me back to the top to slide down again! It's fun, but how many times are we to do this? Oh, yeah! It's the old ask and you shall receive!

We are to continue to do this if the need is there. We are to get cleared of the matching energies we have in relation to the writings on the wall. I don't notice any strange side effects so far, so this is a good way to do this work for ourselves as well as many others on this Planet.

Finally! I hit the bottom and didn't get floated back up. It looks like you are finished too. Yes! We are at the bottom of the pyramid, deep into the Earth. It is nice and cool down here and the humidity isn't too bad either. Let's spread out and see what is in this area. Give a shout if you find something awesome!

Here are more artifacts, but why are they stored down here? I am going to pick one up and see what it is, even though there is a sign that says Do Not Touch. Just a little one. It is a replica of a little person, sort of a garden gnome-looking being. Oh, it came to life. It has a lot of information on what this place is.

Yes, the builders did slide down the stone slide. They were fun but strict peoples. They lived fiercely. Peoples of great passion. From what I understand, they loved the land and the people. The first ones here devolved into the darker aspects of waring and torture to create slaves. They are extremely happy that we are helping to clear this lower vibrational energy.

Once this little guy gave us his information he went back to being non-animated. I think he just had the message to deliver, as if in a time lock of sorts. I am going to touch another one and see what happens. You can too if you want.

I just got the same message again. It must be what was stored to be given to me at this time. Maybe you will get a different message.

My hands and feet are tingling again. The side of the wall just opened into a tunnel and our Portal became active. It is a huge cave-like tunnel with lots of crystals that I have never seen before. They line the walls. They don't seem to be a part of the natural surroundings. Perhaps they were brought here from somewhere else. The Portal is carrying us along this tunnel to a new opening. This seems to be an underground connection between the pyramids.

Which one will be our next adventure? This time we are being brought to the innermost workings of a new pyramid from the tunnel system.

Again, "Ask and you shall receive" is happening. I have no idea what this is about. It looks like a place where we can take care of our needs and our Avatars'. This room has rugs and pillows, and I hear it is for meditation and healing. That is probably a good idea as we just cleared a whole lot of that Victim/Slave/Prisoner/Warring energy. I, for one, need a little time to recalibrate before we explore this next pyramid.

See you tomorrow!

MONTH FOUR – DAY SIX

This is a very lovely pyramid. I am not sure where it is located on the Earth. I have a feeling it is somewhere in South America, maybe in Brazil. I love how the walls have some type of lighting system where they seem to glow. I don't see any torches or electrical systems. This glow is very calming and bright enough to not only see where we are going but also the writings on the walls.

We have come to a T in the hallway. So far, there have been no rooms to enter, just this long hallway which has now ended with our choice of going–left or right. Let's go left. The writing on these walls extends to the floor we walk on. It seems like we can feel their energy of them as we walk over them, even in these heavy riding boots. I notice that this isn't a War or a Sacrifice energy in this area.

There is a room on the left that I feel we should go into. It looks small to begin with, but seems to be expanding as we all fit inside, including our Avatars. There is an altar at the far end with some artifacts on it. There is a candle. It isn't pretty and nice smelling, but it does give off light of a different vibration than the walls. It also contains some metal objects that float in the air right into my hands. They are similar to dowsing rods, but have a different feel. Perhaps these are the type that can be programmed. I don't get a chance to ask. They pull me out of this room, down the hall and into another room.

Here, there are cutouts in the walls with a variety of tools in each one. I recognize that it is time for a lesson, as there is a hologram of a being that tells us how these pyramids were built, and how different this one is from most of the others. It has been hidden from the outside world, so it hasn't gone through the trauma of many of the other pyramids when they were pillaged for their artifacts.

It is time for us to pick a place where there is a wall cutout. We are to pick up the tools stored there, then create a circle to sit down. There is a hologram to teach you how to use these tools for yourself and the person sitting next to you. Pay close attention to what you notice shifting within yourself while you work, then the person next to you, and again as that person works on you. There is a lot of opportunity for a variety of clearing to take place.

Our intention on this journey is to clear Poverty Consciousness created through the power and control of the Slavery-Victim programming that so many of us carry from our ancestors. Remember how you do this and how your partner works on you. This is a technique that can be done when you get home.

Once you have used the tools, you won't need them anymore because you will have a memory of them within you. When you feel complete, put the tools back in the little parts of the wall where originally got them.

We can now move into the center of the pyramid and prepare to be swept away by the Portal to a new location tomorrow. First, take a little time to recalibrate yourself after all that healing work.

See you tomorrow!

MONTH FOUR – DAY SEVEN

The Divine Portal we have entered has been patiently waiting for us. Today, as we are in the center of the amazing energy of this pyramid, remember. Take it into yourself and hold it in your heart. You may draw on the memory of this event any time you feel the need. It is an easy way to bring this energy into the world in which we daily navigate.

I see that we are all ready as the swirling energy surrounds us and sweeps us directly up the center of the pyramid and out the very top. Oh, wait, I thought it was the very top, but we are pulled out an opening in the north side just before we reach the top. We are being taken to an energy, and we're follow it exactly. This energy we are clearing is very precise in how it must be cleansed. Of course, it is, otherwise, it would have been cleared already by someone else.

You can ride your Avatar within the parameters of this Portal as we are taken to … wherever we are going. Even I don't know until we get there, which is about … Now.

It seemed like we were swirling in a northerly direction most of the time. We are nearing the Equator. The pyramids here look so much different from the last one we left.

It contains more archaic energy. Not that it's an older structure, not at all. It's just the energy is not the same as the previous one. It was so easy to be happy and get pulled into the higher vibrational frequencies of the one we just left. I now wonder what this new pyramid is like.

To me, it feels harsher. No wonder we weren't brought here first. I don't think any of us could have handled it several days ago. We had to get some of our stuff cleared before we could venture into this area to help. What? You thought this was only going to be just a fun ride?

As it says in the description, we are here to do some spring cleaning–especially of Economic Slavery energy. To do this, we must clear the energies of War, Slave, Soldier, and Powerlessness. There is a lot of this clearing to be done here. Can you feel the heaviness? Yuck! I am not so sure about this. Oh, remember, we are well supported in this journey and we have our Avatars with us!

Navigating the energy in this one, is going to be a little tricky. I can see how the edge of this one has stairs, and about halfway up, there is an opening. Let's fly up there as it's so much easier than a steep climb. Yes, just as I suspected, torches light the walls this time. This is okay, there are plenty.

We will go through a hallway that slants downward. It isn't too steep. Just as in some of the others, there are many things drawn on the walls. The pictures are terrible. They show how they kill each other and the Tribes that are close by. Blood spurts and heads roll in the pictures down this hallway. It isn't fun to look at, but we are here exactly for this reason, and we can do it.

Take a breath! Call in your Angel or ET team to activate a storm inside of here which consists of giant bubbles that are sticky on the outside to pull negative energy inside of them. Looks like these bubbles come from a bubble machine high above us. This is so awesome! As they touch you they will also clear any matching energies you carry from ancestors or, if you're an empath, absorbed them from the atmosphere on this Planet and the huge mess we walked into.

I know this can be intense, but stay with me. Keep breathing and let your mind focus on the colors of the bubbles floating around and through the tunnels in this pyramid. It appears to me that, as they are broken and eventually get onto the floor, they neutralize the Warring-Slave-Sacrifice energy.

They meld with the darkest of the energies and absorb them. Right behind the bubbles is golden, sparkly fairy dust. It looks like the golden dust from the Creator that heals everything. The intensity lessens more and more with each breath. The pictures on the walls have changed!

We can now walk further into this pyramid and really notice the changes that have occurred. It is lighter and brighter. The walls start to become light as we experienced in that last pyramid. Yes, there is a reason you signed up for this journey! We come upon a large room right off the center point of this pyramid where we can easily recalibrate ourselves. Thank you for sticking with it. We did a lot of work here for ourselves and the Planet! Get some rest.

See you tomorrow!

MONTH FOUR – DAY EIGHT

That was quite an intense journey! I hope you are doing okay today. You may need some time to make sure your chakras and meridians are aligned. It really does help to take a few minutes to do this and breathe!

What will we experience today? Let's get started and find out. I hear we must buckle up. I didn't know that Avatars had seat belts, but maybe it's just a term used to get ready for a wild ride. As we are still in this same pyramid, it must mean there is more to do here.

We are on a path that leads to a lower level toward the underground. To me, this energy feels almost like an exact match to that first pyramid we started on, which means we need to find the root of this energy and clear it as well as we can.

The root is the deepest, lowest point in the Earth on this one. Let's find the center of this pyramid, that can't be too hard. We can make a left-hand turn and see where it takes us. It's leveling out and starting to feel better, just as I had hoped it would.

The energy is getting more excited, or so it seems, the closer we get to the center. The light is also getting brighter and brighter, also hotter! Almost there.

We are in the center, so get onto your Avatar, and let's ride to the lowest point of this thing to find the root cause of the pyramid's strangeness. It may or may not relate to our Divine Purpose within this pyramid, but I feel we must to do this. It seems like there is a direct tunnel from the pyramid's tip to the bottom. Focus to create a light to go before us. Also, if you have flashlights in your pack, bring them out for back up. Let's go.

I notice a lot of nice writing on the walls up here at the top, but as we go deeper, it gets gorier. The energy gets denser. Make sure you have your protective shield from the Creator around you and your Teams to help with this situation we are embarking upon. I am asking for more protection for the group and a specific Team to help us with what is coming.

The bottom is quite dense, and the sounds down here are pretty harsh. As I look around I see what could be called a dungeon. I think it was a form of prison during a certain time. I don't see physical beings here. Rather, I see the spirits of what was once kept here – they are trapped within these walls. I am asking if they should be freed.

The problem is they are not natural to Earth. There are a few human spirits trapped here, but mostly some very strange animals I have never seen before. They are not harmful from what I can tell, but they are in pain. My team says they need to go into a form of containment they will provide to remove them from this Planet and to heal them along with their handlers. We are to hold as high of a vibration that we can to support this.

Keep your shields up as the energy down here is still not good, but we can shift this. Stay with your Avatar and go into a rhythmic breathing, slow and deep. Intake with the nose and out with the mouth. Tone a low OHM with the out breath. Great, you are so good at this. Now watch, as you continue breathing, the Teams assist these spirits and souls out of their cages. There were no physical bonds used in their restraints. It was all energetic, as are our bonds of the Economic Slavery–Victim consciousness held on this

Planet. With our breathing and the intent of releasing these beings, include the Planetary Bondage to go with them to be cleared on all Dimensional aspects accrued on this Planet, since before and after their physical time here. Follow the energy and the Teams as they take this entire situation right up the center of this pyramid to exit the top point and continue off our Planet. I asked if this could be done on the other pyramids at the same time, and I got "Not yet."

Feel that? It's amazing! Now, let's ride our Avatars to the top and exit this pyramid at the very top point. Our Portal is now taking us to a camp being prepared for us to recalibrate and recuperate for little while.

See you tomorrow!

MONTH FOUR – DAY NINE

I hope you are doing better than ever! This is an amazing place. I have never been to a campsite like this before. It is so beautiful and relaxing here with all the food and drink you could ever want. Whatever you need is available to assist in your healing from the great work you just did for the Planet! I could feel a huge change in the levels of light that increased throughout the day. Each person working for the light makes a difference.

Today, we will be using the Divine Portal as a transportation device again to find another pyramid designated to be of assistance to each of us, which of course affects everything else. I am so thankful you are showing so much excitement to be a part of this experience. Let's mount our Avatars and see what is in store for us.

We are getting a little view of the area as we fly over. It is a rain forest that once looked like it was dying, but I can already see new growth since a few days ago. It's a healthy new growth, not the normal direction it was going. It looks like the original DNA of the plants is kicking back in. Also, the ocean has a brighter, more brilliant and energetic shine. It looks like it's spreading the clean energy out, but rather slowly.

Now I see where we are going. It is a pyramid on an island just off the eastern coast of South America, still near the Equator. We are being pulled toward it like a magnet. It is where we are needed next. It looked so small to start with, but, as we get closer, the pyramid is bigger than the last ones.

I am also starting to feel the turmoil which resonates within, and, of course, it is exactly the journey we are on. Spring clearing of the Plagues put on the Planet at the time Economic Slavery was used to control the people.

Let's roll up our sleeves, so to speak, and prepare ourselves for this task. My Dragon feels this energy too, so I imagine that your Avatars are quite perceptive to this trauma, especially in the way of the Plagues. Take a moment to make a call to the Creator for support and protection for yourself and your Avatar. Remember to ask for guidance in how to go about this task we are being called to participate in. Include Teams of assistance and protection for all involved in this journey, and include a request to protect our Avatars. Also, thank you for sending what we need, even when we don't know what to ask for.

We have been circling this pyramid looking for the right door to enter. So far, it hasn't presented itself to me. I am now being told we need to fly through the waterfall on the side closest to the ocean, and that there is a tunnel for us to enter there.

This waterfall is very different. Normally, when we go through a waterfall, it's full of amazing energy to heal us. Today, it feels like we need to set an intention of it being a waterfall of protection for us. Yes, there it is. Now we can fly right into the center of it.

These blind moves are a challenge. I hope my Dragon sees through the water to know if it's clear ahead, or if we need to make a sharp turn, or if there's a solid wall with a tiny opening for us. I also hope my Dragon knows where to turn without my direction.

Of course, he did. He's so good at this. I am told that where he's from, they live–in tunnels behind waterfalls. Wonderful! The tunnel is large enough for all of us to easily travel through. It is also well lit, at least as far as I can see. We are being told to take a headset from the wall as a means for us to communicate. Not with each other, as we already do that quite well, but with the pyramid itself. Our Avatars can communicate with each other telepathically, and they with us. They will also be on the lookout for any danger.

As we go deeper into this tunnel, there are several others that branch off. I don't feel drawn to enter them, and we should stay together for a while longer. I have just been shown a part of the bigger picture from my Dragon. He tells me we're in a tunnel around the perimeter of the pyramid where, as we spread out, we will soon surround it.

Once we complete this grid, we are to stop for a moment and listen to what this pyramid's story is all about. I am hearing it was once a part of Atlantis. It was used for healings as well as experimental projects on those that did not obey the ways of the people. Some were also volunteers to be given more of whatever it was they needed in their living arrangements for themselves and their families. All of the experimentations were done in the name of science to find better methods of activating one's' natural abilities to the highest levels they could create. However, once a person was in the system, there was no leaving. They were held in this situation the rest of their lives. Exactly why we are on this journey. Economic Slavery was going on in this time.

Now, the question is – what are we to do to clear this? Seeing that we are in a grid around the pyramid, we each are to call in our teams of Angels and/or ETs of the highest and purest of Love, Light, and Gratitude to assist in this healing. I see many are gathered in this area at this moment. They seem to be holding hands and chanting and/or praying for those who were left behind to step forward for a healing. The Teams are doing the healings as they hold hands and create a stronger bond of energy. As these souls come out of hiding they have to, and will be, responsible for the receiving of the help.

Here, we just hold the intention of allowing them to receive what they need, to be able to heal from the traumas that have held them in this prison on the Planet. I also see a Team preparing a transportation device for them to continue their healing on a Medical Unit ship.

As they leave, I feel air sweeping through the area, cleaning and clearing it of the traumatic effects that have been held from the past until now. I also feel a golden shower of light coming into the entire area, for us as well as the area's past.

Once complete, it may continue outward from this pyramid. We will have to wait and see if it is possible at this moment.

Breathe Take time to allow it into yourself. For us to bring the Manifestation of Abundance into our lives, we must allow the release of traumas held within ourselves, then receive the abundance ready to flow into our lives. Today, take time to focus on breath – in and out. Along with the inflow and outflow, allow clearing of the old and new to make room for abundance to come into your life, including Health, Wealth and Joy.

See you tomorrow!

MONTH FOUR – DAY TEN

Are you doing okay with this? It's a lot to process in these mini sessions we are creating. I am being told we are assisting in a lot of shifting on the Planet at this time. I had no plans at all of this being so intense, and gathering so much information on how much of this Economic Slavery-Victim energy is being brought up. This is information that had never crossed my mind before this group of sessions. Thank you so very much for signing up to participate in this level of work for the entire Planet as well as ourselves, of course.

Ready for a new day? We seem to still be holding on to the information in this island pyramid. To me, this means that we aren't finished. Yes, we did release a lot of–the hidden information–from Atlantis. Let's tune in to what it is to be done next.

I believe we left off with us holding a grid pattern at the inner base of an island pyramid on the Atlantic Ocean side of South America. I see water is flowing out into the rest of the ocean with a newness to it thanks to the Island's water sources. For example, like the waterfall we rode through.

Let's allow ourselves to be teleported up a level to see what is going on. Oh, this I see, and I feel those who are in power having their meetings here. There is arguing and Chaos energy. The room is filled with maps and charts, bookcases full of plans for the Planet.

We are still in the perimeter grid formation, with energy now running diagonally and across each direction, back and forth. This exact place is one of the major causes of the fall of Atlantis.

Correct, we cannot bring Atlantis back to this Dimension. We have a job of clearing the current level of contention. This is the beginning of the secret societies and their plots against the people to further their own purposes and themselves.

Our grid of energy creates various holograms of information displayed in its middle. As it is shown, the Teams we work with don't delete what happened, as it is history and it happened. Instead, they clear or delete the contentious drama involved that still churns and creates lower vibrational currents on this Planet. I am seeing that what they did in the pyramid held a lot of power in the Earth grid. It holds our Earth back from the ascension it works so hard to take place.

Okay, now on to the other part that we play in this. We each bring up our fields of protection. We should already have them in-place -- this is just a reminder. Call in our Teams which specialize in this type of clearing and shifting for the whole Planet to move out of the political chaos that brings destruction of all.

I see many teams come into the room and sort of erase the writings on the wall which held the energy locked into this Dimensional reactionary state. Other Teams go behind the first group to clear and clean the leftover desires to have old, traditional drama locked on the Planet. They leave a trail of golden fairy dust from the Creator behind them as they usher the old patterns of information into the HAZMAT containers to be carried off our Planet through the star gates, to be dealt with in systems we would call a judge, but on a bigger level, as it has affected the entire galaxy.

We are to breathe this new life force energy being created into ourselves and assist our Avatars to do the same. Notice how your skin tingles as you breathe out the old, heavy traditional programming. Allow the golden fairy dust from the Creator to fill every pore of your skin to assist in your own clearing of these programs.

Reach into your heart and squeeze out the darkness of the old information. As you release it, see it fill with the new Lifeforce of the direction we are to move into.

This is a real heart -deep level of 'Out with the old, in with the new. Out with the old programming of Economic Slavery on all levels imaginable. Breathe in the new plans you have for your soul's purpose, even if you are not consciously aware of them. Just know that you now have made room for it to come in.

You have assisted in making room for the whole Planet to move forward. I would ask you to go somewhere else, but it feels like the grid at this point needs to be held a while longer. We only have one more day to get this done. Thank you for participating in this deep Planetary work that affects all of Earth, Us and the Galaxy.

See you tomorrow for our last ride in the Portal!

MONTH FOUR – DAY ELEVEN

WOW! Already we are at our last day. Yet, here we are in the midst of this huge pyramid still creating changes in this world. Let's see what we are to do with this situation. I must say that I was really hoping this would just be a fun experience, but it turned into quite an adventurous journey. Now to see what today brings.

First, we are to call in our Teams that know what to do next with whatever we encounter. They are very calming and here to assist in this next step. We are to gather our energy as a whole unit, including our Avatar's, with us. Then, with our intention, we are to ascend to the next level of this pyramid, still holding the grid we created. That was easy. You are so good at setting an intention and following through!

We are now at the healing floor. It has been created to keep those who ask to stay in a state of perfect health, but it is locked into the energy of those we just released. It is beautiful. The crystalline structures, the clear, crystal floor, the healing chambers – all have so much potential.

WOW! I've had dreams of this place but had no idea where it was. I thought that perhaps it was on another Planet, but here it is, simply hidden away in this pyramid.

I notice a dullness to everything, like it's all in a standby mode. NO, it is a mode of healing energy sent to the ancestors of those doing the work in the floor below that we cleaned. With the clearing done, we can do what is needed with this floor.

I just heard we are to participate in the reprogramming of it for the Now and for only the Light Workers who operate within the Creator's Truth, Love, and Gratitude. It will no longer serve the dark. We are to help with the reset of the Planet's Blueprint to assist with the reset of our Blueprint, which is to have no residue of Slave-Victim-Poverty-Powerless Energy. The economic poverty created by the power and control of our right to thrive, is to be removed in the frequency of this crystalline healing chamber inside this pyramid.

Are you ready? Our Teams are now prepared to assist in the direction of this clearing and cleaning. This is a whole new level of spring cleaning. They are ready with the HAZMAT team to clear the dark energy, so it can be exploded from here. The reset Team is here. I see the healing floor needs to be powered down completely before it can be re-booted to the Now and Beyond frequencies.

The switch has been turned to OFF. Give it a moment. Just breathe. Feel the drop into the void as it is switched off. The whole Planet will notice this. Now it can be cleaned easily. I see tubes of dark power energy dropping away, disintegrating, from certain control centers. I see replacement crystals for those burned or tarnished being brought in, as well as new, upgraded crystals with the energy of higher frequencies to be utilized in the correct Blueprint activity. The replacement is happening quickly.

Ready? The ON button has been pressed. Feel the rebooting, the revving up? Feel your feet on the crystal floor, and notice how your Avatar is loving this too. This level of clarity and excitement throughout our cells is awesome! Now, feel it in your soul. There should be better communication between you and your soul now.

So much easier to create an abundance of what you and your soul decide is best in the moment and into the future.

Give yourself a little time to recalibrate to this new frequency. For a bit, you may notice a change in body temperature or tiredness. You may also notice those around you who don't know what happened being a little out of sorts for a day or two. They will catch up quickly, as light of this nature is very healing.

If you need to take a little nap in one of the healing chambers, do it. Remember what it feels like, as from now on, you can call on that memory anytime you need to be transported into one. It is now in your consciousness for you to utilize as needed.

How do you feel? Are you ready for the next step? If not, take a little more time before continuing. We are now ready to breathe and let go of the pyramid's grid. We did an enormous job that has been waiting for this exact moment for us to be brought together to get the Planet moving at a higher frequency for the betterment of all.

It is time to get onto your Avatar and enter the Divine Portal once again to be lifted out of the tip of this pyramid. We will fly over the ocean and lands to deliver you safely back to your place of residence. Your Avatar may stay with you in an enlarged or shrunken state to put on a shelf or pocket, or you may leave it in the Divine Portal until next time, your decision between the two of you.

As we fly around this Planet, notice how the water is becoming clearer and the vegetation is taking on a more brilliant sheen. The original DNA Blueprint is being activated for the entire Planet. Of course, it is up to each of us to receive, as this is still a free will Planet. We can only set this offering before those to choose.

Thank you for your help and traveling this journey with me! We may be riding again next month. Where? I have no idea! But I am sure it will be adventurous.

See you next month!

See you soon with Truth, Love, and Gratitude

Pat, The Cosmic Cowgirl

Journal About Your Freedom From Economic Slavery

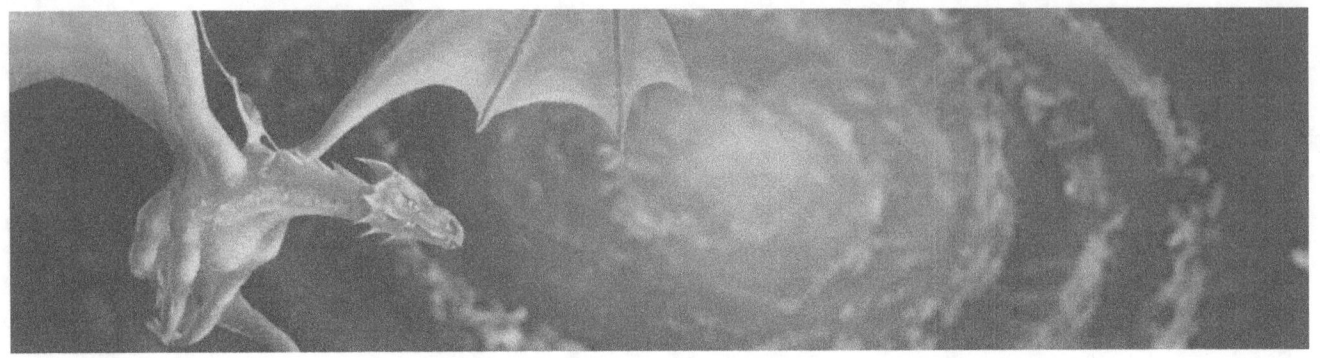

CHAPTER FIVE: CLEANING & REBIRTH

MONTH FIVE – DAY ONE

Hi! It is good to be back in the Divine Portal again. This time it is related to the spring ritual of cleaning and rebirth! Have you noticed how it just happens without having to think about it? The rains which cleans the air and the ground around you and bring about little plants shooting up from the Earth happens without any intent on our part. Of course, if we did add our intent, how much more intense or interactive could it be? I think we are about to find out.

This time we will be entering the Portal in an area of an island in the north Atlantic Ocean. The land here brims with the new growth of spring. The air is crisp one day and warms the next. The Portal waits for us to enter. I am not sure where it will take us, but I have a feeling it will be remarkable.

Before we can enter this Divine Portal, we are given a backpack with new supplies for this journey. This pack includes new clothing and other supplies that appear as we need them. Who would have thought of that? First, we are to go into changing rooms and toss out our now old whatever it is we are wearing.

We get new shoes, stockings, if you want, and more in this pack for later. We only walk out of the dressing room with the new items we are to take with us. Our older items are to be left outside of this Portal. This is symbolic of cleaning out our closets in the spring, as you may want to do in your daily life on Earth as you get time to do so.

Ready? Here we go! It looks like a giant cave we are walking into. There are stalactites and stalagmites everywhere which are beautiful and seem to be giving off a vibration of spring newness. I also notice that, as the Portal circles around us, one moment the stalagmites push up from the bottom while the stalactites hold tight to the ceiling. The next moment, they change positions. What is so wonderful is that I don't feel the rotation.

I don't quite understand how this works. Oh, I was just shown how this is the same as in the Air Ships that go whirling across the Universe. You don't notice how the ship flips around as you go through the sky. It feels like you are upright no matter what's going on. Yes, this is going to be an interesting ride.

Next, we go to the check-in lodge where we are given an orientation of what this Portal is and how it works. It is like nothing I have ever encountered, as I am told. We are directed to the plants. Do not touch them, as many are endangered, and one of our jobs is to preserve the integrity of the land. We will be told of other little things as we go along pertaining to the environment within the Portal.

We are given a guide to take us to our rooms. Let's see where they are. We are taken along a steep path to start with. There's a great view, if you take some time to look around.

We have to walk single file for the moment. Notice how the plants brush against you as you move through the area. Can you feel them clearing the old energy from your body through your skin as they brush your clothing?

As you walk along the path, each time you place your foot on the stones, it feels like they are pulling old, dried up pieces of the layers of hardened energy off and clearing them. These stones seem to know just how to do it easily.

We are led behind a waterfall to our rooms inside of a cave. This is the most beautiful housing situation I have ever seen. We have our own rooms, with a common area that has very comfortable seating to meditate with the waterfall. If you put on the headphones provided, you can hear tones from it which are specific for only you.

Notice what you clear as you are in the presence of this waterfall. Right now, I realize how it changes colors with how I feel in the moment. As I clear one old program, the waterfall seems to pull it into a cleaning phase. The colors and tones change as I do. Then the area where the old programs or information used to be is filled with a healing color for that program and what is required of my body to make the needed changes. After you feel that, you are clear enough to sleep. Go off to your room and let yourself recalibrate.

See you tomorrow.

MONTH FIVE – DAY TWO

How are you doing? I can still feel some effects from the meditation I did with the waterfall yesterday. What I notice is how spacey I have been feeling today. I suppose I still have some more clearing to do, along with recalibrating in this area of Spring Cleaning and Rebirth.

Grab your backpack so we can head out and follow the guide today. We seem to be going out of the cave behind the waterfall on the opposite side of what we entered yesterday. I can see ahead only a little distance. It feels like there's an exciting surprise awaiting us. The tunnel we walk through is extended out into a covered dome-shaped, see through environment. We can view the plants and animals that live here in a controlled space, so we don't harm them, and vice-versa. We must understand how our emotions can affect them and all which is around us in creating our own reality. Even though we are behind the glass, some of our junk energy leaks out through the molecules of its surface. It is time to be responsible for who we are and what we do.

Reach into your backpack and pull out some special gloves to protect you as we leave this place. If you are not wearing long slacks and hiking boots, now would be a good time to also put them on. Yes, they are in your backpack. It isn't that you would be physically harmed, as in touching something would be poisonous. Rather, as these plants touch you, they can clear you so fast that you would not easily know how to handle it. Hopefully, by the time we are finished in here, you will be able to.

During this part of our walk we have been told many things about what to expect within the Portal. The end of the controlled environment is just ahead of us. We have been directed to follow this path and turn right at the crossroad. There, we will be given a surprise.

There is such a feeling of excitement that it's hard to contain myself. I feel such an energy high with the new change coming toward us. The field of change is being created on a grander level for us due to our own anticipation and intent. I also feel your anticipation to get your Avatars!

I see a whole variety of Avatars to choose from in the corral up ahead. Consider your own thoughts and ask your soul to decide what you want your Avatar to be. Of course, mine is still the big Purple Dragon that can fly through the multiple Dimensions we play in as well as others for my work. He can also grow or shrink as needed for whatever the situation calls for. Let your imagination flow and allow your Soul to help decide what is required for this journey.

As we walk over to the corral, notice which Avatar comes right up to you. Is it the one you had in your mind and soul of what you wanted it to be this time, or is it some completely different sweet or fierce being?

Your soul will pick the one you are to work with. Take time to get acquainted. Hugs and treats are always a nice way to begin. I know I really missed working with my Dragon lately. I am sorry I didn't call on him sooner to help with some of the things I deal with daily, including traffic jams. Loving hugs are so healing for both.

Now that you have created the bond, you will start working together with your Avatar in your dream time. It is time to go back to the cave, for there is still some more work to do with the connection to the waterfalls.

Find a quiet area within this room where you can hear the tonality of the falls hitting the rocks as it moves down into the river below. Notice how it almost has a tinkling tone in the background. Is it the same color as it was yesterday?

To me, it seems to start out a darker green, then changes to blues as it shifts with my energy and what I clear. The tones of the falls change too. Sometimes I hear soft, windy sounds while other moments I hear the falls pounding the sides of canyon as it rides itself into the depths below with the water crashing into the bottom. Each moment of change outside brings change within as we are here to let go of the old to make room for the new.

When you have had enough, walk around to get yourself recalibrated or go to your room to recalibrate for the next few hours. Continue with the meditation time as much as you can as there is so much to clear for most of us.

See you tomorrow!

MONTH FIVE – DAY THREE

I have been thinking about this Ritual of Spring Cleaning & Rebirthing – or changing of the old ways to make room for the new. This has played out in my son's life, with whom I recently visited. His baby was born three weeks early in perfect condition in an at-home delivery – a whole new event for the family. Then, a few days later, his oldest daughter graduates from high school, ready to go off to college in the fall.

Of course, there is a lot going on between these two events. There was a lot of preparation for each to take place. The entire process of creating a baby, then the entire process of going to school and working very hard to be able to move to the next levels, the leaving the old patterns of how to interact in high school level with friends that have been there for years.

The preparation for these adventures of the baby and the graduate are whole Rebirthing processes not only in the physical world, but very symbolic for how their whole lives are changing, which changes our lives and everyone else around them. What changes in the moment for one, creates changes for the whole.

Today, we get to go out into the Divine Portal to experience a little more of this phenomenon. I notice that our backpacks are filled with a new weight. We are also dressed in clothing which covers every inch of skin on our bodies. I feel the excitement for the day already. We are clearly ready to make some huge adjustments in our World by each move we take.

Let's start with finding our Avatar. Remember the path we took? Since we walked the main path before, we can now take the shortcut and bypass the enclosed area where we were taught about the plant life that we'll interact with at various times. If you need a refresher of any of it, please go back through it later tonight when we get back.

There is a hidden door right behind that desk over in that corner. You can see it once you get closer. We can go directly to the path to the Avatar corral from there. Ready? I see they are prepared for us and are being led out for you to easily get into the saddle of sorts. Take a moment to feel what your Avatars are thinking and let them feel what you are thinking. Think and feel Love. It is the best way to connect and create a calm interaction. Now we are ready.

Let's take off to the left in pairs so you can help each other if a problem comes up. Now that we are gliding over to the left of the Portal, reach into your backpack and pull out a device to put into your ear. It will help you learn how to listen to what is going on around you. It isn't a magnifier, but an enhanced way of hearing to recognize the feeling involved with the message. It is what the plants do here and how your Avatar communicates. It will make life easier for you out in this environment.

As we glide over the many varieties of plants, notice their color variations. We can get a closer experience of this by landing in that clearing ahead. Now that we are here in the middle of this field, notice how all these color varieties are being emitted from the same variety of plant species. I would like for you to reach into your pack and pull out the treat that has been prepared for your specific Avatar. Notice how their Love for their treat emits a frequency that affects you. Where do you feel it? As the Avatar experiences their treat, what are the plants doing? They too are experiencing the Love frequency coming from not only the Avatars but also you as you feel the Love of your dear friend. I notice how the plants become closer to each other in color and lean in toward us.

Take your gloves off and let the plants touch your hands. By being a part of this Love interaction of three different species – you, your Avatar, and the plants – notice your shifts. How your old, tired, muscles are becoming more youthful just by experiencing the clearing of the old energy and allowing it to be replaced by Love. Isn't it amazing how fast it can happen?

Take a few minutes to walk among this specific plant variety and allow even more clearing of the old energies to be released. It is a very calming healing effect. I notice some of the Avatars rolling around in this clearing area. They know what they need. It is us silly Earth Humans that hold onto our old baggage for too long.

If you are ready, we can now get back onto our Avatars and return to the cave. Once we are there, give your Avatar the rest of the treat from your pack. I know this sounds strange, but take a small bite of what you give to your Avatar. It's not harmful. In fact, you will probably Love it as much as they do. It will also create a different type of bond between the two of you.

Once we are inside of the cave, find a quiet place and allow yourself to do more recalibrating from the old energy you released. Allow yourself to be filled with the Love that came back to help you move into the next level of who you are to become. If you still have some energy left within, take a little more time to sit with the waterfall again. Each time you do this, you will move deeper into the You ready to Rebirth your abundance energy and own it on a level that resonates at your core level. Remember to take extra time to recalibrate within yourself.

See you tomorrow!

MONTH FIVE – DAY FOUR

Hi! I am so happy to be here. While I was creating this Activation for you, my computer decided to download the newest edition of Windows, and there was no way to get out of it, at least with my limited bit of computer knowledge. So, now that I have gone through their process of getting me back to this page, I am very sorry I am a little late in getting this off to you. However, I also see how this month's activations have created a little strangeness.

For those that I know personally, there are a few things happening beyond our control that are moving us out of the old. In other words, we are doing the energy work to clear ourselves of the old programs and emotional traumas hanging around – right? So, of course, there are to be changes in our physical world. Mine just happened to be a computer upgrade I wasn't expecting. I know another person had an office manager who was okay with them doing the job. Not great, just okay enough to not want to train another person. She just gave her notice that this is her last week. Now it is time to find a better fit for the job.

Another person had a situation happen beyond her control which caused her to leave a second job giving her an extra amount of money to have a night out occasionally with her kids. The job had served its purpose for the past year, and it was time to move into the new purpose.

This, like so much Spring Cleaning, rids us of the stuff we hang onto thinking that someday we will get to it or need it. Clearing out the old prepares us for the Rebirthing of whom we really are, why we are on this Planet, and the way that will support us in an Abundantly Prosperous Journey of our Soul's Purpose. I am more than ready to see what today's journey brings. Let's get ourselves prepared for the day.

Take a deep breath and ground yourself from the top of your head, all the way down to the bottoms of your feet, into the soil of which we are walking on at this time. Take it down deep enough so that, when you are on your Avatar, you are still grounded in the presence of mind to be in the space of flying, yet not be too spacey. That feels so much better now.

Backpacks and gloves on to start with, along with the earpiece for communications going on around you. This will help you develop your telepathic skills. Just the knowledge that there is more going on around you than what you normally hear, see, and feel, in the physical is helpful to create your intuitive skills.

The Avatars are ready for us. Mount up! Oh, they too are ready to go. Some were quite frisky with their riders. For those of you that can't see the others around us, there was some crazy activity going on.

We are going to go straight up toward what looks like the top of this Portal where the stalactites hang down. Each of you will go to the one that calls to you. Fly around it, notice how slowly it moves with the vortex. It is sort of hypnotic in how it moves, slowly in a rotation over to the side moving forward. As you near the one that calls you, ask to take a piece of it. Hold out your hand and watch as a small piece is dropped into it. Of course, small is a relevant term. To some, it may be a grain of sand.

To others, it may be a larger chunk. Place it safely into your backpack. You will not be affected by it if you keep your gloves on.

Fly to the next one that gets your attention. Don't think about it, just go to it. You may notice some differences in the two of them – size, shape, color, or how it feels. Ask this one – either telepathically or verbally, I am certain it will understand – for a small piece of it to be given to you for your healing journey.

Take your time and let it drop into your hand. Put this one in another backpack pocket. For now, keep them from touching each other.

We will slowly fly to that landing pad off to our left and then straight down. It will be a safe place for us and our Avatars to just be for a little bit. Once we land, reach into your pack and pull out a small treat for your Avatar, one for you, and water for both. Once your needs have been met, bring your pack into the center where seating has been arranged for you.

It is time to reach into your pack. Keep your gloves on, and pull out the first stalactite piece that you received. Place it on the ground in front of you. In your mind, or verbally, ask it what message it has for you. You may feel it, or you may hear it in your earpiece. Take your time.

Now set it aside, reach into your pack, and pull out the second piece of stalactite. Place it on the ground in front of you and retrieve the information it has for you in the same manner as the first. It may not make any sense at all, or it may be exactly what you need to hear.

Place them both together in front of you. They may touch or just be near each other. Feel how they communicate with each other. Together, they have another very special message for you. Remove your gloves and hold them together close to your center/stomach area and listen to their message. Feel the energy shift they create for you. Notice how you are being cleared in so many areas – mental, emotional, spiritual, and physical.

Once this is complete, put the stones back into your pack to take back to the cave with you. Ground yourself again before you get back onto your Avatar. Give the command for him to go back to the cave. You may be taken on the scenic route or you may be taken back in a moment of time.

When you arrive, take the stones to your room and go through the steps again in the privacy of your own space – one stone at a time, then together. This will take you into a deeper level clearing. Once done, give yourself time to recalibrate to the new You.

See you tomorrow!

MONTH FIVE – DAY FIVE

That was some incredible Spring Cleaning and recalibrating. I can see in your auric field that you are already shifting into a new energy. This is the preparation it takes to Rebirth you as a Phoenix. The most important aspect of this is to learn to be in your Heart Space and easily enjoy it for extended periods of time. Allow the Phoenix to begin to take shape.

Today, we will begin with a hike around this waterfall area. Remember how the water would change colors when you first got here? Let's see what it does now as we go near it. The trail will take us right up to it at the front of the cave, which is the back of the waterfall. It will be very noisy, so utilize the ability of how your earpieces work. Listen for the subtle tones within colors of the waterfall. I will also keep in contact with you through it.

The first thing I would like for you to do is take the water container from your backpack and reach into the waterfall to fill it. Notice its color as it goes into your container, then notice how it changes each time you take a drink. Pay close attention to yourself and how you are now handling the waterfall going internal. At first, the waterfall can be very intense energy to be around in comfortable chairs. Now you are drinking it! This is a great way to shift the emotional energy you carry.

You may wonder why we are going through so much shifting and clearing during these journeys. It's because a person has great difficulty in creating the energy for Manifesting Abundance while carrying deep rooted emotions of grief, sadness, anger, lust, greed, sorrow, and other emotion used to manipulate you and those around you. When you are clear of these emotions on the deepest level, you notice how so much just falls into your lap.

It may be a $20 bill that you found in your pants pocket, or your seasonal jacket, at the exact moment you needed it. Remember the excitement and relief you felt when you found it. Perhaps you walk out the door and you find a $20 bill just lying on the seat in your car, or blowing down a path you are walking on where no one is available to ask if it is theirs. It takes time to stay clear, so you can manifest at this level. This is the Rebirth you should be looking for. Just a little tangent we needed to get off on to clear your curiosity as to why I do some of the things I do.

Now that you drank all the water, do you feel like taking a little hike? I suggest we take the path along the river. It's mostly an easy path, especially if you are wearing the right shoes for this adventure which, with just the thought, you now have them on. Good that you also have on protective leg and arm wear. Remember the power in the plants and rocks within this Portal. You may want a hat or some protective headgear and gloves.

As we walk in a single line on this trail, you might notice which plants lean toward you and which ones pull away as you come near them. What thoughts run through your head at the time? Curiosity, grumpiness about the heat, tired feet? Interest in this part of the adventure, or complete dislike of hiking? Fear as a snake or lizard crosses your path or over your shoes?

Or, do you have an excited feeling. Are you wowed as a hummingbird comes near you? Each of these emotions affects how you manifest. It really is about being able to receive and be in a state of joy versus a state of any form of Victim energy. I can see and hear how that explanation helped. Remember the earpiece? It also helps to let me know how you are doing within this little day journey and within the big journey.

I notice we are in a large area, and it is safe to remove the protective head gear and gloves. If you are afraid of what may happen, don't remove it; but if you are curious and ready, slowly reach up and take off the head protection and your gloves. If you aren't ready at this moment, you can do it at any time within this experience.

Sit down on the ground. Breathe in a slow, steady rhythm. Relax into being in the moment. Close your eyes and allow the Portal to give you what you need. Take a few breaths, relax, and let yourself be taken into the moment.

Now open your eyes. Don't panic. Just breathe slowly. Yes, the plants came to you and are now covering your head and hands. They are like very delicate electrodes touching areas of your head and fingers to help you move to the next level of your own journey. Once you have received all you can for today, they will remove themselves from you and go back into the ground. Take your time to feel yourself moving back in your own shoes before we start back. Feeling your feet within your shoes is a quick way of grounding yourself to return to the now of the moment.

You might want to put your headgear back on as we get back on the trail with a bigger variety of plants surrounding us. Because of the processing you just went through, you probably don't need more stimulus right now. As we go back to the base cave, you can take your time to observe more of this area. You may want to sit on a rock and watch the river as it rolls by. It's tempting to put your feet in for a nice soak, but I would not advise that just yet. Maybe later in the journey, after you have processed on a different level, you will be ready to do that.

Today will probably be the last day at this cave. You may want to take some extra time to review the plants and their properties within this Portal again, or you may want to sit with the waterfall and see what else comes up, or both. Take extra care of yourself with the recalibration process that is going on.

See you tomorrow!

MONTH FIVE – DAY SIX

Today, we are to prepare to move to a new location. Not a big deal, really, as the Divine Portal will take us there since it's moving. From what I can tell, we are going through a wormhole in the cave system within the Earth. It feels like we have been placed into a bubble as a group which are going through the same experience at the same time.

We are leaving behind the waterfall and the intense clearing plants that were natural to the area. I am not sure where we are headed, but it seems like we are going somewhere around Australia. Our Portal is spinning its way through an inner-Earth corridor. We are coming out on an island near Australia yet staying in the Portal. I am not sure why this area, but it feels like we have some matching energy clean up. Oh, the Spring Cleaning job!

I just got a piece of the puzzle. How many of us have ancestors who have been treated badly at one time, forcing them to move to another area of the world? For example, I have ancestors from Ireland and Scotland who were starved and imprisoned by England for not doing various things, like not paying taxes to the English.

Then, they were shipped to America to be indentured servants. This feels like a place where something like this happened as well.

Perhaps it has to do with Slavery energy of all types. Who hasn't felt like they were enslaved at some level to their country, their family, their job, themselves, medicines, drugs, sugars, foods, addictions?

WOW! This is going to be a huge piece of Spring Cleaning in order to be clearer for the Rebirth of the real Divine Blueprint of who we are to claim our Birthright of Abundance.

Are you ready to venture out of this bubble we have been riding in? I see our Avatars were also protected within a bubble in this Portal. We don't get to leave the Portal to venture outside, but we can move to where we are guided to go within the Portal to do what is next. Grab your backpack and let's go.

It feels like the ground is moving under our feet as this Portal hasn't completely settled into the area, but we need to get onto our Avatars to be more stable and allow the Portal to settle down a bit. Yes, this is a very huge piece for us to experience. Mount up!

We are going to lift off to the right this time as it currently seems the safest. Let's go up to just under those pink clouds. We will continue to that outcropping on the side of the cliff over there. There is a cave for us to enter the mountain.

We can build a fire in here and relax for a while. We will get some broth fixed, and add some of the herbs that have been prepared for us from a container on the shelf. I checked, and they are completely safe. They will boost our immune system as we shift out of this strange Slave energy. Oh, good, this broth doesn't taste too bad, I have tried some nasty tasting immune-building broths before. This one is okay.

Some of the local Tribes' people are here to play the drums for us to dance around the fire. This is a very ancient way of clearing the old. They will dance with us to teach us what we have forgotten of the ancient ways. Listen carefully to the words they sing. You may not understand them with your ears or mind, but the ancestral part of you will, and that is where the clearing will begin.

It is time for those that are ready to begin this part of the journey.

Join me in this very important part of Spring Cleaning. Listen and move to the beat. Allow the drums to enter your Soul as your feet move with the rhythm of the heartbeat of the Mother.

Spin, sing, and dance as you allow yourself to enter the realm of the ancestors. If not yours, then those of the collective consciousness – the Morphic Field of Slavery.

Now, call upon the Divine Teams that ride with us to protect us from all harm in every Dimension, to assist in the Spring Cleaning of the energy fields of all Slavery. To clean and clear the Collective Consciousness and the Morphic field of Slavery of all forms. Then, to bring the Golden Light of the Creator to heal all the DNA that was locked into that realm.

Once the DNA begins to heal, we can move to the next level of the New Consciousness of believing and knowing that we can be what our Divine Blueprint and Divine Plan had in store for us when we said yes to coming to this Planet. We are to embody the Divine Beings that we are, and KNOW we are here for the purpose of doing our work with Ease and Abundance.

As you feel the need to rest, find a place here in this cave to sit or lay down to allow yourself to recalibrate. If you want to continue dancing after a break and more broth, just join in the group. There is no set amount of dancing or resting required for anyone. You may dance until you can't move your legs anymore, or not. It is your choice, you are not slaves to any rules. Take your time to embody this clearing and get to know the real You.

See you tomorrow!

MONTH FIVE – DAY SEVEN

WOW! How do you feel today after that huge shift? That was a lot of Spring Cleaning! I noticed a lot of changes happening within the collective consciousness of the Realm of Slavery. It may take a while for you to navigate from the old program you are used to living in to the new You that you are capable of being now.

I just got a message, we are going to be moving again. Not just us within the Portal, but the entire Portal. It is swirling on a huge mission to get us to the European continent. Just stay in this cave with your Avatar until we get to the area of calmness within here.

Before we leave, look in the fire pit. I notice some very special stones in there which hold the clearing energy of what we just did. You may take one if you wish. Just pick one that resonates the most with you. Hold it and notice how it makes you feel. When you are complete, put it into your pack to take with you.

Our landing is very interesting. We are in the vicinity of the Vatican, the representation of a very old Religion on this Planet. This is a place of many years of turmoil, rumors, and control. I wonder what we are to do, or how we are to do any Spring Cleaning here. I understand the representation of this place and what we need to do pertaining to the Spring Cleaning around this time. It is all about Religious control and how it creates the victimization of the entire Planet. The religious wars that have pitted family against family, tribe against tribe, country against country. I am not sure what part we can play in this realm of clearing.

I hear we are to get on our Avatars and ride to a clearing just above this cave. We will be out in the open where we can experience the Earth, Air, Water, Fire, and Spirit elements as they too have been affected by this level of Ego power. It will only take a moment to get there. This is a beautiful area, and it also has a fire pit with beings coming forth to help with the fire maintenance for us.

What we are to learn here is the control of self without Ego being the motivator. We tend to think that the money game is all about power and control. Actually, the secret to having money and abundance is all about being in a state of calm, Heart-Centered, Creative energy. That has been difficult to do with the programming we have undergone in relation to Religion.

How many times have you heard that money is the root of all evil? To be wealthy is a sin. To be wealthy, you must be a ruthless person. When you have money, everyone expects you to share it with them, without their doing anything to help get it in the first place. This creates the fear of it being taken away, including the governmental system of taxing. No one can have more money than the Church ... another emotional trauma.

Now the question is, what can we do about it? As I put this question out there, the answer I am shown is for us to gather in a circle around the fire. It is a huge fire, like a bonfire from some camping experiences I have been on. Within the fire an image is appearing – a hologram of a moving history lesson of what has been, and how we have always been with our ancestors being a part of this creation. We are to watch it for a little while.

It is very hard to watch the trauma, the hardship, the pain that so many went through in the process of trying to make enough money for their families to live on.

Some of it isn't so different from today with wars that have pitted people against each other. It is very intense, but that is the reason it's being shown in the fire.

We are to pick up a handful of dirt and bless it with Love and Gratitude with the intent of it being a part of the healing and cleaning of this old energy. Toss it into the center of the fire, covering the hologram with a film of clearing dust.

The wind comes from all directions – not too strong, but enough to fan the flames back into a large fire again to clear more. Now it is starting to rain, but that isn't dowsing the fire. This leaves us with Spirit to complete the clearing.

On the ground around the fire pit is a tip of what looks to be a bag. Everyone pick up an edge. This is a full circle of lifting this bag up over the fire. As we do this, our Spirit Guides and Helpers are here to assist in bringing the top of the bag together. As the top of the bag touches the other side of itself, there are sparks of the highest intensity that flash within the bag – sort of turning it in on itself!

Notice what you feel as the flash happens. It nearly took my breath away for a moment. It was a form of neutralizing the entire situation of Religious control and Victimization for all of us. I don't know about the entire Planet, but at least for all of us. I hear this will include all our ancestors involved who want this Spring Cleaning for themselves too. It isn't automatic for them, it is only if they want it.

It is time to get back on your Avatar and ride to the main cave for recalibration. The waterfall will help neutralize these intense clearings we have done. Take some time for yourself to allow this healing to take place. Notice if you begin feeling like you are being rebirthed into the new energy of You.

See you tomorrow!

MONTH FIVE – DAY EIGHT

Welcome back. I wasn't sure if you would be here after the last two days of very intense Spring Cleaning. Hopefully today will be a little more enjoyable. Yes, we are going to be moving again. Well, the Portal will be moving again. We are always moving!

I was informed that today would be a journey to an island in the Pacific Ocean, where the islands of Lemuria once were. Just off the coast west of South America. I was hoping it would be Hawaii, but I guess not this time. Hang on to your stomach, as this is quite a quick journey with a different spin going on within the Portal.

It feels like we are going through a wormhole to get us to the area quickly. Wow, that was quick! I have a remembrance of this area somewhere deep inside of me. Of course, we are still inside the Portal, but we can get glimpses of what is around us through the walls, floor, and ceiling. The water is a very specific color that is only right here. There is a special calmness in the atmosphere as well.

I notice the Portal is taking on the island's environment including the plants and animal. It's amazing how it can do that. Breathe in this calming sea air and breeze which is only attuned to this area. This is a great place to find those Abundance Energy Blocks and just Spring Clean them out of ourselves.

What I am being told is that so many of us have experienced some great disappointments. One example would be where we have done all the steps in focusing on receiving the goals we set, including Vision Boards. We start out with great intentions, energy flowing in huge, positive bubbles around us, but we just can't quite hold on to visions of believing we deserve what we ask. Or, we get held back by not believing it is possible to achieve that level of abundance. As a child growing up, how many times did we hear 'Don't get your hopes up'?

So, we learn to create a protective field around our hearts. This level of protection is done from fear, of believing I don't deserve my dreams because I am not supposed to get my hopes up. We protect ourselves from another disappointment to the level of not even stepping out there in hope again. This is another level of that Victim belief. We think we get it all cleared, and it still lurks deep down in the old programming.

Let's take a ride on our Avatars to a very special cave I remember from Lemurian times. I am certain that it was on one of the islands in this area. Perhaps this Portal can create that cave just for us. I am putting in the order as we get our Avatars ready. I know we can find it. Make sure your headset is on, and follow me.

I am being guided to a different area of this Portal. There may be some storms we pass through, but I am certain we will be fine. It is quite a distance from the main base where we have stayed, but what is time anyway? I see it! We can enter it from the other direction if we slow down and make the turn just right.

Yes, we are all here! As we enter this cave there is a spray cleaner as we go through various rooms. It helps raise our vibration as well as gets the dust off. There are three stages of cleaning to go through before we reach the exact room I was looking for.

Yes, it is still here! It is an Amethyst Crystal room. In the center is a crystal table to lay down on. Actually, you end up levitating above it so that you can be cleared on all levels of your being at the exact same time. It is one of the most amazing feelings ever.

There are several rooms exactly like this. I will walk you to the one that is specific for you. Notice when you are on this table how light you feel. There is nothing like being levitated in a healing session. You don't have to do anything this time except hold relatively still and receive.

This type of healing and cleaning is a technique that releases a lot of the thought forms of Needing to live in a state of Power and Control. It helps you begin to go into a state of developing the power within yourself, where there is no need to dominate or be dominated. You can begin to regain your own innate power within. As you are ready to do so, and the cleaner you are of old programs you walk around with, the easier it will be.

As you are completed on the Amethyst Table, you may feel a little lighter or even lightheaded. Take your time. You may stay on there if you would like, especially if you fall asleep. This is a part of your Rebirth process. When you are complete, your Avatar will be waiting for you along with a guide to assist you in getting back to the base camp.

See you tomorrow!

MONTH FIVE – DAY NINE

Great to see you again! How did you like that crystal bed healing table? It is one of my favorite places to take myself when I have a problem. Oh, I forgot to tell you, at any point in time, even after we have finished a Portal journey, you can go into a meditation and take yourself back to any of the places we have gone through to experience it again. The crystal healing table is one I use when I can't get certain things to clear for myself. It is so easy to beam myself into one of the empty rooms and ask my Teams to be there to help also. It is really a great space for me.

Today, we are going to experience more of this Divine Portal. Let's get ourselves ready for a little traveling with hearing and translating devices, backpacks, proper clothing for a great adventure, and riding for a while. Mount up!

I noticed this Portal has several of my favorite things to do. To start with, we will be riding right down the center – if you can tell what the center is as it is spinning. But we will do our best to be in that area for a while. At this place in the sky, there is a wave of energy to just float in that is so much easier to navigate.

We just ride the wave of Peace and Calming. We are now coming to an area that is drawing me into it. Did you notice the ease of which we can just glide? It is another cave on the side of that mountain.

As we enter, there is a place off to the side for your Avatar to stay safely. He will be properly fed and cared for. There are quite a few people in this cave for some reason. We can check in at the desk in the middle of this room, I will ask about the purpose of this cave, what its properties are, and how they relate to us.

Now I know that it's for a specific healing, as are most things in this cave. There are so many aspects to healing that people need at this time, with how fast things are changing on this Planet which, in turn, affects all Planets. I was told it has to do with their own energy as they see themselves, and how they wish to progress on this Planet.

So far, I see this cave as very peaceful. Perhaps the back rooms are more soundproof after a lot of work was done. I just thought this was a strange thing to say, but soundproof is related to the tones of the outside world that influence our being, and we are given the opportunity at this time to help our ancestral family. As we create deep and intentional changes, our ancestors are also cleared. It is very quiet in here, an energy and awareness of how Sacred and important it is to be in this room.

People have slowly gathered the information and have done this work on many levels, but this, I am told, is the fastest and easiest right now. We are going into the Pools of Cleansing. The changing rooms are over there. We are to wear special clothing into these pools. We get to enter this pool all together as it is specifically set energetically for this group. It is time to walk into it.

The water doesn't feel the way I expected it to. It is a nice temperature, and to me it feels slick, not a slippery, falling slick, but a smoothness, like we are sliding into another Dimension. I notice little sparks of light as various programs are removed from us. These are very old programs that have affected our DNA into holding us back and not letting us evolve completely in this time where we are now living. There are other sparks of light helping us continue our easy correction of the DNA. This will only take place on a level you are ready to work with. If you don't want to shift any of your DNA, it won't happen. It is all your choice.

Once we are complete as far as we can be shifted right now, we are led out of the pool and to a room to rest. This is where we can continue with the recalibration – the Rebirth into new beings we are to be at this time on this Planet. Take your time, be easy with yourself, and notice the little things that are different.

See you tomorrow!

MONTH FIVE – DAY TEN

I am so happy to see all of you here and physically okay this time. I have no memory of how I got back to my room at the base cave after being in that pool. I am so glad to see that you are back here as well. We have been through some very intense healing sessions this month. I'm hoping this Spring Cleaning has brought you closer to the resonance you need to Rebirth your Divine Abundance.

Today, we need to have a little fun in this Portal. Let's go for a ride deeper in. Know that where we end up, our base cave of rooms will be there for us. We will need both our communication devices for our ears and our backpacks. I will meet you at the opening where our Avatars are kept.

I get the distinct feeling we all currently need a little chance to feel more fun within ourselves. I also hear that the Avatars are getting a little restless. I have an idea … let's see how fast they want to go and just let them. I used to do that with my horse occasionally when I was growing up. My Dad wasn't pleased, as he thought I would get hurt or the horse would do something crazy like run away with me. She did, I didn't tell him, I just hung on. She eventually stopped, and we had a great day. I have been watching you and see you are great with the connection to your Avatar, and that you will do just fine.

We can go up near the top of the Portal and ride a current of waves which will keep us moving as fast as we want and give us the freedom to do spinning dives and flips. Or, it will keep you as slow as you want.

Woo-Hoo! This is great. I love the feeling of the wind blowing my hair in all different directions at once! WOW! I needed this feeling of freedom.

Oh, look up ahead – a different type of rainbow! It has so many different layers of each color. As I am now in it, it feels thick and gooey. I wonder what it tastes like? To me, each color tastes like a fruit. Some I recognize and some I don't.

So many flavors of each shade of the color of orange, yellow, and red! I think whatever this rainbow is made of, it also does something with a part of our physical being. My tongue feels tingly and my Dragon has the hiccups. Now I can't stop laughing. How do you stop a Dragon's hiccups? It's all I can do to stay on with my laughing and his crazy intense hiccups.

We bounce into a purple cloud! It is incredibly sticky. I can feel it soaking into my skin, so, of course, it is soaking into the Dragon's skin. The hiccups stopped, and my laughter settled down. We are fine now. How did all of it affect you? Maybe you just had fun laughing at me and my Dragon. I, for one, hate being sticky!

Now we need to get cleaned up. I see another waterfall up ahead that we can go into to wash off. However, I also feel a great pull to go into it. I wonder why. This feeling usually means something important is going to happen. I just want to get rid of this sticky stuff.

The waterfall is gentle as it helps melt the sticky cloud off us. My Dragon is feeling better too. Now I recognize what this waterfall is all about. It brings us into a preparation for what is to come. The never-ending easy flow of how the power within works. When we flow with ease, no one has power over us – we are inside the power. That is, Abundance flows toward us instead of us struggling to keep it or grab onto it. When we are in a state of Abundance, we ride the waves of constant easy flow. That doesn't mean we don't do our work. It means that we don't have to struggle within ourselves to do the work we are put here for. It is just easier.

I can tell we did some easy shifting today as we rode the wave of time with our Avatars. Fun and laughter is the biggest catalyst to create what we want from ourselves interacting with the Universe. This was a great, easy way to play as we created some forward movement through this Portal.

The base cave is now ahead. Let's go in early and enjoy the time that we have left in here. You can always ask at the information desk about some extra exploring to do if you want. Just some more time to spend together before we are finished with this Portal.

See you tomorrow for our last ride in the Portal!

MONTH FIVE – DAY ELEVEN

Today, as we gather for the last time this month at our base cave, my heart is so happy that we had this time to spend together. We went through some very deep Spring Cleaning events. I can tell a lot of changes took place and are continuing to occur in the Rebirth process of the power within you to create Abundance you are ready to receive. I am looking forward to continuing our Divine Portal Activations next month with those of you who have found these journeys worthwhile. Or, if not worthwhile, at least interesting and a break from the normal world of events for a few moments.

We still have more to do today as we are not at the exit point of this Portal. First, I want you to notice something. See that trail over there? Remember walking a trail very similar to it when you first stepped out of the cave? You had to have long pants, long sleeves, gloves, and a head covering due to the sensitivity of you and the clearing ability of the plants and stones in here. I would like for you to leave the shoes, gloves and head coverings in the cave. You can wear whatever clothes you want.

Now, as we go out that far door leading to the Avatars, notice how nice it is to feel the ground under your feet and how the plants still lean toward you and touch you at times. They are not as potent as they were to you. That is an example of how much you have cleared and changed in this short amount of time. You can still set the intent of more clearing by these stones and plants if you wish to go to another level, but, for now, noticing where you once were and where you are now is a great step.

Let's get on our Avatars and prepare to find the final wave to ride to the end of this Portal. I see it is taking us to the right of the cave and creating a circle around the area for one last goodbye to those who have assisted us along this journey and taken care of our needs within the cave and the needs of our Avatars. The beings that live here are very excited for you to have worked so hard on your journey.

Now we can glide over the tops of the trees and let your feet touch them. You may get a little tingle for a bit more Spring Cleaning. Take a moment to notice how much more brilliant the colors are today. When I see the changes in the intensity and brilliance of the color of the plants, the sky, and the water, I can gauge how much I have changed. Each time it is richer and more vibrant. So, if you want a little more Spring Cleaning, just let your feet drag somewhat when we sail over the trees and the water on our way through the Portal.

I see another waterfall and river for us to follow. It sort of winds through the trees below us. This waterfall is just calling us to come to it and fly through it sideways. I have never done that before. Actually, I have never even thought of doing it that way before as I didn't want to get that wet. But in here, if we are being Called to do something specific, I think it's a good idea to do just that. So, here we go.

Oh, it isn't as bad as I thought it would be. I am hardly getting wet at all, but I do feel something familiar, yet different, happening. I remember now what it is. There have been times when I have taken my car through a special car wash where, after it is clean, a sealant liquid is sprayed onto it for a protection against things like bugs and weather.

This seems to be what is happening to us. We are getting a sealant of some sort poured over us as we fly through the waterfall going from side to side. It is to help us hold this frequency longer once we enter the real world again. It feels very nice, not sticky or heavy. It is breathable as well as protective. I like it, and I can see how we will need it to help us keep the Power Within frequency moving with the wave of abundance flow.

We can now follow this river to the end of the Portal. It really winds in an interesting pattern. It seems to flow through a vortex type of path that seems like inside of a tornado. I feel the entire Portal now shifting itself back to the place where we entered. It always gives me a little funny feeling in my stomach when it moves like that. It's just an awareness I have of knowing what is happening around me. This is good, because we can easily recalibrate back into being in the world of where we must follow our purpose on this Planet. It should be easier now that we have gone through that level of Spring Cleaning.

I see the exit station. Also, there is a landing space where we can leave our Avatars and pick them back up next month as we begin the next journey. They will be well taken care of and transported to the next Portal for us. Or they can be taken with you with a pack full of special food and a shrinking potion to fit them into your travel bags, plus a recipe of how to create more for later. You have a few minutes to think about it as there is a waiting line. We are not the only ones here.

We are now ready to say our goodbyes and go our own directions. I will miss you! See you next month!

See you soon with Truth, Love, and Gratitude
Pat, The Cosmic Cowgirl

Journal Your Cleaning & Rebirth Levels

CHAPTER SIX: SUMMER SOLSTICE & USING FUN AS A MANIFESTATION TOOL

MONTH SIX – DAY ONE

Welcome to the Divine Portal of Benevolent Abundant Activations happening on the Full Moon, which happens to also be on the Summer Solstice. That just sounds and feels like the most FUN a person could ever have within a Manifesting Portal. Manifesting is easiest with the frequency and the experiences of Fun, Happy, Laughter, and Joy! Are you ready to experience any of or all of what is possible for this amazing journey?

I have Portal rev up for about a week. To me, that signifies it is going to be a very powerful experience. To begin with, you need a critter, a being, or what I call an Avatar – mine being my Purple Dragon – that you can get onto, fly, or be used for some form of flying.

Take a moment to find that very special one for this specific experience, and meet me on the landing pad with the painting of my Dragon on it.

I will wait for you and everyone else signed up for this journey. After all, there's no rush. It's all in Divine Right Timing. Things happen when we show up!

To manifest what you want, you have to Show Up! This is so exciting. I can feel the anticipation within this Portal. It is so charged with Manifesting energy! It must be the combination of Full Moon energy with Solstice Energy. WOW! I am nearly vibrating out of my skin.

Now that we are on the landing pad, or maybe I should call it the launching pad, get ready for the ride. I see the Portal – I guess to some it may look like a tornado moving in this direction – but notice it isn't windy around us, and it doesn't sound like a freight train, so it must be something greater. Get onto your Avatar, hold on, and, of course, Breathe! If you remain calm your Avatar will remain calm. It is time to enjoy this next eleven days. Wow! What a take off!!

This is so amazing. We are being taken to the Moon, or at least what the Portal would calls the Moon within itself. The energy here is highly exciting yet calm. It is like we are floating up easily while, simultaneously, it feels like we are slowly spinning around the Portal's vortex. I think we are moving much faster than it seems.

As we ride these waves of energy, it might be wise to let go of the old, you know, thoughts of responsibility or what happened yesterday or this morning. Let the old ideas or ways of doing things melt away and slide back to the landing pad. You don't need them in here. They can wait for you to pick up later, or you can just tell them they are no longer a part of your new life.

That feels much better for me. Sometimes I forget to let go of the old while I am on a new journey. How else can we embody the new if we still hang on to the old, right? So, take a deep breath and, as you breathe out, let all the old programs you have been running just slide off and out of your consciousness.

Just in time to land on the Moon of this Portal. We can walk around for a little while and just notice what you can. For me, the ground looks sort of white and feels spongy as I walk. I don't get the sense of sinking down. It is like walking on a foam mattress that tickles my feet. Each step seems to be doing a deeper clearing on me. Sometimes I wonder if there is an end to this clearing thing, but here we go again. I do feel lighter with each step. Also, the Moon's soil isn't sticking to my feet. It is staying in place. Just another observation coming to me.

It's time to start gathering back as a group toward that direction, just to make sure we are all here for the moment. I realize we are still within the Portal while on this moon, but I felt a strange shift or movement under my feet, sort of like a bulging up, then back down. As if I stepped on a live critter.

WOW! That sort of unnerved me for a moment, but it also made me giggly. I am not sure why, but it is sort of funny when the ground plays with me.

We are all together now. I want to hand out a new tool you can wear around your neck that helps with communication when we are out of site. It works with spoken words as well as intentional telepathic thoughts. We don't need to know every thought that goes on in each other's head, but if there is a need it will create a definite intention to be used for getting mine or someone else' attention like the Portal helpers. It can be used to get questions answered as well as a need fulfilled, such as if you forgot your water bottle. You then you get a water bottle delivered to you.

Oh, I just felt the bulging again, getting bigger and opening a hole. Now we are all sliding down into it, sort of like a bubble in the sand is giving way. It also feels like a slide at a water park where we are spin, drop, spin again, and drop, but not get wet.

The last drop brings us into a large ball pit. That was really fun! I think our Avatars liked it too. Maybe more like a ceiling opens and easily brings us into the underground room. Pick up a ball and take it with you. We will find out why later.

That was great! I see this room is like a giant hotel lobby of sorts. The floors look like polished marble that reflects symbols you get as you walk on it. I am not sure what activates it. Maybe we will learn that tomorrow.

Now we get to follow a leader to our own space – again not exactly like a hotel. You can create your own space room – a practice in 'ask and you shall receive' Also, it's a way to get the food you want. Get some rest. It is safe to explore within these boundaries.

See you tomorrow!

MONTH SIX – DAY TWO

Greetings for the New Day! I hope you had a great evening. For me, any Full Moon experience can be wonderfully strange no matter where I am. The colorful vivid dreams came again, but this time not as scary. They were full of brilliant activity of the Universe, with me getting to participate in the creation of what is next.

I love the room I have been given. It had a whitish vibration, but it was more of a pearlescent glow. Not a corner in the whole place. It had an oval shape to it, an oval bed, oval window, oval bathtub, even an oval space for my Dragon to sleep. It was sort of like being in an egg ready to be reborn each new day. I also felt the rotation of the Portal throughout the night, also like an egg being turned around once in a while. I am not sure of the meaning of all of this, but I am certain it will show itself soon.

As we walk into the main room of this hotel, my attention is brought to the symbols on the floor. They are always there, just under the shiny marble tiles. They look mostly like normal angelic writing, until it's time for them to activate the person that steps on them. Then I see them change. Sometimes they glow or start spinning and turn a different color like gold or silver, sometimes red or blue. I have also seen them whirl into the air at a frequency that looks like a fire which activates something needed by the person that steps on it. I have been watching them as they get stepped on and activated.

Then it happened to me. It was very pleasant, but this doesn't even come close to describing what it feels like, with glowing energy flowing through me. I could feel my stomach being tickled all the way around and straight through to my spine. It was just a little strange for me at the time, but it then turned into a huge belly laugh. This was such a giant release of some old programming. I think it was programming of how I am supposed to behave in a place such as this. Probably something I was taught when I was a child.

Just as I recognize the energy of how I used to behave, and how I can behave now, I feel so light. The floor of symbols suddenly turned into a musical chairs type of floor. Instead of sitting on a chair, the symbols move as we do. In regular musical chairs, humans walk around the too few chairs to see who does or does not get a one when the music stops. This is where the abundant symbols rotate around the floor with us standing above them. When they stop, whomever they are under is going to be activated with a symbol of what the person needs for the moment! Each of us get activated all at the same time! This really creates a lot of laughter within the group. The more we laugh the lighter we become. I can see the dark globs of energy fall off us.

Oh, that felt so good – all of us laughing uncontrollably together!

We are being led into another room full of bubbles. We are given a beautiful bottle with bubble liquid in it and a wand to blow to create more bubbles. At first, most of us blow a few bubbles to see how this works. Yes, it is fun, but it can be more. As we hold the bottle in one hand with the other hand on the bubble wand dipped into the solution, do a quick focus on what you want to create. It may be basically more money, or a job you enjoy, or a family, or a house, or something entirely different.

Now, lift the wand with this focus in mind, inhale, and blow this intentionally-created bubble. How did that feel? Do it again and again until it is easy for you to think about what you want as through the simple act of creating an intentional bubble through a bubble wand. Follow your bubbles out into the room and let them burst over your head. Let that manifestation flow from the bubble into your head, arms, heart - your entire being.

My bubbles have risen too high for me to reach. I will get on my Dragon and fly up to them. Now I can poke a hole in them and let the manifestations flow into the top of my head and absorb into the rest of my body. That feels wonderful. I can feel the old beliefs and programs being removed as this new lovely information flows through me.

I see you decided to join me near the ceiling with all the bubbles while riding on your Avatar. What kind of a game can be created up here with these bubbles? Maybe we can bat them across the room into a container, sort of like playing Quidditch in *Harry Potter*. I will let all of you play whatever game comes to mind while I watch.

I feel like it's time for me to go back to my room for some recalibration. You can stay in here as long as you like.

See you tomorrow!

MONTH SIX – DAY THREE

Are you ready for a new adventure today? We are going to do some exploring within this Portal while still on its Moon. The Portal's air outside of this building is just fine for us. It may be on the verge of being so good that we become more alive within ourselves. Take a deep breath and get into riding gear safe for what may be ahead for us today.

As we leave this building we will go through a shield that protects the environment in which we are in right now. It looks like it is solid, but we can go through it without any problem. It is an interactive smart shield. It knows what to keep in and what to keep out – anything or anyone that is a pollutant. As we come back in here later, it will clean the debris that collects on your skin and clothing. It will not hurt you. In fact, you will probably feel better after you get all of that 'not yours' stuff off you.

As we take off, you may notice it is quite nice out here, or maybe not. The environment seems to shift with what you think it should look or be like. At first, I was thinking dry, dusty, dark, and that's what I saw. Then I started thinking about this place as lush and green with lots of plants and water with all the critters that go with it. By the time I got through the shield, the terrain had changed into a beautiful place.

It reminded me how much we think of our lives. Do we go through life thinking that our bank account is dried up, dark, empty, and a place we don't even want to look at? Or do we think or feel that our bank account – not just one but many accounts – are overflowing with lots of money ready for what we want to use it for. This is a world where we create what we think and feel deeply in our soul.

I see some interesting colors up near the top of the Portal – let's investigate them. I also wonder if they are really a part of the Portal or a manifestation from one of our group, or even me. I am learning that sometimes things get manifested with just a quick thought which hasn't had time to be evaluated yet. Not always the best results, but always interesting when that happens.

Oh, the colors and textures of these clouds, or are they clouds, is very interesting. They look smooth and soft, but when I touch them they feel almost like sandpaper and very firm. They don't feel like they look. This is very interesting. As I ask about them, I am told to hold out my hand – you too – and a small piece will drop into it.

Okay, now it feels cool to the touch, still a little like sandpaper, but when I examine it closer it is the smallest of glittery diamonds. That is how they are created on this moon. We are told we can take what is dropped into our hand home with us. It does have a frequency and a message within it for each of us. You can hold it close here to receive the message or put it into your pack or pocket to examine it closer when you get back to your room. I am waiting until I get back to my room as I feel like that is what I am to do at this moment.

I had no idea how vast this place can be and still move like it does. Did you feel that? It's like we are getting ready to go somewhere else. Well, maybe not yet. But I think we need to head back closer to the center where we are staying.

That doesn't mean we can't get a little sidetracked. I see an event that might be a lot of fun to stop off at on our way back. It's a sort of a waterfall on the outer sides and the center are stairs for our Avatars to walk down in with lots of fresh food for them along the way, even a grooming salon for those that like to have a little pampering.

We can start at the top. I am told it will be a form of body surfing all the way down. Let's go! Oh, my goodness – this is sort of like being in a pinball machine. Every so often there is a flipper thing that bumps us back up to another level where we can slide down the same way or take a different route. I think if you are really good and don't want to do that you can slip past them all the way to the bottom.

I guess I'm not that good, as I'm being flipped back and forth all over the place. Each time I hit a soft plant or rock there's a dinging noise and I get downloaded with another piece of information I need in this Abundance learning journey. I can't believe I like this. I find myself laughing each time I get flipped around. I even go flying past the Avatars onto the other side of the whole event, then get flipped back and forth a few times. I will meet you at the bottom. Enjoy!

I think I've had enough fun for one day. I am ready to head back to my room for a nap. I forgot we have the shield to go through. Wow, that feels really good. Now my clothes are clean and dry. It also reminds me of the diamond cloud stone in my pocket. I wonder what message I will receive from it.

See you tomorrow!

MONTH SIX – DAY FOUR

Well, well, well ... Strange way to begin. Today we are in for a real journey! The Portal is moving. We have spent the last three days bathing in the Earth's Full Moon Solstice's intense energy while working within the realm of what it represents and assists us in, for each being within Earth's incarnation. Take a moment to inhale deeply a few times as this can be a little on the roller coaster side of fun. It will help if you can become at ONE with the Portal as it does the moving, like being inside of an airplane with a sliding gravitational floor.

I feel the undocking from the Full Moon's energy field. So far, very nice and light, sort of like I am drifting in space but with my oxygen cord attached. Maybe I better get back inside the Portal. I didn't realize I had taken a door to the outside. I thought it was just another room to explore. WOW! That was sort of weird for a little bit there.

While we are in the conference center, our headquarters, we can explore a lot of different rooms. I am going online to find the ones that are the most fun for Earth Human s. I guess not everyone has the same sort of humor experience that we do. That is okay, we are unique to the rest of the Universe.

I found a place where we can go for starters. As we walk into the room closest to the ballroom, everyone is in a costume related to their interests. They all turn and look at us as we walk in with our Avatars! I wonder what they are thinking, not that it matters, but since there are so many of us in one place, we definitely didn't go unnoticed.

I did a quick scan and notice buffet tables set up with a variety of foods for us to experience. I do mean EXPERIENCE. I touched a chip, and it turned into a butterfly. The rest were quickly taken away as they began a fast process of cocooning then hatching into beautiful various types of butterflies. Someone must have brought out the wrong tray. There are a lot of other interesting foods for us to sample.

Try the frozen balls of icy slush. There are a lot of intermixed flavors. I notice that it makes my tongue tingle in a very interesting way. It's like having a type of candy that my kids used to eat called Pop Rocks as it made a popping and crackling sound when it hit the moisture on the tongue. The difference is that this icy slush creates that feeling in all my cells.

I had to find a mirror to see if I was starting to crack open in places or morph into something else. It doesn't hurt, but sure feels funny. I wonder what is it doing to my DNA, as I notice the wrinkles on my hands become less pronounced. Also, my skin feels smoother. Maybe this is the fountain of youth! The icy slush is the fountain of youth! That would be a great moneymaker. Who in the group can do that?

It certainly took my mind off the Portal moving into another realm. I think I better check to see where we are going. Well, it isn't back to Earth yet. We are headed toward the constellation called Orion's Belt. I had no idea we could travel so fast. I am told that, as we combine our Portal with a wormhole, anything is possible. I find this journey to be quite exciting as we zip through the Milky Way with so much flying past us.

I see a Star Gate spinning ahead that we will be going through. It has a time machine on it. We are going forward ten years. What will we find out about ourselves in this time that will assist us in our Quest for Abundance? Remember, what we see in the future is changeable. If it isn't what we want it to be, this is giving us a chance to make the changes needed in ourselves to create who we can be differently. Or, it may be exactly where we want to be, and we can learn from the experience to make sure we follow the path to this or something even better.

As we land in this period we can call our future selves to us and interact with them. You might want to have a pad available to take notes as you interact and have an interview asking what you can do, what you want to be, and where you want to be in ten years. Are you still alive? If not, find out why. Do you want to be? Look around at the lifestyle here. Is this what you are willing to work for to stay on this Planet?

I find myself in a self-driving vehicle. I can program in my destination and it gets me there safely in a blink of an eye. My family is healthy and happy and enjoying their own lifestyle with ease. My purpose is being utilized on a regular basis with vacations to explore other areas of the Universe. Yes, I do want to be here in another ten years. I also look as young as or younger than I am now and am in great shape to be able to explore the mountains, valleys, and waterways that are more beautiful every day.

Once you have gained the information you want or need, make your way back to your room, as you will be given a chance to assimilate all of it before our next experience.

See you tomorrow!

MONTH SIX – DAY FIVE

I see we are still traveling through the wormhole into Orion's Belt. The time-traveling Star Gate must have brought us back to where we started. It was a great glimpse of what may be in the future. Now is also important. We were put here to enjoy the journey, which is why we are on this Divine Portal of Benevolent Activations of Abundance. Abundance can happen when we least expect it. Let's see what this Portal has planned for us today.

As I walk around this center – I had no idea how huge it is – I find it branches out in all directions from the main hub of the Portal. Today, we are directed to walk into a hallway where some old music plays. The songs are also a part of what is going on the room. The one that I recognize is part of "Stairway to Heaven," or is it the Disney song "When you wish upon a Star?" I'm not sure, but it is something about stars.

Right in front of us are stairs to climb with glittery stars all around, including sparkly Star Dust falling as the Portal spins into its path. This is a winding staircase that keeps going and going and going. How far do you want to climb? There are lookout ledges every so far to step out and look about.

I think I will see what this one is about. You may come with me or continue on, and I will catch up later. I view a circus from this ledge, or it's what may seem like circus music with big tent colors and flags from what I remember as a child. Lots of laughter, jugglers, high-wire walkers, and balloons!

Lots of balloons and cotton candy! The people are really having fun entertain those who stop to watch. There is carnival music, food aromas, and people laughing and having fun in every corner of this place.

The animals can talk! The horses, bears, elephants ... All are there for the Love of Interaction and Entertainment. They even make up their own routines and love the reactions they get from the actors and the crowd. They especially love the healthy treats as everyone gets to be creative with mixing their own. There is no limit to much they can have.

Time for me to climb further up the stairs to the stars. The next ledge of incredible views has waterfalls. They are the most incredible I have ever seen. I call my Dragon to ride on and explore them further. Come along with me if you so choose.

The wind currents to get there are visible. They look like written music with the notes to carry us into the gushing water. The base of the note opened for us to sit inside where we float through the waterfalls without getting wet. Yet, their essence flushes through us, so breathe it in. This is a place of peace and clarity. I feel like I could be in here forever. It's a great place to become clear on how to take some moments to have fun and still have plenty of time to devote to business and family. Maybe there is a way to have fun with all of it combined. Breathe in the knowledge of how it can be.

The next waterfall has me back on my Dragon, flying through it and feeling the invigorating energy as it flows over the top of the rocks and down. So far down. I choose to ride the falls all the way down while on my Dragon. I go really fast to the crashing waves at the bottom. I always wondered what it would be like to be in the middle of crashing waves as they hit the bottom, and then rise back up to flow on down the valley. It was literally breathtaking.

I am so glad I took a big breath of air before we went under. I am surprised I wasn't afraid, but enjoyed every second of the life-giving energy of this experience. WOW! That was amazing. My skin is all tingly from something in the water. It must be another download of some of knowledge. Now to get to the side.

There is a ground escalator to take us back to the center. It's slow, so this gives us time to dry easily and view the interesting plant life as we move through. I love these Portal journeys where I get to see plant life only created for a specific area, and each plant has its own purpose. Some are for beauty, some for medicinal purposes.

As we near the center for our own exploration and recuperation, I want to remind you to ask any questions you wish about this, and there will be someone to answer them for you. Take your time to soak in all that you experienced on so many levels today.

See you tomorrow!

MONTH SIX – DAY SIX

Great to see all of you again! This is going to be an exciting day. It is day six of this Divine Portal of Benevolent Activations of Abundance. We are just over half-way finished with this journey. I have noticed a few shifts in my life since this one began. They have all been beneficial. I hope they have been for you as well.

Today, I am being drawn to find out what the Portal is doing in Orion's Belt, or maybe the reason we were brought here. Let's ride our Avatars out that door and see what is out there. I think we have oxygen masks of a special type in our packs. Be ready to use it if necessary. Our Avatars are quite capable of breathing anywhere.

Oh, it is beautiful out here. We are still within our Portal, but outside of the center in an area where we can see through the Portal Boundaries but are protected so we don't accidentally cross over into the outer realms. I can see we are winding through the "stars" within the belt, back and forth and around each one. I am not being told any specific reason, except we had to wait for a certain wave to come along before we could go back to Earth.

Something beneficial to do was to interweave our energy into this system as well as us pick up its energy to take back to Earth. It's a good thing to do to benefit all Mankind. Well, we are all for doing this type of energy work, if it is benevolent.

Since we are all on our Avatars, let's explore this Portal a little more. I see a wave coming. Do we surf it or just ride it? It looks like the wave of a current to take us from this side to the other side of the Portal, but it isn't a straight-line type of a wave … it swirls.

You can go upside down, sideways, then right-side up all the way across the Portal. I hope I don't get a stomachache since I usually don't do well with real spinny rides.

It is a new way to learn how to ride and trust ourselves. Our Avatars also learn to trust we can stay calm during these situations. Mine is somewhat calm, just get him to quit giggling each time we change positions. Once I start giggling it starts a whole rhythmic wave throughout my Dragon's scales. Then we both have a fun time rolling in the wave energy. Much better than being sick to my stomach. I love these changes!

Now that we made it across, what do you notice? I see there are caves we can explore. Our Avatars can wait out here for us or can also come in and find us if we can't find our way out. These caves are nothing like I have seen. They are very interactive with our thoughts. As we walk into the first one I see a slide going down and around over to the next open area. We didn't have to walk, and it was much faster.

Oh, this room is all about full-circle rainbows. Some are vertical, others are horizontal. These rainbows are different colors. Instead of each being a full spectrum, each one here is all one color of many levels, including fluorescent and sparkly aspects. I wonder what each one feels like. I am going to find one to sit in and feel its energy. You can, too, if you are ready to experience this type of frequency.

I am so glad we get to be a part of this. It makes it so much easier to differentiate the frequency of the blue spectrum from the red. Now I can feel how red plus blue moves the energy into a purple spectrum and all the in-between fields. Now that I feel it, I can let myself absorb it into the parts of my body which needs it. Each cell needs different spectrums of light as it processes events it has to attend to within the body. The sparkly and opalescent colors are so different now that I get to feel them all separated. It is on the level of comparing a delicious apple to a crab apple. Still in the apple category but its own identity.

I see all of you are filled up with color! Some of you are filled with a little too much color in certain areas. You may have needed it for the moment and your body will process the excess out in a little bit, so no worries if you are little more orange, purple, or green than normal. Let's go into another room and do a some more investigating while we are here.

This room has many bottles of various shapes, sizes, and colors. They're full of what I am being told is an elixir of what a person may need. Some have a scent, while others don't. Go inside of yourself and feel which one you might need to take back with you, as they are gift to us from the Rainbow Caves.

Each cave within this area is filled with items of various colors for most anything you need help with. Since we are on a journey of Benevolent Abundance in the form of Money, let's ask if an individual elixir can be made specifically for this purpose for each of us.

Yes! Wait a few minutes or seconds for it to be given to us! It is also in never-emptying containers, so you can use all you want, and it adjusts itself to each day's need.

This is a very special gift for each of us! I will take extra care in packing it into my saddlebags, so I don't drop it.

Now, how do we get out of here to find our Avatars and then make our way back to the center? Just ask and there it is – the door opened right to where our Avatars are waiting. The way back to the center also lit up like a glowing golden path through the airwaves. We begin to receive the 'Ask and receive' part of the Divine Abundance Portal. Let's follow it – it's so smooth, like glass – to guide us back.

This has been quite an eventful day for each of us.

See you tomorrow.

MONTH SIX – DAY SEVEN

What an exciting way to start out today! The Pathway to Earth through Orion's Belt has just opened. The Portal we are now in is headed back to Earth. I am quite happy about it. Don't know why, but the energy of going back home flows through here – very nice and smooth. I wonder what new adventure will be coming our way.

We just zoomed past the space station. The look on their faces when they saw us is priceless. I guess they don't see Divine Portals zipping around space very often. I did wave, but they just looked at me like they couldn't figure out what we were. That's okay, maybe we will broaden their minds by being in our 'space' for a few moments.

Hmmm, I just heard we are going to land in the Grand Canyon for a little bit. Maybe there's a refueling station for Portals there? This will give us a whole new area to look at as we explore the inside of the Portal.

It is still moving and morphing around everyone and everything, including the Canyon ground. I am being told we can explore the canyon while staying within the Portal. It is in harmony with us.

As we walk toward the walls, they move in the direction we go. We will be completely safe as we experience this area. And, it's temperature controlled. This time of year, the canyon floor can get very hot.

I see a path that is drawing me toward it. Let's see where it takes us. Be aware of your surroundings. You never know what you will find here. For instance, look at this rock wall. It's smooth to look at and touch it. Run your hand over the area and focus on what is beyond this wall. Did you see the glyphs light up? Do it again with more focused intent from you heart. Now more glyphs are lighting up and moving in a sequence. The wall is disappearing. We now see a cave opening lit up with the glyphs on the walls. This is an amazing discovery. I was told of a place like this being in the Grand Canyon, but wasn't sure if it was true.

Since we are in the Divine Portal of Benevolent Activations of Abundance, we are on the edge of something amazing. We just walked into a historical civilization that was abundant in this area of our continent. As we continue through the cave- perhaps it is more of an underground city – we see the straight walls are covered with a pure, hard material. This is not a cave that has been recently dug out and supported with rickety beams. This looks like it was made in the times of the Egyptian Pyramids. At least some of the writings are similar to what I have seen in books about them. There are statues in various cut out areas that I am certain mean something to those that lived here at that time. It feels very sacred.

I hear different tones coming from the walls as we walk into the larger room of a circular shape with more wall cutouts with paintings on them and statues in the front. Since we are within the Portal, we can look and hear, but we can't touch them. There is an altar in the center of the room with writings and glyphs on the sides as well as the top. As I glide my hand across the top, the glyphs light up with a message for us. We are to sit in a circle and meditate for a few minutes.

As we sit, I feel a presence here in the room with us. It is a Benevolent being from that time. There are two of them, male and female. They glow golden white energy. We will receive an activation from them that will assist us in being able to bring Abundance to ourselves and the communities we live and associate with.

There is a stream of white golden flecks within a pillar coming down over each of us as we sit around this room. The two beings hold their hands out to send energy from them and their hearts around us as each pillar is activated to fill us with Activations inside ourselves from their advanced civilization. The flecks are being absorbed into our bodies. Once the pillars are clear the activation is complete. Now, we can go back to the center of the Portal to allow this activation to recalibrate all our bodies.

See you tomorrow!

MONTH SIX – DAY EIGHT

Today, the Portal is traveling to another new location. It feels like we are going to be flying around Earth for a while, which is actually pretty cool. We get to simply be in the Divine Portal of Benevolent Abundance. That sounds so nice. Maybe it is because we are still absorbing the information from yesterday and are not ready for a new place. We just need to experience what we can within here.

So, let's explore more of what is in here. We can ride our Avatars outside of the center and just see what we find today. I love how we have these new devices to put around our neck like loose headphones to communicate with each other and anything else within the Portal. There is a perfect level of translation for us too. This includes the plants and animals that live here.

As we skim above the trees I hear them greeting us with excitement. They are inviting us to join them in a clearing up ahead. This is a marvelous opportunity for us to learn more about what is in this Portal. The landing pad for our Avatars is plenty big and there are attendants for them. I see we have picnic lunches prepared for us at the large circle where we can learn about those who brought us here. We can sit at the large picnic table, or on the benches around the edges, or cushions we can place where we will be the most comfortable.

The information coming into the headphones is very helpful. I am learning that this Portal has been in existence since the beginning of time. It has been inactive for many years as there hasn't been the belief we could be safe within it. It has been working very hard to let people know about the Abundance and how we can manifest it ourselves from within our heart and emotional beliefs. This journey we are on is one of the few that have been taken in the last years. We are to get the word out to others that this is possible, and this method of being activated within the Portal on levels we have experienced is available to everyone who wants it. Abundance, including Financial Abundance in a more fulfilling lifestyle, is available by being Benevolent. When Abundance is benevolently created, there is no chance of bad karma being generated. It's for the benefit of all.

The trees and plants around us tell me how wonderfully unified this group is in its heart. This group is being prepared to do more for this Planet than ever thought possible before this time. I agree, this is a very special group of beings that have been brought together for reasons I can only imagine.

There is bowl of stones on the table beside the food. We are to each pick one to take with us. If we want to wear it as a necklace, just think it and the cord will be on the one you pick. Or, if you want to keep it in your pocket, you will probably pick one for that purpose. They are all charged with what is needed for our Abundance Journey of Financial Freedom. These stones are not necessarily from Earth. Some are from the Solar System and brought here for what we need.

The trees are creating an opening for us to find a special place to meditate with our stones before going back to the business of the Center. As you receive the information from your stone, you might want to journal about it. Know that each time you meditate with your stone you will get more information as you are ready to work with it. Keep notes, as I have found that sometimes there is just too much to remember.

While you meditate, don't be surprised if some little critter comes to you with more information. It may be in the physical while in the Portal, and it may be in an etheric form when you are back home. It may be a critter you will not recognize as it may be from another Planetary system. Then again, it may choose to show itself to you in a familiar form. Sometimes that makes accepting their information easier.

It is time to find our Avatars and get back to the Center. Time is so different here. As the Portal has been traveling it seems to elongate in some areas then shrink in others. Today it seemed we traveled a short distance to this area, and now it has stretched out to where we have a longer ride back.

Maybe we can find an energy wave to ride on to cut our flying time in half. I see many going away from the Center. Oh, there is one just up ahead. Yes, we made it and this one is smooth. No whirly areas to play in, but that is okay this time.

I think I want to take more time tonight to journal about all the information this Portal holds for us. I want to remember all that the trees told us.

See you tomorrow!

MONTH SIX – DAY NINE

Welcome back. I hope you are well rested. I see the Portal hasn't landed into one specific spot yet. Maybe it will before we are completed here today.

This Divine Portal of Benevolent Activations of Abundance is cruising right along. We are entering a new phase of our Activations. It may not be from a specific item, location, or action for a while. It may just happen as you are in the moment of receiving as you may need a soul nap or just get a download while you brush your teeth. Of course, we can always enjoy the fact we are being downloaded or our DNA is shifting into another phase, which is what these specific activities have been doing. Even today, as I hold a stone, I can feel it activating me with its information, and this creates a DNA shift. Some ideas have been floating around that a DNA shift must be something huge. It can be as simple as shifting from unhappy to happy. It is the change from decay to regeneration. I choose regeneration! Regenerate me, regenerate more laughter, regenerate more money! See how that works?

Let's see where we are taken today. We can get onto our Avatars and include them in our journey. To start with, I am passing around wands. Everyone gets one. Look at it.

Does it look the way you want it to, or is it too generic? Focus your mind and heart on what you want it to look like. Some may want it to be white, gold, or purple. You may want to include some scrolling on the handle or a specific design or writing.

What do you need to do to make it a part of you and your heart thoughts? Mine is creating itself into a blueish-purple dragon with black claws, pointy tail, trailing beard, and perfect scales. It's perched on a vine with green/brown stems and leaves. It has bluish white flowers with yellow-orange centers. There is a lot more, but I want you to get the idea of how the details are important in the manifestation process. You might not get data on how it is created, but you can get information of what you want it to look like when it does show up. WOW! These look great!

Now we can fly around the Portal. Just be cautious to not create big changes in the Portal itself. There is such a thing as respecting other's property. We can practice with that waterfall over there. See how it flows?

Let's focus on what we want to create. Maybe a small stream with brown, round rocks we can walk on as we cross it. Now, hold your wand toward it and feel/see in your mind what you want it to be. Create a direct point in your direction of focus. Don't forget to breathe.

That was easy. Now, return the waterfall to what it was. Same way. Hold your wand toward it, feel/see in your mind what you want it to become – exactly like it was a few minutes ago. Remember it. Focus the point of your wand going into the waterfall's center, and if you want, wave it around to create the dramatic effect of change. Of course, remember to breathe. Wasn't that simple?

Let's try something else. See that outcropping of rocks on the side of the mountain? Let's turn it into a statue of a dolphin, or three dolphins. We all know what a dolphin looks like, so this should be easy. I want to see what you can do – I will watch. Remember, that you have communication devices available to speak with each other and come up with the same idea.

Very good! Two of the dolphins look great, but this one looks a little disjointed – he has a fin on his nose. It's an easy fix. This is a great lesson in creating the focused intent and how to work together. The energy field shows that, by the time you got to number three, your group focus was a little tired. I will return it to the original outcropping of rocks and we can go on.

Let's try one more thing. Hmm. How about a golden path of energy going back to the Center where we can continue this discussion? I will help. Got your focus on the point of your wand? Notice how your thoughts/what you see connects with your Heart energy, what you feel, and the loving, benevolent energy going into your wand. Allow this to continue out to the energy waves of the path to lead us back to the Center and create it with a color of gold. YES! That is wonderful. Our Avatars will have no problem gliding along on this light path all the way back. We can meet in the small room just off to the side of where we come in from the stables.

What we have done so far is manipulate the form of one item into another. It is a great way for you to learn to trust that you can do what was once thought impossible. To actually manifest Money ... that takes a larger thought process.

First, do you have a job? Do you need a raise or more hours, or a job that pays more, or more clients that tip better, or more time to create? The process of manifesting Money is about creating the means to do it. It isn't like you manifest it out of thin air or manipulate the numbers in your bank account. That would be sort of nice, however, it would throw the whole system of exchange on Earth out of whack, and I think it has something to do with Universal Laws and karma. Perhaps the part about fair energy exchange.

I want you to realize that, in the Portal, it is easier to create rapidly so you get instant results to help you understand what it is you are doing. Out in the real world we do this level of creation, but the results aren't manifested quite as fast. Then we get discouraged thinking we did something wrong.

We tend to go into an emotion of doubt and start the process of unraveling your creation. Then we try again without the full trust in what we can do.

Are you doing it wrong in the real world? No, time is just different. We also need to add into the mix a little bit of patience as well as work on the speed of the manifestation. While on Earth, it helps if we connect to the Creator of the Universe and align with all our Heart and Seeing/Brain/Thought energy.

As you go on your way, you can bring out your wand and use it, or your finger, or, when you are ready, your thought patterns. Practice manifesting a few things, maybe the exact meal you want tonight, or winning the game you are playing. Maybe changing the color of the shirt you are going to wear. Let me know how it works for you.

This was a little bit of a different journey today. I wanted to make sure it was the right message, but this is what my Team wanted me to tell you. I hope it helps.

See you tomorrow!

MONTH SIX – DAY TEN

Great night! We learned how to manifest with the heart and sight/feeling/mind. The wand is a great prop. However, it has a Morphic field around it to magically create your commands. I am sure it was helpful in some manner for you to start with it. Just keep practicing until you don't need it anymore. You may step down to using your pointer finger, then your energy field. You can always use the wand. It is very cool to point it and create what you want.

Now, back to the Portal. We have only one day left before we get booted out of this spinning vortex called the Divine Portal of Benevolent Activations of Abundance. I wonder what journey awaits us today. Once we ask, the answer comes rushing to us. The Universe is ready to fulfill our questioning wishes.

We are headed to Alaska. I am certain that the Portal has not been here before. We are going to land at the highest point possible, the top of Mount Denali! It is the highest peak in North America at 20,310 feet above sea level.

Let that sink in a little. I am from Colorado, and we have many mountains of 14,000 feet or more. Mountains I have no desire to climb. For one thing, I don't like the cold and, at that altitude, it is probably cold, no matter what season. Right now, I am very thankful we are in a climate-controlled Portal. I also like to breathe without being oxygen deprived.

I am asking my Team why we are here. This mountain has volcanic action going on inside, like many areas along the Rockies. It isn't something we tend to worry about, because it isn't in the forefront of our everyday lives. It isn't in the news very often, but it is really happening. Occasionally, there are reports of earthquake activity but not the volcanic aspect. Maybe we are doing something within that realm, I am not really sure.

Okay, I just saw what we are going to do. The Portal found an opening into the volcanic neck of Denali. We are going in to bring the "Fire in your belly" part of manifestation education to you. The Portal is sliding down the inside of the volcano where we can see and feel what she is thinking. I never have thought of a mountain being a she before. Some people think the inside of a volcano is angry fire. I don't feel that at all. I feel that when she laughs, she jiggles the Earth to create the quakes.

Let's go on into the mountain's belly and see what we can learn. As the fiery molten lava swishes around, it creates sounds and glyph-like signs for us. It has a language of Mother Earth. Let's listen with our translation devices, and perhaps we can get the bigger message.

Laughter, joy, love, and play are the most important aspects to benevolent creation. That doesn't mean some toes don't get stepped on or you need to be the doormat and get yourself stepped on. It means you stand up for yourself.

Look how tall Mt. Denali is! She stands up for herself and shows the world what it is like to be the most majestic mountain. She uses the fire in her belly to create, and it activates all around her. She creates the Love of animals and land to give them nourishment in Abundance. Sometimes, she shakes places around her with laughter to keep everyone on their toes. No laziness survives in this territory. She doesn't do the shaking to be mean with the intent to destroy. It is a part of a movement of creation to a new level.

This is really important information for our daily lives. We can use it to conduct ourselves on a regular basis within our families and our work areas. Do you get the same message from her? Take your time to connect with the forces of this mountain's belly and feel what the message is for you.

Once we have all made connections on some level, we will leave this sacred place. We must remember to give thanks to this extremely sacred mountain. She gave us very important information we are to take back with us to our homes to integrate into our lives and teach all those around us.

The Portal has found another way out. We are squeezing through a very small cave. It is like we were put into a container that molded into the size it needed to be to fit into the cracks and crevices throughout. That was an interesting experience even for me.

The Portal is going to circle the Planet again while we integrate this information. You might want to journal about the personal piece you received.

See you tomorrow for our last ride in the Portal!

MONTH SIX – DAY ELEVEN

I realized this is our last day in this Divine Portal of Benevolent Activations of Abundance. Time has passed by me so fast. I love learning and clearing everything I need for the next phase of manifestation in my life. I always want to make sure that what I do is in the energy of Benevolence.

We are all here for a purpose. Each and every moment we are on this Planet is for a reason. We may not understand what it is every moment, but even if we don't get out of bed we are still shining our light from within to be of assistance. Just being here is helping the light on this Planet shine brighter. Being in the Portals, as we have been for the last several months, has helped us, and the Planet, clear old programs and activate all of us to move into higher vibrations of learning, and assisting each other as well as ourselves in becoming more abundant.

Since we are still within this Portal we may have experiences of divine magic to play with. I use the word magic as playing in a world of the unseen. If you can't see it with the naked eye or under a microscope, I consider it magic.

By playing in a Benevolent Portal, our magic is also of a benevolent nature. I hope that clears up some of the terminology for everyone.

We are magical creators ourselves. For example, what would happen if we couldn't heal injuries like a broken leg or a cold? Perhaps we would die the same as a broken tree branch or a plant with a disease.

Most of the time, the affected area of a plant dies. We are magical. We can create our lives to be what we want them to be. The question is, how much of yourself are you willing to give to the process?

Sometimes it takes a lot of our energy and focus to heal something like a broken bone or a disease. Since we are in a Portal about Abundance ... I don't mean you have to be a workaholic to get rich, but I am sure you have heard the phrase "You have to put your heart into it." What part of you is invested in this creation? We know that it isn't just our 'heart' we talk about when that term is used. As with our wand experiences, we utilize our entire being of manifestation when we use that term.

Have you noticed that when your heart is in a project how fast it goes and how there are very few flaws or areas that you have to fix? When you are frustrated, or tired, or it is a project of someone else's creation, how do you feel about it? How fast is it finished, how well is it done? How hard is it to complete? If you are in service to someone to create for them under a contract, you may be able to put your heart into it easier than if there weren't. Is everything making sense now?

We are creators/manifestors of each and everything in our lives. We are to learn to stay present in the moment of manifesting to complete the project. Remember the dolphin that ended up with his tail on his nose? That was a lapse in staying present. It takes practice as we become more and more involved in our evolution.

Now for our last day in the Portal! We are still circling the Planet and preparing to land as a plane does. While in this pattern of movement, let's take a final flight on our Avatars through this whirling place. You may still wear your translation/telepathic devices if we are in here.

As we fly on the right side, can you feel the Portal's energy pulling and pushing you along? This is how the waves we ride work. Let's get our Avatars into a wave of pulling us quickly along through here. It may feel like a roller coaster at times, so hang on!

I love the information coming through our devices as we move past some of the vegetation. I hear, "Don't forget us." We are nearing one of the waterfalls. Yes, we can go through it sideways! Feel the refreshing, new water wash over you. It feels like it's clearing out some old programs of how we look at a waterfall. Perhaps they aren't as dangerous or cold or hard to be in as was once thought. They can be renewing. I never felt the laughter come so easily until I flew sideways through a waterfall. I am really going to miss doing this.

Let's continue our journey, because soon we will be landing. Oh, there is a cave we didn't explore. I think we have time for a little stop. The big entry room is brightly lit with several rooms branching off. Pick the one that calls to you. The one I am in says to create the stone I want. Hold out my hand and it will appear. I want a diamond of perfect shape and color. I just got three – a clear white one, a clear brown one, and a clear blue one! This creating as you think it is getting more fun and easier each time. I hope you got the one you wanted.

We need to get moving as we are running out of time. I feel the intensity of the Portal as it enters Earth's atmosphere. Of course, we are safe in here and can still gather information as we move along the Portal's left side as we head back. Let me know if you see something you want us to stop and investigate. Yes, I see it down there among some fern-like plants.

We can land near it. It looks like a baby plant-eating dinosaur. I hear this Portal picked them up when the Planet was going through one of its extinction periods. This is the first one born since then. It's a very special moment. Send it the love it needs to survive the new world it is being brought into. Thank you!

Are you ready to land? It's departure time. We can check our Avatars into the Center to be taken care of until we're ready for them again. Once we need them, all we have to do is call to them and they will come, no matter where we are.

I just learned that the translation devices we have been wearing have a component that fits into our home computers. We can take a digital recording of all that passed through them while we have been here. It will help you to remember some important clues.

We have now landed at the pad with the purple-blue Dragon image on it. This is our place to go back to the real world. This is always the hard part for me, as I will miss you. It is time for a big group hug!

See you next month!

See you soon with Truth, Love, and Gratitude

Pat, The Cosmic Cowgirl

Journal Your Use of Fun as a Manifestation Tool

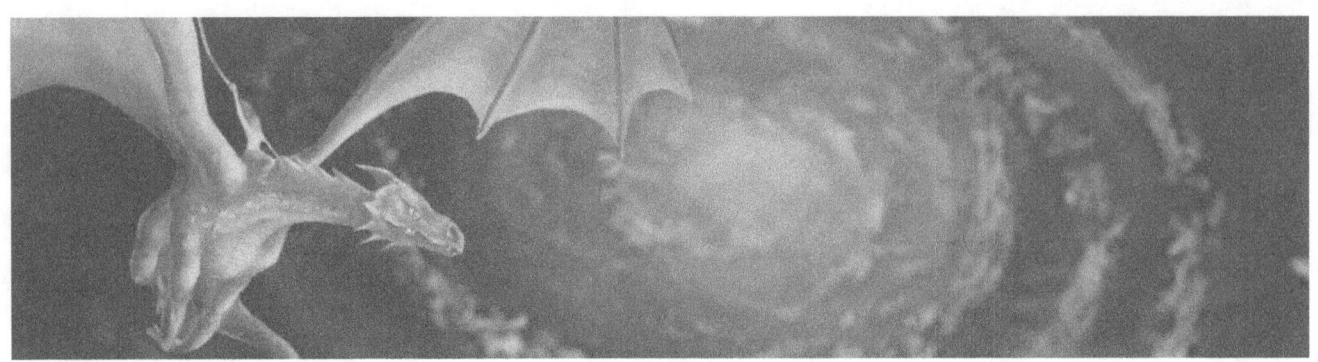

CHAPTER SEVEN: ELICITING HELP FROM THE FAIRY REALM

MONTH SEVEN – DAY ONE

Hello! Today we begin another eleven-day journey. This one is through the Divine Portal of Abundance Activations. Since it is summer, and so many plants are blooming and thriving in my yard thanks to my communication with the Fairy Kingdoms, I decided to see what that realm has for us. They are just so exciting to be around, and they teach me something new every day. For example, they help my plants be wonderful without much water, even in this 100-degree heat.

I know I'm not nearly as knowledgeable in this realm as many others are. I just play with those who show up in my world for the moment. Most of the time I have no idea how to categorize them and call them the wrong name or words that represent who they really are. I am told it doesn't matter. We are all here for the Divine Purpose of just being on this Planet for all its needs. In other words, to create an environment of thriving.

Let's begin in my backyard. There has been a gathering of Fairy Peoples around my fire pit and medicine wheel, both are next to a lot of green plants. I saw them throw all types of sparkly things into the fire pit to create a lot of sparks for the atmosphere and the Earth. It was being prepared for us and to be turned into the Portal. We are to gather, lock arms, and jump into the Portal. Ready? Let's GO!

There is no bottom. It is a vortex which takes us to the first of the realms that we get to visit. I see each of you as we swirl around in the tornadic winds that take us into the main Portal where we will be routed into the larger one for our journey.

What I find is the Divine Portal we journey through each month is huge with various off-chutes designated to be frequencies of what we work with at the time. They have an intelligence of their own which seems to communicate with what we call our own intelligence.

This one is the Fairy Realm. It includes what we call the Fairy folk as well as Dragons, Unicorns, Pegasus, Elves, plants, stones, and crystals – all of the magical beings many cannot see. Of course, we make this stipulation: all we are interact with is of the Benevolent nature.

The transition was flawless. We are now in our own Portal going inside the Emerald Forest. Of course, this the first place I thought of as magical, with the Fairies and Enchantments of this Benevolent world. Just to clarify – Benevolent only means good stuff. It doesn't stop our fine friends from being funny or playing games with us, which I am certain we will experience later.

As we step out of our Earthly realm into our Divine Portal, we are greeted with very special guides. You might not think of this as the Fairy Realm, but look closer at your belief system as to what this realm is. Yes, this does look like a plant from Dr. Seuss' books, but feel it. Yes, it is of the Fairy Realm.

It is very animated and knows exactly what each of us needs. It divides itself into copies so each of us gets escorted at the same time. It also communicated in a language you can understand.

We are being shown our living quarters within the Portal. They look like little Hobbit homes – rounded doorways and windows and set back into a hillside. They are the cutest little dwellings I have ever seen. They are made to fit whatever size we are and seem to morph into what we need. They are supplied with our desires and needs. They are totally upgraded with technologies we like to amuse ourselves with during downtime.

Oh, the Crystal bathtubs are amazing! They vibrate to what our needs are and bypass our wants. It provides a vibration of what is needed each day. You will find other items in here for both what you need as much as what you want.

We will meet each morning at the Community Center. It is much bigger and provides the various supplies we need for our adventures.

As you have probably noticed, your size fits the surroundings. Perhaps something happened while we were traveling. We are being prepared for a great adventure without having to eat or drink things like in the Alice in Wonderland adventures. We are to be of the size needed to communicate on an equal level with our wonderful Fairy friends. It may be a little surprising at just how we relate to some of the beings in this world. Have you ever thought of the size of a dragonfly or a Praying Mantis compared to the size of a Fairy? That is just one example.

As you walk into your little dwelling, pay attention to your surroundings. To start with, as the door opens, you will most likely get a surprise shower of sparkling energy to help you find your laughter. After a wonderful bath in your crystal bathtub, your energy will be better aligned with the next phase of expansion awaiting you. You may take your bath inside, or the tub can be moved to the outside deck. It only takes your desired thought. Each bed is created for your individual needs. It may also change depending what you need each day.

It is time for us to follow our plant guide to our own … I am not sure what to call these places. I like the word cabin, but it doesn't quite fit. Maybe we will know later. Get yourself settled in for this journey. Relax. It will be an experience which benefits you in an area you are ready for. The Divine Purpose of this Portal is to assist in the alignment with

Abundance. There are many types of Abundance, including Money. This is the exchange we all use on this Planet. Money is Spiritual.

See you tomorrow!

MONTH SEVEN – DAY TWO

Welcome back! Today we get to venture within the Magical Realm of the Fairy that has been created for you deep inside this Portal. We will be walking, so make yourself comfortable. Bare feet are a nice option for me as I am not a big shoe person on any given day, and the path we will be on is of lush, soft, mossy grass. My feet will love it.

We have a guide that is so cute with his extremely large pointy ears and beautiful large eyes that can see everything on many levels. I'm certain he can hear our thoughts. If you let yourself within this Portal, you can also hear and see more than you do on the Earth plane. I do not know this guide's name, but I don't think it really matters as he knows when I have a question and will automatically answer it. I am certain he will do the same for you.

As I thought, this path is wonderful. We can choose to walk on the mossy grass or the stones. Oh, my goodness – these stones talk, so step lightly and listen to what they tell you. The one I stepped on said to believe in yourself. The next one said pay attention to what is ahead. Remember what you hear and what it means for you.

We get to cross a stream with an arched, wooden bridge. There is a large tree beside it with what looks to be a mossy-like vine hanging over the entrance. It is sparkly – it really gives off sparks of energy. This is our first activation for today. I hear it will help open some of the blockages we have. Each one of us is different, so we will not be receiving the same activation as the person in front or behind us. Somehow, it is created to individualize the activation message for each of us. That is truly wonderful, as we are all gifted with our own knowledge and methods of receiving. Take your time. If you feel like you need to stand in it a few minutes, just do it. Time is not an issue here. Let yourself absorb the entire activation created just for you.

I feel the mossy vines wrap around various areas of my body. My legs and arms receive something different than my back. It doesn't feel like I am bound to stay here, or I'm restrained in any fashion. As soon as the information is transmitted, the vines fall off. New ones grow from the tree for the next person. I feel like parts of me that were tired are now awake and ready for better movement, both physical and mental. Maybe a better word would be ... Alive.

As I cross to the other side of the bridge, I am greeted by a group of Fairies carrying a filmy substance that they wrap me in as they fly around me. It's really refreshing and is just absorbed into my skin. It seems to adjust to my body temperature for this Portal's climate. I can also feel it nourish my immune system, lungs, and blood. This is such a gentle way of getting vitamins into my entire body – much nicer than having them go through the stomach or being injected into a vein. Must be what I needed now. Perhaps it is a method of teaching us how we can take care of ourselves easier. Or, perhaps one of you will invent something like this to use in our Earthly lives.

This path has been very enjoyable. I have also noticed the greenery – so many different shades in this area. It seems like everywhere I look the area is covered in plants of so many different sizes and shapes with some having tiny flowers. I am told this is to help purify the air and us as we walk by.

We are foreign to this environment, and it helps bring us into alignment to be here for several days. Not simply for us, but for all that live here.

It is like being on another Planet! Lots of new adjustments on all levels as we allow ourselves to be prepared to receive the Spiritual Abundance of Money, which can also be thought of as receiving the Golden Token to put into the slot for a gate to open. As it goes through the chamber it is just the right size to release the locking pins so opening can take place.

I feel like it is time for another soak in my crystal bathtub; then a nap on my ever-changing bed to prepare me for another day.

See you tomorrow!

MONTH SEVEN – DAY THREE

Amazing how fast time speeds by in this world. Today, we are meeting in a room with a variety of doors. I have never seen so many different doors, and in front of each one is a unique individual holding it closed. Let's just walk past them and feel which one we are supposed to enter. The first being, wearing a green hat with a feather in it, is very polite. He greets us with a deep bow, but he doesn't open the door.

The next one is a Dragon-shaped door greeter. He is also polite, greets us with a fiery puff of smoke, but doesn't open the door. It is as if the greetings mean "Welcome, but not today. Move on to the next door."

This next one is held closed by a Leprechaun. He holds it so tightly he doesn't notice us. As soon as he loosens his grip, the door flies open and pulls him and us into a wind tunnel. It is like being inside of a vacuum, as if I knew what that feels like. It is hard to breathe because we are being pulled through this hallway so fast, and there is nothing to hang onto.

We come to a stop where we are flung against crash mats on the wall. There is a tiny hole where the wind is coming from. As we get up and look around, we see the whole room is covered in crash mats. They were ready for us. There are stadium seats up higher, but they are not for us. We are the entertainment, or so it seems. I also see a first aid station off to one side. That makes me really wonder what we are in for.

Here comes someone who we can ask what this is about. It is time for us to learn to ride the Dragon Fly. Yes, they are bigger than we are, and their wings are quite different. They stick straight out. They do not fold back, so we must walk around them. Their heads are enormous, and those six legs. I never paid that much attention to what they looked like when I was bigger than they were.

The wonderful Fairy people have equipped them with a special type of riding gear that we can hang on with. I am on a gentler one. It is just tricky to get our balance as their wings move strangely to cause them to be a little jerky sometimes.

We can do this. Who wants to go first? Okay, I will. I am always up for learning something new. It is a little tricky getting onto them as their wings seem to be moving a little even when they are holding still. Up I go! And Down I go! I am so glad we have crash mats all around us.

I know there is a pattern to their movement; I just have to get into it. That wind tunnel is creating a pattern for him to follow and gives a little resistance, so he has to slow down for me. I am so happy this is a nice easy Dragon Fly to practice on. Oh, I see now, my Dragon's body tends to move up and down while this guy tends to move all directions at once. Sort of reminds how some Rodeo bucking bulls just wriggle all over when they move.

I really hope you are watching and learning from my many ups and downs because you get your turn in a few moments. I am starting to get the idea of how to stay on this critter. It helps to keep my knees and hips loose, not locked into a specific position, as it makes it easier to follow the random directions we are moving. I also have to let my spine shift with the directional flow of the wings and body combined.

Have I given you enough hints on how to do this? Your turn! Yes, I know it is hard. But the falls aren't bad, just surprising, and they carry the memories of how hard a fall is on Earth. This is a way to let go of some of the Fear of falling. It isn't failing each time you fall. It is a safe learning experience that you will master. You are doing better and better – hear the crowd cheer you on? Use their encouraging energy to pick yourself up and get back on! Yes! You did it! We did it!

When everyone has mastered this practice Dragon Fly, we get to pick our own for a little part of the journey in here. I think I want a blue one. On Earth I am always fascinated with the blue ones. Take your time and pick the one you feel the most comfortable with. Once picked, our animal-tending Fairies will prepare it for a ride. Yes, we must get on them right away before you forget the pattern of staying on a perpetually moving critter.

Ready? We will take a short flight around this area and then meet back here. I am certain that, if they are not telepathic, they know their way back here if you tell them to go home. Let's try to stay together, but I am not totally sure how we can do this with the randomness of how they fly. I will meet you back here at some point in time.

WOW! They are fast! I can see why they used the wind tunnel's resistance to teach us how to ride. We move so fast over the tops of the plants they are a blur. I can't describe the many aromas coming from each plant we skimmed. It was beautiful and exhilarating.

That was so fun! How did you do? You might want to take some notes in your journal so you don't forget how you did this. I know I will need to. I just hope I am not too sore tomorrow. I used muscles in my back and hips today that I didn't even know I had. It was all worth it to conquer the fear of being near a giant insect, plus learning to ride it. Amazing experience!

I am so ready for a long soak in my crystal bathtub.

See you tomorrow!

MONTH SEVEN – DAY FOUR

Looks like everyone is doing fine after the Dragon Fly ride yesterday! I hope you remember all of notes you took, as today we are going on an excursion riding the Dragon Fly you picked out and stayed on! It will be so exciting. Of course, everything in this Emerald Forest is exciting.

You might want to keep in the back of your mind that this is the Divine Activation Portal of Abundance within the Fairy Realm. Also remember how Abundance can be anything you want or need including health, wealth, and love. They're all activated here in Magical Benevolence.

This is so wonderful. You look great, like you have been riding these insects forever! I think magical dust was put on the saddle to help us stay magnetized to the spot we are supposed to sit. There is no way I could be feeling so comfortable up here without it. Set your intent for the day's journey, keeping in your heart why you are here, Health, Wealth, and or Love, or just to have a phenomenal experience.

Our guide for this journey is so magical looking with his long white beard and an immense twinkle in his eyes. His energy is so comfortable while in charge of his Dragon

Fly, yet also happy and full of energy. He is an excellent rider. We are to follow him on jour Dragon Flies. They move so fast and not in a straight line that it would be hard for us to steer them.

I find it quite fun to not have to worry about how to get where we are going. It gives me time for a closer look at this realm's plants. Magical plants have always been interesting to me. You know, plants that are used for so many things. Like how the flowers are for one thing, the leaves for another, and the roots for even more deeper health needs.

That was fast! We land next to a waterfall and are being directed to get off the Dragon Fly and walk on a trail that is narrow but usable and goes behind the falls. It is quite a different sound than I expected – musical instead of roaring. Or, is the music coming from somewhere else?

My eyes are getting used to the dimmer light, and I notice we are inside the mouth of a cave. Right here is where we can put on miners' headlamps. There are gloves and kneepads available if you want them.

It gets darker as we go deeper into the mountain, and I hear more music. I think the rock walls are singing to us. Occasionally I see gold flecks falling from the ceiling over people I know who need the gold. Meanwhile, music referring to the gold plays. Silly songs like "Goldfinger," "Goldilocks," and Disney music – I didn't even know there was music to those shows, but the music is here, and the picture of the movie pops into my head.

Lots of gold flecks falling from the ceiling again. Maybe it would be a good idea for us to catch them and put them in our packs. Yes, that is what we are to do. Now some of the flecks are turning various rainbow colors to represent the changes we can create with proper usage in our upcoming lives. Looks like someone in this group has some big plans moving forward with gold assistance.

As we come around the corner, I now see miners with picks, shovels, and neat hats working very hard but keeping clean. How is that possible? They are singing along with the stones. It's like a party in here.

Large and sacred gemstones appear in the walls next to us. I hear we are to take the ones calling to us. Rubies, emeralds, diamonds, sapphires, and some I have no idea what they are called. Wow, they do shine! The cave can just create more as needed. Take your time to get in tune with the music and your wants and needs, then pick the gemstones calling to you or singing your song. Put as many as you want in your packs. Remember to say thank you to our miner friends, the singing cave walls, and our guide

Time to venture back to the entry and get back on our Dragon Flies. They are plenty strong enough to carry however many of the stones you decided to bring with you, so nothing to worry about. This is so fun to hear each of you sing along with the stones you picked. The magic of music is wonderful.

I see no problems in getting back to the center and checking in our amazing Dragon Flies. You might want to give them a special thank you treat which you will find in the bottom of your pack. When you get back to your rooms, place your stones around the walls and windows. Let them harmonize for your life's needs. This helps you come into a harmonic resonance of where your life is going. It also helps you bring into yourself vibrations of what you prepare to manifest. Manifestation is getting faster and faster.

See you tomorrow!

MONTH SEVEN – DAY FIVE

I hope you enjoyed being in the harmony of the gemstones you took home yesterday. Mine shifted the energy of the room so much that I had a little difficulty getting to sleep. However, for some strange reason, I feel completely rested today and ready for a new adventure.

Just a reminder for your brain. We are meeting in the center building of all our dwelling, and I still don't know what to call them -- cabins isn't quite right, but Hobbit house is close. If you have a better word, let me know.

Last night I was at a fun energy group and one of the people there actually saw a little being flitting around my head. It told her she was a Sprite, and not the kind you drink. She is from this realm of adventure, and her showing up at the meeting was a great reaffirmation that I don't make this all up. She may be helping with the direction we go today. She said, "Of course she is, why else would she have shown up so visible to other humans?"

We are to walk toward the big green house with what looks like glass. It's a more ecological product than glass, but I have no idea what that could be. We are meeting an old friend of mine. I am so excited as I have not seen this being since I was a child. Don't be frightened. He's big and green, but the gentlest soul I have ever met. I don't know if he has a name. He is in the form of what we call a Praying Mantis or Walking Stick.

There are many varieties available on this Planet, but this one is the most common in my area. He is an amazing teacher. He really is from another Planet and in charge of the whole production in this building.

As we great my dear friend, we are given a delicious green drink to assist our immune system. I must admit, I do not like most of the green drinks I have tried. This one is amazing! I wish we could get it on Earth! We can have all we want as we walk around in here, but we can't take it home with us. Oh, I do know of a way that we can!

I realize this is a sort of pretend event for most of you, but I want you to learn how to create from your mind exactly what you need. It's also a part of learning how to create abundance.

Hold your water bottle, coffee, tea, or whatever is your preferred semi-healthy beverage. Go into a prayerful state. Drop into your heart, feel your breathing slow down, and feel for a moment. Perform an energy focus on your drink with your hands on or around the container. Imagine it's a delicious green drink which is exactly what your immune system needs at this moment. Say thank you, then drink it! Take a moment and feel it enter your mouth, go down your throat, pass through your stomach and out to all your blood vessels. Thank you for taking a moment to experience the way which you can create for yourself at any time, every day. Now back to the Portal.

This is the warmest energy from a greenhouse I have ever been in. The plants seem to reach out and clean you as you walk by. They know it's their job in this Portal. I hear they're being prepared to be on Earth again to help us someday. In the meantime, we get to experience them in our moments here and in our dreams. Our dreams help bring them to Earth.

This is the flower room. Oh, my! Have you ever smelled anything so wonderful? They're so perfected they do not cause allergic reactions. They seem to be at every stage of opening. As we walk by, a little Sprite sprinkles Pixie Dust to help them open just for us. They go back to their original stages after we experience them.

My favorite – Foxglove! I always thought of them as being Fairy hats in my garden. I just love how it feels, and so many varieties of it here!!! There are also lavender and lilies! Maybe this is why I have these in my gardens and help them work within our Earth. There are so many more varieties and colors here. It's truly heavenly.

The vegetable building is next. You may continue to as many buildings as you wish. I want to show you what you walked through as we came into this room. See that mister overhead? As we went through it we were gently sprayed with a light mixture of Victim-clearing spray. Not that any of us are true victims, but I bet each of us have moments when we wonder "Why?" about something in our lives. Not simply to learn something, but why did this happen to me or someone else. As we learn to not stay in that state, the easier it is for us to manifest the Abundance we are here to learn about.

As you leave the flower house to go out or into another room, you will probably notice the misters. The ones going out of this building will also assist us in other areas we may need help in. Enjoy them. Stand in them as long as you want. They feel so wonderful as they help everyone's old stuff just slide off me.

See you tomorrow!

MONTH SEVEN – DAY SIX

Get your hiking boots, because we are going to hang out with some other Elementals today. Of course, you can go bare footed if you want. I thought it would be cool to say that since it was the first thing that came into my mind as I opened this page to type.

We are going to explore a huge rock mountain. It called to me saying it wanted to be first on the list for us to do. It isn't very far up this nice path of moss with so many flowers lining it. We have Flower Fairies tending to the pollination process of the multiple species along the way. The Fairies are so beautiful, and they seem to be the color of the plants they tend to. Their wings are see-through and iridescent – they just sparkle all over. The pollen floating around them is also sparkly. They are always so happy, and this keeps the flowers happy. Together, their energy creates such an uplifting attitude along this path.

I think we made it here in record time. Not that time matters in here, but it felt like we danced all the way with music from the Fairy's wings. Notice how the path ends right at the base of these huge rocks. Look at these boulders. I mean really look at them. Can you see the spirit in each of them? If you can see the face on each rock it will give you a hint of who lives in it and the interesting personality it holds. You can climb on them – they aren't going to be offended. Get to know them, including those at the top. Each of them has a specific job. Some are guardians of this whole Portal, others are here to support the guardians, and others are here hold the energy of what Rock Spirits do.

If you listen real close you will hear their messages to you. We don't have to stay together. Take your time and I will meet you at the top.

I am meeting some amazing Rock Spirits. They have quite a sense of humor. One actually said, "Ouch! Get your foot out of my eye!" as I stepped on it. It was loud enough that I nearly fell off him. Then he apologized for frightening me. My foot wasn't even near his eye! He was actually very happy we took the time to visit. Not many come this way as these rocks aren't as sparkly and glamorous as the other gardens and paths are in this Portal. They get a little lonely, but they know their job is to hold grounding energy for the whole Kingdom. If it weren't for them, there would be very little order, and the level of Air Headedness would increase dramatically. Of course, it would increase with all light Fairy energy. A little grounding is necessary.

Is everyone ready to take a new path back to the center? I hear a stream a little way over there, and feel a need to get my feet wet. Yes, it's right over here, and it's okay for us to wade in it. We are mixing the Water Spirits with Rock Spirits in this little place. It feels so amazing. As the water flows over the rocks listen to it whisper to you. It has a very special message for each of us. It sounds like various pitched musical notes at times. If you don't want to listen that is also okay.

Walking over the smaller sparkly stones with the water flowing at various speeds is clearing old programs we have held onto. I can feel them being pulled from the bottom of my feet all way up to the top of my head. These programs have been here a long time, so it's time to release them! Yes, it feels so much better, and my brain is working better now as well. The cool water and the slippery hard stones were just what I needed. I hope you enjoyed it too.

Our guide motions for us to head back to the Center. It is movie and popcorn night. My favorite! I wonder what the movie is!

See you tomorrow!

MONTH SEVEN – DAY SEVEN

We get to experience the Water Beings in this realm on today's Portal journey. There are a lot of names for these beings, but I think the main one we will learn about is the Mermaid/Merman. This is one of the Fairy Realm beings I know the least about. I am very excited to experience this group.

I have been told there is a changing place near the pond and stream we will be playing in today. I, for one, am putting my swimsuit on under my clothes. I have been dunked one too many times to not be prepared for the rest of my life around water. Even if it isn't on purpose, somehow, I end up in the water before I am completely prepared. So, this time I will just wear everything I need all at once, except for the towel. I will deal with that as a separate piece, and it will probably get wet, too. However, it turns out I am certain it will be a lot of fun.

The pond is a bit of a distance for us to walk so we will ride our Dragon Flies. I hope you brought treats. Sometimes, when they haven't seen you for a day or two, they can be a little stubborn. Mine was easy to get to come to me this time. I love the feeling when it happens. He remembered me!

We do have a guide again, since this place is not located where I thought it was. We will land in an area where there is assistance to take care of our Dragon Flies, so they don't leave us. These critters aren't as loving as my Dragon Avatar. They can just take off and not even think about leaving you at their last drop-off location. I'm sure glad we have help. It makes it a lot easier when it is time to head back.

This is a nice easy flight so far. I see we are taking a detour. We will meet a few of the Fairy Realm inhabitants for lunch before we give our attention to the lake. I guess we need a few pointers of safety around this realm's water. Yes, the Mermaids are very nice and helpful, but there are some beings that like to control the water.

I have heard the world Undines in relation to some of them. They can be a little temperamental and unpredictable like so many people on Earth. The problem is that water can be unpredictable as well. It can be controlled with thought easily and, if one is not aware of their thoughts, strange situations are created. I hope you understand this is not to instill fear. It's for educational purposes and to help remind you that you are Great Creators of what happens around you.

We are now ready to get into that refreshing water and meet some new friends. The water beings can remember so much because water retains information. It is easily programmable. That is why it is used in ceremonies for many special occasions, including a variety of blessings. It is also used to physically and energetically put out a physical or energetic fire. Fire and water information is just as important as the beings who reside in them.

Oh, yes, the water in this Portal is so nice. It's not only refreshing but it contains the knowledge needed for creating the Abundance you want. Let it soak into your skin. And it is okay to drink. It is the purest water you will ever find, even though critters live in it. Sorry, just had to remind you not to swallow a tiny fish or Water Sprite.

There are floating devices here! I'm not normally a water person, but this is healing. Getting into and out of the water on a timed basis helps to give yourself the time to take in information, and then to get out onto a floating device to absorb the information on another level. Don't forget to stay hydrated, for drinking this water brings in information on a totally different level from the skin.

As you meet the beings that live here, listen to them. Learn all that you can about why they aren't visible to most of us on the Earth. One of you may be able to write a book on this.

I am ready to head back to my home away from home and climb into the crystal bathtub to help my body recalibrate all this information I have taken in. I know that part of it is assisting in the regeneration of these cells and the telomeres of DNA. I also want to journal some of the conversations I had with these new friends. You may want to as well.

See you tomorrow!

MONTH SEVEN – DAY EIGHT

I am so excited, I can hardly wait to tell you! We get to meet the Pegasus, the Unicorns, the Centaurs, and the beings who are all a part of the Fairy Realm. It will be a little hike to get to their area. I thought about riding the Dragon Flies, but decided against it, as I have a feeling it is time for something else to happen. We can meet at their holding pen in just a little bit.

It is time to thank the Dragon Fly you have been working with and set them free. They are not used to being kept in a state of captivity for very long. We learned a lot working with them, and had so much fun. Search in your pack to find a special treat given to you for your own ride. The bond between a rider and the insect realm for that purpose will not be forgotten on either side. It was a very special few days for us getting to experience riding the Dragon Flies! Give them the biggest thank you that you know how to!

Now we get to go for a small hike up the side of the Portal. It's another lesson in being not only on good behavior and keeping your excitement contained, but also an opportunity to experience a sacred event.

Today, the Unicorns, Pegasus, and Centaurs let people see them and participate in their space.

There are also some special treats in your packs for each of them. I hope you didn't eat them thinking they were yours. If you did, it won't hurt, but they probably didn't taste the way you thought. You will be given more when we get there.

That hike wasn't too bad. Mostly flat until the last half-mile where the Portal began its daily turn. A little feeling of sea legs, but now everyone is looking quite grounded.

There is a line. I did not expect this. Sorry, I guess we should have started earlier. It is moving fast, and we have a person coming around to give us some basic information about them and how to be aware of their behaviors. They are very similar to horses in their temperament. For instance, if their ears are not straight up and down, or they're wriggling back and forth. If they're flat back against their head, be careful and do not approach especially from behind. Also, just like our horses, they have a very powerful back kick. They are very similar to horses in their temperament. Just be aware of your surroundings and you will be fine.

It is now our turn. It is quite interesting how a Centaur guides the tours. It is probably a great way to create a bridge to ease the energy around everyone. We are not the only humans in this Portal. Plus, the beings in here respect them so much they just want to see them and thank them for their service in here. I think we are the last group going on this tour.

We are so lucky. We get to be up close and personal with these amazing magical beings. Remember your treats as we go into the area of the forest they live in. Oh, my goodness. As I watch each of you, I am in awe of how you are treated by these magical beings. I wish I had my camera! I am being told the one that you are feeding now will give you a ride back to the Center when we are ready to go. Did you notice the baby ones? Their Mothers are really showing them off to everyone. Look how they prance around the meadow.

And the Pegasus are learning to fly here as well. Sometimes it takes a little fairy dust to help get those that can't fly to do so. I have treats for the baby ones; I will also share if you want to help feed them. Aren't they just the cutest little pieces of Magic you have ever seen?!

I am impressed with the Centaur being so friendly. In many of the books I have read, they seem to be more to themselves. This group must be the first to let outsiders so close to participate with them.

Are you ready for the ride on your Unicorn? They are so much nicer to sit on, even without a bridle or saddle than the Dragon Fly was. I have not experienced such a nice, sweet, magical energy in a very long time. Plus, they are so soft! Now I understand why the stuffed Unicorns that kids get are so loved.

Wow, magical for sure! We are teleported back to the Center.

See you tomorrow!

MONTH SEVEN – DAY NINE

I still feel the Unicorns' magic. They are one of the most special beings that live here in this Magical Kingdom. Their tears heal a surprising list of situations. Remember in *Harry Potter* how Unicorn blood was used. It is of course wrong on all levels to kill a Unicorn, but just to know how you feel in one's presence is quite a testament to their Purity of Magic. They are Benevolent Beings that work in Light, Love, and Gratitude.

Enough about what was – we are here for what is today. This swarm of Fairies flying around my head, are telling me it's time to have a question and answer session with them about this Portal and who they are. It will be held this evening in the Center's garden. The time starts when you arrive.

Right now, it is time to call in your Avatar. Think of the most magical creature you can work with and ride at the same time. They are best if they have a personality of wanting to help humans before taming them. As most of you know, mine is the Purple Dragon. I have really missed having him around in this Portal, now that we can bring him on board, I am beyond happy. Mine is the bluish-purple one. What are you going to call in for yourself? If you have worked with a certain one for many of these Portals you know exactly how to do this, and you can always change to a different one if you feel so inclined.

Get into your Heart Space and feel what an Avatar of your choice might be like. Focus on its look, smell, and size. As many ideas that you can come up with the better. It helps to call it in if you make the visualization.

Let your heart open a little more and just know it will be here when you open your eyes. You might want to do this slight meditation at least once a day. Keep it totally positive, because it helps the connection go better.

I see many Avatars arriving into the pens outside. Mine can shift into a size so he can be in here with me. Oh, I have really missed this big guy! Let's go outside and see what has arrived. There is a lot of commotion going on out here. We need a little Pixie Dust to calm them all down. I think some loved being together and have missed seeing each other for a while.

The many wonderful beings in here that love to work with these mystical Avatars are getting them ready to ride. I had forgotten that it takes a little bit of time for them to also adjust to the Portal. I will just send some of this Magic Dust that keeps reappearing in my pouch over to them to signal that we are on our way.

Are you ready for a short ride? I think the Avatars ready. I am so excited as my Dragon is a lot easier to ride than the Dragon Fly. I hope you will have the same experience with your Avatar. Let's take a short ride over to the stream and pond where we can investigate the falls. Follow me! We need to be a little patient with our Avatars. Being inside of the Portal was a little strange for us the first day, so it is for them as well.

I see a huge sparkly rainbow we can experience without taking our Avatars too far in their first Portal run. I had never noticed the top of this rainbow before. There are Fairy beings flying around it sprinkling sparkly dust on top for it to slide down and mix with the colors being painted by another group of Fairies.

I am told we can fly through the rainbows on either side or near the bottom to be able to absorb the color frequencies and activations of the Fairy Dust! We can also sit in the rainbow as long as we want or however long it decides to exist in this space.

Take your time. It feels like this is what we needed. Looks like we aren't the only ones participating in this activation. I think this is how the beings here get cleared of crazy old stuff. I even see a Giant sitting at each end with the colors really absorbing into them. I hadn't thought of the Giants being a part of this realm. Very interesting.

I am heading back to the Center as I do have a few questions I want to ask the Fairies. You may stay as long as you wish.

See you tomorrow!

MONTH SEVEN – DAY TEN

Since we have our Avatars with us, we can explore another part of this Portal. One area our guide told me about, but couldn't venture out to today, is the Land of the Trolls. I remember a story I was told called Three Billy Goats Gruff. In it, the Trolls were going to eat the goats, but the biggest goat butted the Trolls away. Well, I really don't think Trolls are all that bad. The ones I have met have been extremely polite and very helpful. I am ready to find out if the ones who live here are truly like those in their homeland.

Our guide gave me a map we can follow to the Land of the Trolls. It looks pretty simple. We can do this! As we fly over the trees and streams we are keeping low, so we can see the landmarks that are on the map. There are areas where the canyons are quite narrow, but we can fly in single file if we need too. We have all day to get there.

Oh, here is one of the landmarks. That ledge over there must be the same as the one right here on the map. We have time to give our Avatars a break to get some water and rest. We can also benefit from some downtime. I see a great spot right near that stream where we will all fit. I guess our Avatars were a little hungry, they are devouring their food. You too? I see that we have a nice amount of food packed for us. Dig in!

I, for one, want to put my feet in the water and just relax. This stream is so nice, and the beings I see around it are the Flower and Tree Fairies. They keep the plants happy and growing in a pristine environment. They said it was okay for me to wade in the stream but to be careful as the round rocks are not only slippery, but they are alive and sometimes bite or move out of the way if you step on them. Well, I would bite too if I got stepped on. Moving out of the way is the best. We can just be careful where we step.

I also see a Mermaid family in the pool on the other side. We don't want to disturb them, so we will stay over here. The water does feel great. It is relaxing to me in a manner I know as detoxing. I can feel it pulling the toxins out of my liver. It is incredibly strong, it doesn't hurt, it's simply an awareness. Everything here is so pure that it is ready to help us be that way.

Is everyone rested and ready to journey on? The map shows that we are to follow this stream up to the huge round boulder that blocks the water off and causes it to go into two different directions. At that point we turn left and follow it to the Land of the Trolls. Not far now!

Do you see them? They are waving for us to come join them. They are excited to see us and to share their lives for the afternoon. I love campfires with gatherings around them.

Thank you, whoever packed for us today. We have our ear translation devices! We also have another device that looks like an ever-evolving blue ball. It floats between people to also help with the translations. I had no idea they would talk this strange language. To me, they sound like the Ewoks from *Star Wars*. They also have a similar walk/run gait. I love this family! Once they realize we can communicate with them, they are so happy to share their stories. I think we will spend most of the afternoon here. I am certain that our Avatars can find their way back to the Center in the dark.

This has been a very long afternoon and it is still light out, but I have the feeling that something is about to change quickly. It is hard to leave these wonderful, misunderstood beings. We do need to start our journey back.

As we get on our Avatars, I see a whole group Fairies coming with lanterns to help us find our way back. They also know a shortcut. We had to follow the map to get here as it was easier having the landmarks and the stream, but I am all for shortcuts! Ready? It's nice flying in the dark. It is so peaceful.

Now I see why we had to be escorted back so quickly. A party has been planned just for us. Oh, how interesting ... the Trolls were told to keep us busy so the party could be arranged without us knowing! That must be why our guide couldn't be with us. These Magical beings are amazing in so many ways.

I wonder what Magical 'feats' we will get to witness and be a part of this evening! I hear music, and my feet can't stop moving. I think everyone in the Portal is here to participate in our final night adventure. They have games for those of us that want to participate and so much food! Even the food sparkles. It is also delicious.

Just fair warning, the food is spiked with magical fun! Laughter is not an option, or lack of may be a better way of stating that. If you aren't laughing, the food will help you be in that state. I want to watch and take it all in, but the food ... Oh, my goodness ... Belly laughs for the entire night! Plus, dancing!

See you tomorrow for our last ride in the Portal!

MONTH SEVEN – DAY ELEVEN

I hope you all got a little sleep last night as that was some fantastic Magical Party. If you didn't believe in Magic before, I bet you do now! The crazy thing is that with all the magnificent food I ate and strange things I drank, I feel just fine today. This is going to be one of the hardest Portals for me to leave.

I don't know if you could tell, but in each area we experienced, and each Amazing Being we participated with, we were helped in our ability to Receive Abundance. This Abundance is all around us and in each choice we make. It is up to us to receive it and bring it into the existence we want to participate with. Learning to ride a Dragon Fly was a great lesson in understanding that we can do anything we are willing to participate in. Sometimes, it is hard to step into the roll we are asked to be a part of. Just remember, each experience makes it easier to bring in and accept the Abundance in your life. Sometimes it is Money and what it can help bring to you and others. Sometimes it is better health, or a happy family. No matter what, you are to be an active part of the equation.

Since today is our last in this Magical environment, let's see what else we can do. We were able to be in the presence of all the wonderful Beings that live here and sort of said our goodbyes at the party. However, we didn't get to say goodbye to the Portal itself. Let's find our Avatars and go for one last ride through here.

Amazing how telepathic this place is. Our Avatars are prepared and waiting on us. Let's start at the far-right side and circle around over the top, probably swirling down into areas we want to experience one last time.

I already feel the rotational swirl in here the closer we get to the sides. I feel it doing another activation on me, and, you if you choose, you can also receive the activation of Receiving Abundance in every Fun activity experienced in the real world. I can feel it move through my spine on out to my exterior muscles, bones, head, and abdominal area. Lots of vibrational increases in all areas of my body. It is a good thing my Dragon doesn't react the same way as I do to these activations or we wouldn't be flying right now. At least all I have to do is hang on as I have already given directions to him.

I love how the vegetation and land work together here on the sides of Portal walls. No matter the position of the rotation, it settles where it is supposed to be and the Nature Fairies and Land Caretakers all work together for the betterment of the entire Portal. I think we could take some of that wisdom home with us. Our Earth most certainly could benefit from this energy.

Along the upper edge, we can see how the sky rotates yet maintains the seasonal aspect of the how the stars are located and the energy emitted by them. It has its own way of creating a flow like our Moon. Generating currents in water and wind elements. These keep the place clean of debris beings like us bring in, and it also keeps the Portal fresh every moment.

I look for the sparkly rainbow, as I want to fly through it again. Sparkles just keep the flow of change happening, reflecting new opportunities that are available in each choice.

I see it over there and, yes, they knew we were looking for them. I see the Giants and Trolls. Instead of sitting at the bottom absorbing what they need, they stand in a circle around it.

The Fairies are riding the Pegasus ponies and spreading more sparkle, while the flowers and trees are trying to fit underneath to be a part of our farewell ride-through. This is really a part of the unconditional Love we have experienced in here. I think they will miss us as much as we will miss them.

This was such a wonderful feeling, being in the presence of such Pure Love and getting sprinkled with all the colors of the rainbow as we rode through them.

It is now time to find the exit. We need to be at the Center for it to find us. It gives us time to say goodbye to our Avatars or help them get into the Portal of their own so that we can be with them again another time.

The exit point is right in the middle of the Center. We each have a round plate to stand on with our name on it. We will be beamed up into the larger Portal and taken directly back to our location on Earth.

Ready? I will miss all of you and this place. I want to remind you that, if you want to experience this again, just go into a meditation and take yourself back to this place. Of course, you can re-read any of these messages as many times as you choose.

See you next month!

See you soon with Truth, Love, and Gratitude

Pat, The Cosmic Cowgirl

Journal What You Learned and Experienced in the Fairy Realm

CHAPTER EIGHT: HARVEST & REGROUP

MONTH EIGHT – DAY ONE

Welcome to our ending of the summer/move into the fall Divine Portal. This is a time where we shift from the busy long days of doing. When we play in the sunlight, even if it is called work, we participate in soaking up the rays of sunshine as much as we can. Though we may be in an office all day, we have an anticipation of wanting to be outside in the sun. The sun helps us be healthy and grow in many ways.

Have you noticed we have to buy new clothes for kids going back to school as they seem to have suddenly outgrown everything they once wore? We grow in just being, soaking in, radiating the spiraling rays of the sun combined with the Earth and all the elements we are made up of. We grow in the Ever-Changing of Earth. Our jobs, our families, and how we are ready to make a move into the next level is called Regrouping.

The Divine Portal we are to experience this month is a spiral of energy preparing us to begin harvesting from the play and work we have engaged in for the last eight months. As we stand in the light of the sun for a moment, we can feel it beaming down its warm energy and providing the life force of renewal each day.

We can look into it and gain the knowledge of what is needed. We can do our breathing and stretching in preparation for the next step of what is to come. As we stand in this ray of sunlight, allowing it to fill every cell with Divine Love and Life Force, we are now able to shift our being into the ray to be taken into the Divine Portal of August.

This Portal is filled with a calmness of knowing what it is we are to do in the moment. Just as you walk to your garden and look over it, you see what needs to be taken care of today. The beans need to be picked, the carrots are nearly ready and need a little more water, the cucumbers are ready to be harvested, some of the corn is ready to eat, and that zucchini plant is exploding with a harvest that can be shared with neighbors. It is all related to how we live our lives in the cycles of the Planet. We are also stages of the garden plants.

As we stand staring at our accomplishments we can take a little pride in how much we have also grown and learned. Is it ready to share with those that can benefit from it? Or does it need a little more refining, more water and sunlight?

I see this Divine Portal will help us with this aspect of the harvest. The start of separating the wheat from the chaff. A form of lifting the entire harvest into the air and allowing the wind to blow through it. After several times of working with the wind, the stems and leaves are blown away, leaving the ripe wheat to be cleaned and dried and stored properly for use as needed. For those that don't know, I grew up on a ranch with a nice garden. We did this type of separating with several items of the harvest.

For us today, as we enter the Divine Portal, we will experience this separation of ourselves. We stand in the entrance of the Portal with the golden rays of light shining on us and the wind of the tunnel blowing through every cell of our body and our clothing.

With each step we take into the Portal we are greeted with a new level or frequency of wind blowing through us. There are five of these channels we are going to walk through. Take your time as you begin this journey. Each area may take a little longer than another as there are so many different areas to begin the clearing. For example, the first one may only be able to affect your hair and the dust on your shoes. The second may be able to flutter your jacket and jeans or skirt. Third is a little deeper so we can get to your underwear. The fourth can perhaps enter your emotional day to day drama. And the fifth, if you are ready, can start clearing your heart.

Remember to take your time and allow yourself to be cleared. Once you have gone through a level of clearing you will be given a room to recalibrate in.

See you tomorrow!

MONTH EIGHT – DAY TWO

We are now ready to enter the Divine Portal of Harvest and regroup, at least that is what it is called for now. We shall see what we find in here, what we are ready to harvest, and if we are ready to regroup for the next phase of our year.

As we walk out into the Portal itself we are greeted by Divine Beings in golden robes ready to escort us into the room of choice. They open the door for us to enter while they wait outside. The walls are at different angles, some slanted to the ceiling, some doubling back into the one before it, some are full of windows without a door. Do you enter this room, or do you stand beside the beings in the golden robes?

I am going to enter and find out what is new in this adventure. It's so interesting in here, I think I will do a quick look around before I jump into something. In one room, a person can play in the mud to make mud pies, have mud fights, roll in it, and rub it in your hair. So many ideas!

Another room is for painting on an easel with lessons taught by an expert painter, or painting walls, or floors, or painting on yourself.

This one is a waterpark with slides and pools. See how fast I walked right past that one!

Gardening is in this next one, with a controlled environment – no mosquitoes or flies.

Oh, this one is a room to meditate with a place to sit comfortably and listen to soft music, birds and butterflies, Fairies and Unicorns. It seems like each room is a way to fulfill a piece of summer that one isn't finished with. Take your time and enjoy each room if you so desire.

I guess I am ready for the next area of the Portal. If you want to come with me, we can walk with a guide while another will be left for the rest of the group as they are ready. I am certain they will have to go through a cleaning process again before they can join us, mostly to rinse off the mud and paint.

The path we are walking on feels like a cloud. Oh, it is a cloud. We are coming up to an area where we get to enter the Divine Portal. This was just the entrance. We have a slide to take us all the way into the center. It does have a way to secure us in, so we don't get hurt, because I have been told this goes quick. If you didn't get your roller coaster thrill this summer, you will get it now.

That first turn was a little surprising, and now a rolling over and over and over and over, then rolling in a sideways direction for three times, then the other sideways direction, and a dive down to the landing pad. WOW! That one could be in Six Flags, and I probably wouldn't ride it. The rolling in different directions is a little crazy for my stomach. However, in here I am okay, so far.

The building before us looks to be like a harvest party. It is shaped like a giant pumpkin with lots of lights and cooking aromas. Oh, peaches. Yes, it is peach harvest season right now here in Colorado. Pies! County Fair time, too. There are horses, cows, pigs, chickens, rabbits, llamas, judging, ribbons and the hay. Plus, there are lots of carnival noises, kids laughing, and dogs barking. All the sounds that fill the air just before school begins. Of course, we can't miss the rodeos – my all-time favorite thing for this month. I guess that was my secret wish to finish off the season, and I didn't even know it.

Okay, the rooms with things to do didn't get my attention, but this one did. Now it is my turn in the cleaning process of the wind machines. Yes, that is refreshing. I do feel much better and am ready to proceed.

We are going to get started in this harvest event by entering the pineapple fields. You will find gloves on the bench as we enter. We are given a special type of knife to cut the pineapple from its root system. Take your time to find a wonderfully ripe one. Cut it from its root system – only what is ready to be utilized. Then smell it, look at it, and notice all its aspects. How big is it? What color, how spiny? Now, as a token of friendship, the Portal is giving this to you to take to your cabin tonight. It also symbolizes those intangible assets we can now appreciate and the many we have accumulated over the last few months.

It is time to follow our guide to our own cabin. If you need anything at all I am certain it will be found for you – candles, robes, food. Take time to find the exact place to put this pineapple – by the door, center of the table, or cut it up and eat it. It is yours to do with as you choose.

See you tomorrow!

MONTH EIGHT – DAY THREE

I feel so much excitement to be creating more forms of harvesting. Cutting the pineapple from its roots was really empowering. The way it reminded me of how strong we are as we work, learn, and attempt new ways of understanding our growth was exciting. When it is time to harvest, we must be ready to cut loose from the roots, and, if you wait too long, the fruit will over ripen and become useless. Sometimes, the way we do things becomes obsolete.

This is the hard part – knowing when to cut away the part holding you back. Those roots can keep on growing deeper and deeper to hold all the old information that was perfect at the time it came into our lives. Sort of like what is often called the perpetual student who ruminates over the first class they ever took as if it were yesterday and using the same information every day for the next twenty-five years in the exact same way it was delivered. The information is just as valid today – well, sometimes it is – especially to the student. But is it still worth teaching? Evolution of so many aspects of ourselves and the world around us has changed.

But what do we do for ourselves? Are you still exercising to the same program that you did years ago, or even yesterday? Maybe taking the same brand of vitamins that have been a part of your routine since you started taking them the last time you got sick? How does it benefit your growth and reason for being on the Planet right now?

This Divine Portal of Harvest and Regrouping is a great place to notice and hopefully get some ideas of how we can create a better World for one another.

Today as we slowly venture out of our cabins, ready to climb aboard what is new for the moment; look at what you are wearing. We are going to go for a hike. What is the first thing you think of needing? My thoughts went to hiking boots, rugged clothing, maybe a hat or jacket, first-aid kit with band aids for the cut and scrapes. I didn't think to ask what type of terrain we are going to cover or where we are going. My mind was already pre-programmed into it being this one way. So, that is how I am prepared for the day. I am ready to hike a mountain trail.

Remember, we are in a Portal of where anything is possible. I am directly behind our guide who is taking us away from the ideas we have been programmed with. We are going to have another idea of what a hike can be.

We are on an escalator going up through the clouds. It is one of those clouds that are really puffy and huge. This is a new way of getting to the top of a "mountain." We step off onto a landing near the top. The view of this Portal is like nothing I have never seen. I think I could just hang out here for hours.

I hear it is time to grow wings. This is interesting. I have no idea if this is about us or the birds or butterflies. The landing ramp we are on is starting to get smaller and smaller, and our guide is gone. There is no one available to ask. Now I realize we better quickly figure out how to grow wings.

Suddenly, we are falling through the cloud. Well, sort of drifting, as there is a density to it, but nothing to hold onto us or stop the falling. There is nothing in my consciousness of ever having had wings before, but this is information I need right now! Time to go into our subconscious and tell our bodies to quickly grow wings.

It is working. I can feel a tingle on my back between my shoulder blades and spine. My shirt is tearing apart and they are coming out. They automatically connected with my brain and started working. I think it is a level of working just like the heart beats. It just happens. The cloud is gone, and we can soar over the trees all the way back to the Center where we are staying. Wow! That was a real test of creating a new program in just seconds.

How does this fit in with Harvesting or Regrouping? Did you grow your wings? Or, did you find another way of working with this situation? Again, we are in the Divine Portal, so there were other options. Did you ask for a parachute? Did you call for your Avatar from the other Portals using the telepathy we have worked with? So many options are available to us to utilize within our Harvest time. I realize some of you are new to the Portal experience and may not have been taught these amazing ideas on how the Portals can be what you need them to be. So, you were probably better at growing the wings than any of us.

As we enter the Center we are greeted with a new set of teachers. The class is titled "What to do With Your New Wings". It starts tomorrow. For tonight, they are helping us fold them back up and stick them inside our shirts.

See you tomorrow!

MONTH EIGHT – DAY FOUR

I found it quite interesting trying to sleep with wings tucked into my shirt. They most certainly kept me aware that they were there, and I definitely did not sleep on my back. I also wonder what they have to do with the Harvest and Regrouping part of the Portal. I guess we'll find out in the class 'What to do With Your New Wings.'

I see we really do need this class. We can't go around with wings half-tucked in and sticking out at strange angles. Also, the amount of space they take up under our shirts is quite uncomfortable. I am really ready for this lesson. It is nearly time to start.

Oh, the Guides in the golden robes are back. Lesson number one is how to be in charge of our bodies which, at this moment, includes our wings. Yes, we all know we are Earth Angels in disguise. or sort of. Not all Angels have wings or else they know how to conceal them pretty darn good. I guess I am a little impatient today as mine are super itchy and that is a hard spot to scratch. I just want to know more about how we did this and what to do with them next.

To start with, did we create/force our bodies to generate the wings from hidden memories or DNA? It was under a stressed-out situation. It was either do it now or die.

So, instead of dying, we quickly created the wings. We learned that we could do unexplainable things under these levels of stress. Now, what to do with what we created?

Can you see how this is related to your last eight months following this Divine Journey within the Portal? Planting, watering, taking care of your garden? Working, learning, marketing, saving, and creating your life or business? The Harvest is what we do with what we create. It is also a time to regroup and make some little changes as needed.

What do we do with our wings? The Guides help us hold the space within ourselves to go into a deep focus on where the wings grew from. A big reminder is to not freak out, just breathe. We have a choice: completely un-create them or move them into a different form or place. The Regrouping and Harvest are in a realm outside of what you are used to. Our new wings are a part of the learning how to regroup our own energy and utilize our ability to create within our Harvest.

The first step is to decide if you want to keep them. Is what you created too far outside of your comfort level? Do you want them to show, or is there a way to shrink them back into your body but still be accessible for use as needed or wanted? Creating a more manageable plan to work with your creation is a great way to flow with your journey. You can also just have them removed completely. It is your choice.

One of the problems on Earth is that we tend to conceal our identity. How visible do you want to be? Are you ready to show yourself and SHINE? Is this the real You, the business You, or somewhere in-between? How do you want to Be and be seen?

Let's go back into breathing ... Just Breathe. Look at your wings. They are beautiful. Mine are starting to feel better. I just saw the little switch where I can have them shrink back into my back. When I BREATHE, I can access the switch and collapse them into me. There is also a switch right next to it where I can make them invisible. Take time to breathe and practice with these switches. I see they can become fully unfolded under certain stressful times. Is there a way they can be accessed without stress? Yes, just focus on feeling them being there and they are.

Step Two, taking care of the wings. They have to be cleaned and combed. A special shampoo and brush are provided. Just like your lives, what you create has to be maintained if you want it to continue to work for you. The brushing works like the standard coming out as the new comes in to keep everything in Divine Right Order.

Each step in our lives works on the same principle. If care is maintained daily, there isn't so much to do all at once. Just like Harvesting. An example would be the green beans or zucchini in the garden. If they are checked every few days and harvested, then there is little to do as we go along. If we wait and only check once a week or month, they become dried out and on the verge of dying, or are overgrown with weeds, or the beans and zucchini are too big and hard to be eaten. Those clients you work so hard to help at the first will fall away without the completion of why they came to you. The same works with every aspect of our lives.

Now is the time for the bigger Harvest of the hard work we have put in over the past several months. It may include cleaning or weeding, a closet, files, or clients, then Regrouping for the next level of what we are preparing for in our lives. Have you been able to create the Abundance you were hoping to? Does there need to be a course correction? Are you following your Soul's Passion?

That was a lot to cover in one day's journey. Let's take a little walk over by the waterfall and pond. You can either stroll under and into it or just enjoy it from where you are the most comfortable. This is a good time to meditate and journal about what you have experienced. Are you following your Soul's Passion?

See you tomorrow!

MONTH EIGHT – DAY FIVE

For me, it was a lot of journaling last night. The wings are still a little hard to believe. How to work with them is something to fit into my day. Finding my Soul's Passion is the easy part, allowing or finding the time for it is the hard part. Today, I think we need a little exploring with some exciting fun.

As I stepped outside of the Center I had a little difficulty remembering that this is a Divine Portal of Harvest and Regrouping in our quest for Abundance. The path is beautifully maintained with so much greenery and flowers to top off the contrast. It is truly an abundant place. I don't sense our Avatars are here yet, so we will be doing a little walking.

The cliffs with the larger waterfall seem to be calling to us. It isn't too far. I can hear the rushing water from here. I am assured we will be safe. I tend to worry when it comes to water. It is one of the elements that I have not been totally comfortable with.

WOW! This cliff and waterfall is set up like a water park. The tubes are on a conveyer system, so you just have to take one from the pile and get in line. It feels so good. The water spraying up and around us is continually clearing so much of the energy.

Who is going to go first? Yes, it is a waterfall and not a tunnel with edges, or is it? I can feel the edges, I can't see them, but they are there. Our tubes will be guided for us, but we still have to hang on. Of course, I am the one looking for life jackets, but I am being reassured that I won't need one. "Trust the flow," is what I hear. Here we go!

This is extremely fun. There are different levels of how steep you want to go. I am taking the back and forth one with a slight downward slant. It is going under the waterfall at each turn, a nice refreshing and clearing moment at a slower pace. You just take the one that is best for you, and I see there is an escalator at the bottom that you can ride back up and do it all over again as many times as you want. Of course, you can walk the trail or walk while on the escalator if you want another ride faster.

The slower paced one was perfect for me as I was able to do a lot of clearing of old energy and emotions still attached onto my shoulders. They feel much better and I can think more clearly.

I see a picnic area at the bottom where we can eat and float around the river. I also see a meditation area with paper for note-taking. I am drawn to two different colored papers. One is for making a list of the harvesting I'm doing. I may need more than one piece There are so many areas of harvesting right now. For me, it is family, household, and business. These lists will help me use my time wiser as I tend to go into one job and end up letting it take me to another one before it is finished.

I also see another colored paper for the Regrouping. I think I can multitask this one. As I am Harvesting I am also Regrouping. I am reminded of what a teacher of mine from many years ago taught me. It was about spring and fall cleaning. She told me to pay attention to how you have things arranged.

How do you move your furniture and the items you have on the furniture or shelves to make room for the events you are working with? For example, when you plan a party, how do you move your furniture to make room for the guests. Also, what is the color of the candles you set about, or where do you set a food bowl. Then, for Christmas, you may move the furniture again to make a place for the tree and gifts. What you are doing is re-gridding your space to create the energy of the flow for the event you are planning. This is what we are doing with the Harvest and Regrouping. We are re-gridding our lives. Everything is energy. Take your time getting back to the Center.

See you tomorrow!

MONTH EIGHT – DAY SIX

Hooray! Great to meet with you again today! We get to examine how this Portal works. I have been told that it might help us to understand the Harvest and Regrouping aspects of this journey in the Divine Portal of Activations for Abundance we create moment by moment.

To start with, we get to find the stables to pick our Avatar. It is easy for me – having spent my childhood on a cattle/horse ranch. The only way to make sure you are going the right direction is to "follow your nose." Critters have a distinct smell. Some people say they can't deal with dogs or cats, and what they say is true.

Every critter has its own scent. Chickens, cows, pigs, sheep, dogs, ferrets, Guinea pigs, bears, deer, elk, to just name a few. They all have their own smell. I realize my Purple Dragon may not smell as nice to some of you as your Unicorn. No matter how clean you keep the pens, cages, or corrals, there is still a distinct odor that is not human. Follow your nose!

Now, you may notice there are many types of critter containments. Take your time and pick the one you want. Of course, because they're magical, they wouldn't normally allow themselves to be penned in, but, due to your perceived safety, they agreed to be within these areas while some of you get used to the idea of being this close to the various species. Just notice which one gets your attention the most – you don't have to know why. It will be the one that helps your heart open. Talk to it and see if you can work together. Once you decide, one of the caretakers will help you pick out some riding equipment.

I usually ride my Dragon, but today I think I will ride the Bear. It can also fly, even without wings. Today I like the feel of his fur. It feels magical, sort of electric and magnetic all at once. I also really like his powerful paws and claws, and, of course, those huge teeth. We are ready for what we are to experience today.

It is time to Mount Up! We are going into the basic workings of this Portal. See how it spins? We are to do our best to stay in its center. The colors in this area are so pure and vibrant. It can also be hypnotic and intoxicating. Breathe and stay grounded within yourself. Remember, we are here for a reason beyond just enjoying how it feels. That is why, if we stay in its center, we are safer from being pulled into its function.

See how there's a constant flow of New coming in at the top and moving to the right in a clockwise direction? It's being sorted into various categories as it spins around to the bottom. As it flows on over to the left, there is more settling into spaces where information and items need to be, then the old is picked up and sorted, as if it is still working for betterment of the system. Once the information or item is no longer useful for the forward movement of the Portal, it is pulled into releasing waves which carry it on out, to make more room for the New.

This is what we are learning to do in this Portal. It is how best to live our lives. If we are not working with the flow of the Harvest and Regrouping, we become stagnant and create a backward flow, or stall out, or just sit in the void. We as humans are meant to continually move in a downstream wave. It is also easier than battling to stay in the same place or reverse upstream. The same is true for all aspects of life.

Once your heart shows you how important this is for the Portal and how it relates to you and your life, turn your Avatar to the side of that mountain over there. Yes, the reddish colored one. There is a landing space where we will all fit. I will meet you there.

There is food and water for you and your Avatar. There's more to be responsible for besides ourselves now. It is also dehydrating and draining being at that intensity for very long. A big reminder to take care of yourself.

That was an awesome experience in understanding why and how we live our lives instead of just existing. A part of the Harvest is looking for hidden fruit within your space. It may be a penny on the ground, a client you forgot about calling back that really needs your information but is so lost they can't call you, or it may be a special book you bought that you wanted to read then put it on the shelf for that moment you had for it. Then again, it could be something entirely different from my World.

We are going to take a leisurely flight back to the Center. Take time to think about what you saw and learned. You may want to do some journaling about how this relates to you in your real World, or you may just want to soak in the tub!

See you tomorrow.

MONTH EIGHT – DAY SEVEN

Are you ready for some clearing? This is the day for it. Call your Avatar to you. Again, mine is the Bear. He smells so much different from my Dragon. I was asking him why we chose each other for this experience this month. It is because this is my birth month, and, in some traditions, Bear is my power animal for me. Also, he is here to help me clear some of the Earthly stuff I have been hanging onto. I just know he is so warm and easy to be with. He knows my every thought before I recognize I'm thinking it. He's also a great protector, not that I need protecting. Maybe it's a Parenting energy for me at this time.

Ready? We are going to the Red Mountain area. If you tell your Avatar, "The Red Mountain area," they will know where to go even if you want to take a nap on the journey. The Red Mountain is a vibration of so much similarity to that of Earth. It feels like a good fit for our next step. So, what is our next step, I ask the Portal?

We are to dig in the earth of the Red Mountain. I have no idea how this contributes to our clearing, but that is what we are to do to start with. Yes, we are given gloves and shovels. Let's spread out and see what we can find or harvest?

With my first shovel-full of dirt, I uncover a red crystal. It is nothing like anything I have seen on Earth. It is a Portal Crystal! It is beautiful, about six inches long, and thin like a wand. It is amazing I didn't break it with this big shovel. I love the vibration of it. I put it into my pack and it settled right into the lowest part of my back the pack would allow. It really feels like it is attuning my chakras. I hope you are finding some amazing treasures as well.

My next shovel of dirt reveals a golden coin. This is quite a surprise, sort of like a pirate treasure, but only one. I find this interesting, as I have a Pirate Ball to attend this fall. This may fit into the costume somewhere.

The next shovel of dirt brought up a lovely pale purple crystal. The vibration of it is so fine-tuned it makes a ringing sound in my ears. These are going into my backpack, so I can carry them more easily while riding my Bear.

I hope you found some more wonderful treasures. Let's take them to the pond by the smaller waterfall where we can clean and clear them. I find that the red dirt/mud is not coming off as quickly as I thought. That is okay, as it creates a longer connection with each of them as we work together to achieve clarity and a bonding of energies which help to move us into the next phase of our journey and the Regrouping.

That took a little longer than I expected, and I got incredibly muddy. I am ready to sit under that waterfall and let all its wonderful liquid energy clear me of the old energies that came up within me as I worked with my treasures. There were moments of not feeling worthy of such a wonderful find, a gold coin coming to me, a little fear of not knowing how to move forward with these new tools, and a fear of what is to come. Will I be ready to help those that come to me for the work they need? These are from the really old Me and are ready to be cleared in the waterfall. There is a lot more than what I am stating here as well.

You may join me at any time if you would like. The waterfall brings up some ideas for the New Year or maybe even this fall. I will see what I can implement into my life. I feel so refreshed and ready to start a new journey. Of course, it will take more thought than just this moment, but the refreshing clarity is so helpful.

Now my Bear joins me in the Crystal Waterfall. I hope it doesn't make him smell like a wet dog. Oh, this is nice. The crystal aspect of it is really clearing out the strange smells on him. Be aware of his shaking as he gets out. That is the same as getting soaked by a wet dog!

I hope you get what you need from the magical red dirt and that crystal-clear waterfall. I am ready to ride back to the Center. Take your time.

See you tomorrow.

MONTH EIGHT – DAY EIGHT

Yesterday was fun. I love the treasures I found at the Red Mountain. I am still feeling the effects from being in all that red dirt and the Crystal Waterfall. It was great!

I wonder what the Portal has in store for us today. Oh, a store! Yes, it is like a storefront of sorts. As we go around the Portal clockwise, starting at the Red Mountain, we end up in the Mines. I guess this is where we are going!

This is a new way to travel for us. We get to walk into the door at the storefront of the Mines, pass through a hallway, and open the door at the end. We are on a landing, ready to descend some stairs. A posted sign says, "Hold On TIGHT To The Railing!" We better do that. The stairs are moving sideways and down at the same time. There, it stopped, so now we can continue down to the bottom and open the door.

WOW! Here we are, ready to enter the Mines. Oh, which ones do you want to explore? Gold, Silver, Copper, Diamond, or Crystal? Or how about others on down the trail that I can't see the name of just yet? I am going to go down the trail just to see what my other options are. Just as I suspected, the Mines down the trail are more about the physical body.

I see one that is about Mining Beauty. I guess that is possible. I see one that I think I want to investigate. It is about the Heart.

Since we are in the Portal of Harvest and Regrouping, I now understand what this means. Yes, I need to go into the Heart one. Here, I get to experience harvesting the Love I sent out to others to assist them when they were in need. Now, it can come back to me in the fullness of what my heart needs right now. I can feel it filling back up with Love from the Creator as I had given out my Love to others. I had no idea how much I had given out. There is a measuring device which shows how full a person's heart is. Mine was down near 1/16th. That surprises me, because that's nearly empty!

I am amazingly thankful I get to be in this place.so I can feel my heart fill back up. Once it reaches the halfway point, I can feel a mass to it now and it beats deeper. At the three-quarter level, it's even fuller and heavier in mass, not heavier in heart like the term meaning a level of sadness. This is a level of Joy! Yes! Full! I feel so much Joy and Love it is hard to contain myself. I am ready to run and play on a whole new level. I have more HUGS to give away!

What did you find to experience within the Mines? Once you are complete with your exploration, let's meet back at the stairway.

This is wonderful to see how each of you had a different experience! I see backpacks filled to overflowing with wonderful treasures. I love hearing the stories and laughter from all of you. If you need or want more time in this area, there may come an opportunity later when we can come back.

Right now, we need to catch the stairway back to the Center as they do have a schedule to keep the Portal running smoothly.

See you tomorrow!

MONTH EIGHT – DAY NINE

Today is a very important one for this Portal journey. Why, you might ask? I am shown it is the day the Portal is making a new rotational spin as we get close to the end of our journey. There is still so much we need to experience in here. To Harvest more for what we need, we must let go of what no longer serves us. Only so much fits on the hard drive of humans these days.

We are to go back to the storefronts and find a new one to enter. I see one that looks like it has balloons in the window and pleasantly-colored ones painted on the door. Let's go in and see what it is really about. There are several different rooms and each one looks to be for a different purpose.

I just learned that these are not the kid type of balloons we are used to. These are for special purposes. They can be used for many different things, and they are programmable. This can be a fun process, if we let it be.

First, they just look like balloons. There are several rooms where bright colors explode out into the hallways. The first one is very important. We are to walk into it and just stand over a vented area. There are many "balloons" in here, so pick the one that calls to you.

This feels funny. A "balloon" is going up around me, leaving several inches all around away from my skin and the top of my head. It is sucking old stuff out of my memory banks, then deciding with me if it's important. If it is, it is being put into a smaller unit of measure and returned. For example, one I saw come off my skin is where I had fallen and scraped my knee. Sure, I can remember it, but I don't need the whole trauma of how I felt as I fell and hit the cement, what happened to my roller skates, the blood that remained on the sidewalk, who came to help me get cleaned up, and even more. Yes, that is one file which doesn't need to be stored on that level.

Another is where I was in the mountains with my little brother and we got lost. The feelings of not knowing where my parents were, how we took off running up the mountain looking for them, the fear of what might get us … So many things in my head in those few seconds. Then my parents coming back over the hill with the water jug from the pickup and the lunch cooler, the reminders of what they had told us they were doing and how long it would take, and to stay within this certain tree boundary. Yes, this is also one that I don't need to remember all the details on.

I am shown each of these events in a flash and many more as they are pulled off and out of me with a choice of keeping or deleting. When they delete, they just sort of explode with a popping sensation. The ones I keep are put into a pinpoint file then sent back into the same area it came out of. Now, the "balloon" lifts off by being pulled up through me. It is getting every little piece as it goes.

I feel lighter now. We are directed to rotate to the left and do it again. This time it goes into deeper details. We are to do these three times to remove debris which no longer serves us. Then we are directed out into the hallway. I feel so light I could float away like a balloon.

The next room is of our own choice. I want the Yellow one. Strange, as I never even think in the terms of anything being yellow. Maybe that's why I am to go into this room.

Maybe I need a balance of Yellow within me. You may go into the room that you need. I really do like some of the other colors, but I guess I am to work with yellow for the moment.

What is happening to me in here is I hear a noise. I'll say the word it sounds like to me which manifests a paintball sort of thing. It is mostly yellow and is shot at me from a wall. It doesn't hurt! It bursts just as it touches me, and the stuff in it oozes into my skin. It really feels nice. I don't know how long I am supposed to do this, but each one feels better and better. This last one put me on the floor giggling so hard that I have tears running down my face. WOW! I am ready for the next room.

I get to into the Blue room. As I stand there in the doorway, I feel a coolness of the air. It is raining blue "balloons" with a liquid in them, which splats just above my head each time. Some of it pours down over me, some of it I walk around in. I let my entire being decide what I need to Harvest and clear today.

I realize this is a part of making way for the New in the world of Regrouping to receive the Abundance of the rest of the year. This Divine Portal has so much to offer, as we are able to receive it.

Tonight, we need to take some re-calibration time for all of us, depending on how intensely we went into this. It's the reason why we are on this journey. I will be heading back to the Center soon.

See you tomorrow!

MONTH EIGHT – DAY TEN

Our Avatars are ready for some exercise, are you? It is Green Mountain Day. My Giant Bear wriggles all over with excitement about this. He must know more about where we are going than I do. I only heard that some of it may be a little bit like a rain forest, but I guess we will see as we get closer. I understand there will also be a dinner prepared for us at the place we are going. Mount Up!

This is such a magical place. You can just feel it in the air as we glide over the forests. I see a rainbow! I am going to try sliding down it, after all, just how many opportunities does a person get to slide down a rainbow! My Bear isn't too excited about it, but he can do it on his own if he wants to, or meet me at the bottom. It is filled with the excitement energy of the Fairy Realm. Wow! I want to do that again, but this time I will see if I can collect the energy of each color on one giant slide. My Bear is happy to take me back to the top as long as he doesn't have to slide. That felt much better. More balanced in the color field this way.

Now off to the Green Mountain. I have never seen so many shades of green! This is truly the most beautiful scenery I have ever experienced. The whole mountain vibrates with this shade. You can see the auric field of it emanate above and around it. It is wonderful. Oh, it is starting to rain. Of course, this is a rain forest. I don't mind getting a little wet, besides, it will dry soon.

I wonder what we will find here in relation to the Portal of Divine Abundance on the Journey of Harvest and Regrouping. As I came around the corner, the rain changed into musical notes. As it touched the leaves or me, it made a different tone. It played a song for us, and it changed as I changed my way of thinking. When I was concerned about getting to the area where we need to be, it played music that felt concerned and sounded like a dramatic play. Once I recognized what it was doing I shifted my thought patterns to a happier, joyous idea, and the rain music did as well!

It was like walking in the music. The energy of it was of a type that filled my cells with a new vibration at each moment. Bear is actually dancing. He loves it too! This is so wonderful. It helps release old stuck ideas to make room for the changes that are to come.

There is the picnic area. Let's see what has been prepared for us. There is always such amazing food in the Portals. This gives us time to discuss with each other what our experiences are and how our Avatars are reacting to each change. Both the changes within us as well as the changes within the Portal. It seems to me that the happier and more relaxed I am the more Bear is happier and relaxed. The ease to work together with our telepathy is happening the more comfortable we become with each other.

Let's climb to the top of that mountain. We don't have to ride, but you can if you feel more comfortable doing so. Our Avatars will be with us, in fact, they may beat us to the top. I think we may find some very special treasures for our individual needs as we walk. Pay attention to the ground once in a while as there will be things only you will see if it is meant for you.

I just found a ruby ring! That is so amazing. I never even thought about having a ruby ring before. It is very beautiful and fits perfectly! I also found very special ear tips for Bear. They are gold and fit his ears perfectly.

He loves them. I am always as excited about what he likes just as much as he is. Who would think a huge Bear would get excited about music and jewelry. I guess we all change when we are ready, even Giant Bears.

At the top of the mountain I hear a waterfall. Ready? We can jump off and swim a little at the bottom. The Avatars will meet us down there. Have you ever actually done a cliff dive before? I've only done the ones in the Portal. It feels really safe here. There are life vests available if it helps you feel more comfortable. Of course, I am using one. I will meet you at the bottom. Bear made it there before I did!

Time to dry off and get ready to head back to the Center. You might want to do some journaling to tell me what you want to do on your last day of this adventure. It will help you manifest what you want to bring into your life.

See you tomorrow for our last ride in this Portal!

MONTH EIGHT – DAY ELEVEN

I have been attending a Matrix Energetics Conference where I was reminded of a lot of concepts and tools I had forgotten about, as I hadn't used them in a long time. It reminded me that I started practicing with certain techniques I was taught to perfect my skills. I planned on practicing with another one after I got this one down but forgot about the many techniques I wasn't using.

For me, this is a time of Harvesting and Regrouping the rest of the technologies' tools I set aside and forgot how valuable they are. I don't need to take another workshop until I get this one down. I will be Regrouping some of my skills and utilizing them better.

Now, off to the Portal that we are in for one final day. I think we have time for a little more exploring before we get kicked out. Let's call our Avatars for one last ride. I am really going to miss this sweet Giant Bear. I love my Dragon, too, but I have also grown to love this Bear. Ready? Let's go to the river. I want to see if they have a fun ride we did one other time in a different Portal.

Yes, they have the see-through bubbles we can fit into with our Avatars. We can float down the river within the bubble and be able to see all around us and under us at the same time. They are climate-controlled and puncture proof! If there is something in the water you want to bring into your bubble, just reach your hand through the self-sealing edge and get it. It is also made of a product that will help you get clarity as you float down the river.

I don't know how it does it, but as I float along and have a question in my head and heart about how to create a better experience within my business or family, the answers just flow to me with great details on how to do it.

This is so much fun. My Bear also likes it. He is rolling around in it making it go faster in some areas and slower in others. I also see how it helps him create a more luxurious coat. His inner desire must have been to get his fur better, after all, winter is on its way. It is creating a shine and thickness really fast. Maybe I need to focus better on what I want for my life when I get back.

I just experienced a whole new way of understanding this. I took a nap on my Bear, and somehow, maybe through some other form of communication from him and the bubble and the river, I was able to obtain some clarity. There are so many new ideas coming to me right now that I have to find a way to get them into a format for family and business. You just never know where you will be when that inspiration gets downloaded into your being.

How are you doing with Harvest and Regrouping aspect of this time of year? I really hope this journey is helping. We have one more thing to do before we go back to the Center. We get to ride through the big waterfall and let it do a clearing on us. It will help with all of the intense energies we have experience with the Full Moon and all the amazing treasures you found. Each treasure consists of a specific frequency to help you on this journey. Since they are in your backpacks they will also get cleared.

There is something really special about this waterfall. We have to go into it at a specific angle. Make sure you follow me exactly at the right angle or you won't get through the first time.

Yea! We made it. This is an amazing cave right behind this waterfall. We can leave our Avatars here to dry off. Notice how you are not wet? It is a part of the clearing. Now we get a very special luncheon that consists of foods that taste amazing and are good for us all at the same time! Our Avatars also get some very special treats.

Let's walk through this cave a little further as I think there is a surprise for us. Yes, as we enter one room we are each given a little present to unwrap just before we walk through that furthest door. Take your time as this is really awesome. It is so easy. There is time for hugs and, of course, I will miss you.

Once you unwrap your gift, take a bite of it, and you end up back at home! You don't have to go through any of the difficulties in traveling back. It is complete teleportation just for you! I will be last, as I want to make sure each of you are okay with this process of travel.

See you next month!

See you soon with Truth, Love, and Gratitude
Pat, The Cosmic Cowgirl

Journal What You Learned About Harvesting and Regrouping

CHAPTER NINE: THE FALL EQUINOX & DIVING INTO THE FLAMES OF TRANSFORMATION

MONTH NINE – DAY ONE

Welcome to the Autumn Divine Portal Activation of Abundance. I have felt the energy of this group building for about a week. With this level of intensity so soon, it is going to be amazing. I can see we are all eager and ready for a little fun after a very busy summer. We have so much energy building up here! WOW, my heart is bursting with this Love of Life coming forward for us.

I see the Portal swirling just off in the distance. It looks to be moving our way rather quickly. We are meeting on a ledge of a cliff where it will be easy for us to be picked up with the wind currents. While we wait, I want you to pick an Avatar to ride upon through this Portal. As you can see, I am back with my wonderful Purple Dragon. He is also extremely ready to dive into that swirling mass of energy.

It swirls in a direction to assist us in moving into the next level of what we are to achieve within ourselves. We will be activating all the work we have been doing this year to prepare us for our abundant Harvest.

I feel the excitement peaking as each of you pick your own Avatar. When I ask you to do this, sometimes I get a little worried about you picking one that can handle what we are going to be doing on this journey. My mind goes to the *Harry Potter* movies where some people got anything from an Owl to a mouse. Just pick one that can support you on an adventure.

Take a moment to go into your heart and ask for what you need on this month's journey. Go with the first being that comes to mind. Ask for it and you can have it be any color or size you want it to be for what you need. The Avatar that you pick knows what you need at all times, even before you do.

I can see the Portal is starting to open. Get onto your Avatar and form a line behind me. Feel the wind push and pull at you as the Portal comes closer. Here we go! Just be comfortable in the seating you chose.

This is great! I see some of you actually chose an Avatar that support an easy chair to sit in! Some of you chose riding gear to hold you in place like on a roller coaster. Lots of secure harnesses that look to be really safe.

We will be staying in the center of the Portal as the entry is very strong. The energy creates a curtain of mist that we will be riding through. I see it is a decontamination entry. I guess we need it after the year we have worked with. I notice a tingling within me as the mist pulls some toxins to the surface. These toxins are not only chemicals we eat and breathe, but also thoughts which run through our minds.

The next is a rinsing of sorts as the wind and moisture feel like they're going through every cell of my body. This actually feels quite nice, very gentle and soft to the skin. My mind is becoming clearer as well.

Oh, hang on! I see the blowers. This looks to be like a spin cycle in a washer/dryer combo. The spin and blowing are like being on an amusement park ride. Now I see why you are harnessed on your Avatar.

I have never seen this form of clearing in a Portal before. It's a way to get out the last speck of goo. It is like an old-time washing machine my mom had. I also saw this on some cartoon my kids watched. There are three sets of two rollers to go through which sort of flatten you out. It doesn't hurt but sure looks and feels strange as I entered it. Yes, I popped back into my original shape as I came out. Wow, what a strange feeling.

I am so glad that my Dragon is good at keeping within the center for me to experience what I need at this time. He didn't seem to mind that part at all. Perhaps I feel better for him too once all of this goo has been cleared. It seems to have helped with the telepathic communication between us.

My hair is flying around me and seems to be changing colors as it is also cleared while we enter a deeper part of the Portal. Hair holds a lot of memories and toxins. It is the first to show signs of wear and tear created by how we process our air, food, and life in general. We try to cover up these imperfections in our bodies with clothing and makeup.

For our time within this Portal, we are going to clear these out, so we can get a fresh start on our Transformation toward the completion of the many projects we have created this year that have brought us into this state of Receiving Financial Abundance.

I see the landing pad up ahead. There will be Avatar handlers waiting for us to take good care of our wonderful companions.

See you tomorrow!

MONTH NINE – DAY TWO

I am impressed with how you handled yourself in that crazy entrance. We will be leaving our Avatars with the handlers at this point for today. I don't know about tomorrow, as that hasn't been shown to me yet.

We are being directed to enter a building through the middle door, the one that is painted red. Red is a great place to start. After all, the color is what many consider to be the root chakra within ourselves. I look at red and see the wonderful fall leaf color that is a great accent to all the others on the trees and bushes. Perhaps it is representative to both. I have to trust that what I see and say is what we are to experience at this time. Ready? Let's go!

Interesting that this door widened so we can all either enter as a group or as individuals. Either way, we only see ourselves, but we all take the first step at the same time to clear more of the group energy which continually builds. The first step takes us into an underground chamber. Think of a very fast elevator to the ground floor. I was not expecting that, but here we are, ready for the next step! This is really testing our trust instincts with a capital T. The floor has vents in it. It isn't solid like wood, tile, or concrete.

Okay, we are here to experience what's in store for us. WOW! The flames coming through the vented floor should clear us of our fears and old programs. It can be quite intense, but not hot, and the colors are very much of the fall leaves. We have red, orange, yellow, some white and blue, and, as always, green, and there are so many tones in-between. Yes, I did say tones, as the vibrational aspect of each color also puts out a tone.

I feel them move through our feet and on up our legs, into our sacral area, on up to the stomach. Keep breathing. Yes, it is intense but necessary to help us to move into a clear state of Manifestation and Completion. If we could have done it without this, we would have already done so.

Take the next step up and stand there a moment to see where we are directed. It is another level of flames with purer colors of red, orange, and yellow. There is also the purest green and the clearest blue, purple, and white. They are now being flushed through us. Let the flames and the tones of the colors wash upward through you, clearing and cleaning out the old programs, opening doors within for the alignment of Yourself and the Transformation you are ready to experience. Remember to BREATHE deeply!

As you experience this, notice how we no longer stop at the center chakra. We are clearing and aligning your entire being above as below. WE can't be anything without the entirety being activated in a balanced and harmonized wholeness of self. The caterpillar cannot be a completely whole butterfly without the entirety of it being transformed or transfigured.

Ready for the next step? This one is easy. Step up. Notice how light you feel. Are you pulsating with the tones flowing through you? Now the door opens for us to walk into a room full of leaves of every color you can imagine. As you touch them, they can assist in filling you with a new energy. The energy of Fall. We often think of Spring as the newness, but we are experiencing the newness of Fall. This is a room where laughter and fun will help realign you into the new energy.

I can see piles and piles of leaves. They are clean, not dusty, and they promise to not cause an allergic reaction. There are various forms of devices to lift you to top of the room where you can dive or fall into a pile of the various colors or you can pick piles of just one color. The opportunity for you to jump into these Leaves of Activation piles is now available for you. I see a rope that has a place where my foot can fit while I hang on to the upper area. I am going to try that first.

Oh, my goodness, this is crazy fun. I haven't done this since I was a little kid. The rope let me release when I felt I was ready. I just landed in a huge pile of multi-colored leaves. I can hear the crunch and feel my body tingle with activations. This is an amazing feeling. This time I think I will take the escalator to the high dive.

Take your time in here. Let yourself receive all the activations you want or that your body, mind, and spirit want. Each activation in here will be benevolent and specific to your needs only. Then you will be directed to a room to lay down and allow your body to recalibrate.

See you tomorrow!

MONTH NINE – DAY THREE

I hope you found yesterday's experience helpful. It was a lot of fun for me and brought back childhood memories on a whole new level. From the feedback already coming in, I am learning how much you also needed to experience an old activity with a different outcome.

The shifts we make during these experiences assist us not only having a little fun but also letting go of the old ways of Doing and Knowing. The old ways that are stuck within us keep us doing the same thing over and over and expecting a different result. The clearing out of the Old to make room for the New is how we bring abundance into our lives. It is through our transformational growth which gives us Manifestation capabilities in this new World.

Let's gather outside with our Avatars. I realize that isn't the right word for them, but that is what I was told to call them. We can meet at the building where they are pampered and prepared for us. Yes, they are ready to get some fresh air and want to have some fun. Mount up!

We are riding to the top of that huge, very old tree which seems to support the Portal. It is right in the middle of our location. So far, this is nice and easy flying. No wind currents to create any drama, just easy gliding on the airwaves. There are still quite a few leaves on the tree for this time of year. I have not ever seen a tree with so many different leaves. Some are shaped like an Oak or Cottonwood. There are pine and spruce needles in another area, and there also are fruit tree leaves. I have no idea what type of tree some of them represent. This tree must be the origin of all the trees from across Earth. It is much bigger than I realized. I am certain the answers will be given as we move along.

We are being directed to fly to that large branch that has a flattened surface where we can all land. This is amazing, the areas we are in are sacred, and yes, they were a part of creating the various trees on Earth. This tree carries the seeds and DNA codes that helped create the trees, but also all of the plant life on our beautiful Planet. It seems to be a huge storehouse for many forms of life. I wonder why we are being shown this.

Of course, this Journey group is caretakers of this Planet. We need to know where and how to help our Planet regain itself with the original blueprints that work the best in certain areas and the various climates. There is usually a reason for the people to gather with their energy in these groups. Yes, we are here for a reason beyond the abundance of money for ourselves. This is a part of the preparation for the service we provide to others around us. We are creating the abundance codes for the Earth to be activated through us, and what we do.

We are being directed to a way inside through a crevice in the crack in the bark. You would never see it if it weren't for the wood elves that live here. We are able to walk along a path just inside the edge of the tree. There is no damage done to the tree to be inside of it, as we are within a Dimensional space of its growth process. It is like a whole different world inside of here. It is like something out of a science fiction movie. The path we are to stay on consists of various rings of color. As we step on these rings I feel a download of information. The next step helps me to translate this information and store it away safely until I can do something with it. Then the next step gives me another download. I am not sure how we are to utilize these bits of information just yet. If you step on the same step as I did, you will get different information that is just for you.

Some of this information is related to where each of us live and as we just walk on this Earth it will be transferred to where it is needed. I can see how we walk through an airport leaving little bits of information for that area. Also, as we hike in the mountains, the information is sent into the ground at that point, as it is needed to spread throughout the entire mountain range. Another big change we will be creating is just walking through a store or marketplace. Here we will be leaving the codes in the tiles for others to also pick up into themselves and create the changes wherever they go. I see that some of these codes are so original that they can bring back the seeds and water to their original state that is for the area they are in. There are so many ways that we create the new world without it having to be hard. There are some codes that will be held in our bodies the rest of our lives for the exact moment of being in the exact place for their release.

For us, these codes are also for our health and wellbeing. They can be used to bring back an original hair color if you so choose or to give more freedom and flexibility to your body as we live a longer healthier lifestyle. In a sense these codes create a form of youthfulness within us. We maintain our wisdom and knowledge to be utilized as we walk among the plants and animals and other people. I can feel a change in myself already.

I am also being told that these codes can be used to manifest what our heart's wish is. They may be for manifesting a new business, or a new way to run the business you already have. Perhaps it is a way to educate our children or a way to stretch time to get a project completed. They are a way to utilize the magic that surrounds us at every moment.

We have been offered to be guests tonight of those that live within this tree. The Woodland peoples have asked for us to stay over and participate in one of their nightly ceremonies around their campfires. It is a night for a party of dancing and telling stories.

See you tomorrow!

MONTH NINE – DAY FOUR

I must say that I had a great time last night. I learned a lot of history presented through the art of dance and stories. I just wish I could remember it all! There was so much information my brain couldn't contain it along with the dancing. I am certain that if I need to recall it at some time, at least part of it will come to me. Perhaps I can remember more if I am doing the dances as they were telling the related stories. Or, you can remember them and send them to me. That would be so much better.

Now for today! We get to tour more of this Tree of Life. It is like a whole civilization in this place. Everything a person needs is produced in here. There are floors with rooms dedicated to specific species of plant and all of the variations of it needed according to the climate it may be dropped into on Earth. The seeds are collected, then as the Portal moves over an area, some of those seeds are scattered over the lands.

There are floors of just laboratories where the seeds are inspected to be of the right caliber of DNA for the areas they are going to. There are laboratories where animals are also checked for how well they digest or grow on specific plants that are being created for the new Era that is coming. I think it's amazing they are working that far ahead to help all of us on Earth. As one plant becomes extinct, there is often another one needed to take its place in the food chain.

I just found our floor! Can you imagine, a floor just for us? I see where we have the opportunity to assist them in their research. You don't have to, but I am very interested in what their ideas are and what they want to know about us. They want to bring in our Avatars! I think it's okay.

They want to know why we picked the ones we did. What reason is behind me picking a bluish-purple dragon? I don't really know. He just came to me one day. Now they ask him why he came to me. The answer he gives is that he knew I really loved him in another lifetime and saved his life. This time, it is his turn to keep me safe on my journeys. That is an amazing answer! I actually got tears in my eyes. Your turn if you want to participate in this type of an experience.

Once we finish helping on the research floor we are directed to a way of refreshment or a treat. The Woodland people get to blow bubbles at each of us, and each bubble has a program within it that can help clear some of the emotions we carry.

Yes, we all carry some emotional baggage. That is the main reason we hold back on creating our thriving businesses, our true love, or our unlimited supply of money This is such an easy way to clear these stuck emotions. The bubbles get blown and land on the area where the stuck stuff hides.

The experience of having the gooey bluish-green bubble burst in my shoulder was quite different than what I expected. It melted into my shoulder really fast and caused my whole arm, neck, and part of my spine to shiver. Then my body just relaxed into a more fluid ability of moving my arm and shoulder. I didn't have to know what was being cleared or why. The bubble knew exactly where to go and what I needed. I now have a completely different idea of what refreshments and treats are. I love it. I think we all can benefit a lot from this. I am ready for another bubble!

The laughter is contagious within. Okay, I am now slimy and have tears running down my face from so much laughter. I am ready for a shower. I wonder what floor the showers are on.

It is all part of the "Ask and you shall receive" thing. Yes, I will get on my Avatar, and you can join me with yours. I am shown the signs of where to go. Fly down the side of the tree circling inside, near the staircase. I am almost at the bottom where we now see the directions to the other side of the stairway. Here we all get to fly right through a nice warm shower. I can feel myself recalibrating right here in the shower. I think there is more to do once I go back to my room. But for now, this is really amazing.

I asked how to get back to the area where our rooms are supposed to be with all of our belongings. Another "Ask and you shall receive" shows up. We are guided with lanterns floating in the air back to our original rooms in this Portal. Actually, I don't remember being in my room here, but I now have one.

See you tomorrow!

MONTH NINE – DAY FIVE

We get to explore a new area of this Portal today. It is all about the Transformation and Transmutation of ourselves along with Planetary changes we experience every year. Even if we are in an area that doesn't go through huge seasonal changes, the systems in our body react to the length of daylight we receive. Of course, it is much more noticeable when we have the four seasons to experience it with. That is one thing I really like about Colorado. Every day is something new with the seasons.

Our Avatars are ready for a little more exercise. It was pretty easy on them as we explored the Tree of Life. However, today may be a little bit different. We will be heading into a more rugged environment in the higher areas of this Portal. What is higher up when it is constantly rotating? I think it is the altitude. We are being asked to be in more rugged clothing, like boots.

Looks like everyone is ready for some new experiences! We will be going nearly straight up toward the highest peak, so hang on so you don't slide off the backside of your Avatar. Remember to breathe once in a while.

Yes, we are going to the caves of the volcano. Even if it is active sometimes, it seems to be rather calm today. We have our spelunking gear in our packs, and if we need something else, I am sure we can manifest it quickly or there will be people there to help us.

There is a smooth area near the top that looks to be the best place for us to land. There are no trees close by, and the ground is a dark color, as if the volcano's heat burned it. I see a cave not too far up the mountain, let's start with it. Turn on your headlamps and grab your pickaxes.

Oh, this is a tight fit going in here. Actually, it is rather a strange cave. I see that it creates the size of the entry related to who is crawling in. It gets smaller for tiny people and a little bigger for larger people. Very cool. It is a way to make sure we stay on the trail and don't fall over the ledge into the molten lava. That is a great safety feature. I have no idea how far we have to crawl through this tunnel.

We are coming into an area more open for us. I think we are in the belly of the volcano. I see we have the people of the Volcano here to greet us. I love their headdresses and the way they apply their face paint. I am sure they would not appreciate how I try to figure out what is going on by what they are dressed like, but that is what us females do sometimes. We are being directed to sit in a circle as they dance around us. Their dance is of the Fire Ceremony. Fire is a very deep cleansing to the core, and we are in the belly of the volcano with fiery molten lava just beyond that wall.

Let yourself feel it and understand the words as they are spoken in a familiar language understood through the resonance of it. As they dance, I can feel the rhythm of their feet on the ground in tune with the heartbeat of the Volcano. It creates a rhythm in the vibration of my body, even how my blood pulses through my veins. As they sing, I can hear the song of the Divine Portal of Abundance. It will resonate within you in the areas of Abundance that need to be cleared and brought into resonance with your entire being.

As I feel the beating of their drums, I feel my Spirit coming into alignment with a Passion and Purpose to be carried out soon. Take your time to experience this gift they are presenting us with. This can be felt at a very deep primal level as you allow yourself to shift into who you really are, and why you are here at this time.

The dancing has stopped, the singing has stopped, and the drums have stopped. We can open our eyes. They are gone, but have left each of us with a very specific stone necklace to wear attuned specifically to what we need at this time.

This has been a very powerful gift to experience. As we are ready to move a little, I think we are to go out the same way we came in. Yes, as I scan the walls with my headlamp I see that there is only one exit in this cave.

I am really thankful for the tight walls protecting us as I can feel the heat of the volcano on the other side. Not far now, I can see the exit.

Our Avatars were well taken care of while we were inside the cave and are ready to head back to the main building. It is quite a distance, but we have a choice. Either an easy ride back with one group that may take a little longer, or a steep dive that will only take a little bit of time. You can choose. I think I will take the long way back and just enjoy the ride. I also want to experience what my new stone necklace has in store for me.

See you tomorrow!

MONTH NINE – DAY SIX

We are moving right along within this Portal. As we slept, the building we are in is moved within the Portal as it spun through the space of this location. It seems to have taken us in the direction of the next adventure we are to be aligned with in our process of the strange way of Transformation we are engaged in.

It is as if we – and I mean the whole building – just got dumped over the edge of a waterfall that is also spinning. This is a little unsettling for my stomach as I am not fond of spinning on this level, but I am willing to see where this takes us. We and the entire building are spinning and tumbling end over end down this huge waterfall into a raging river. The waves are enormous as they fling us about and cause us to bounce against the other boulders and sides of eroding bank. The river is out of control, or so it seems.

At first, I was a little afraid, but I also felt the Rage. Perhaps the Rage on that level is what helped to ground me into knowing how to be within this situation. No, I am not actually going into the Rage.

It is not mine. I just noticed that is what it felt like going on around me.

I remembered that the biggest thing to do is to just breathe calmly and notice what is going on around us. Strangely enough, everything is tumbling, except us. We are perfectly normal in an upright position while our building tumbles down a crazy river. We are safe within the storm around us.

It is calming down a little. The more we just breathe calmly and don't go into the emotion of what is going on around us the faster it all calms down. The river is slowing, and we are not being tossed around like a kernel in a popcorn machine any more. We are slowly floating along with a feeling of searching for the right place to settle down, and find the perfect place for our building to land.

I hadn't thought of that as being a method of relocation for us on our journey. I see it as a normal thing for this Portal to actually engage in once in a while, probably on an as-needed basis. I know it took me a little bit to not go into a panic mode and freak out because I really do not like water on those terms, besides recognizing the danger of the situation.

This must be one of those things where we have to learn how to stay in our center of the storm – the place where it is calm, and you can see everything going on around you. This is where we learn to not react, but act after thinking it through. We may get a short opportunity to practice this journey. Actually, I guess that is what we just did.

We need to find out where our Avatars are and if they're okay. Let's go out the side door, as it is the closest to the shore at this time. Maybe they can hear us if we call to them. Try calling them telepathically. Nothing, try again, and again.

On our fifth try to call to them, they now come over the ridge. I think they are just as excited to see us as we are to see them! I had no idea some of these wonderful creatures could act like a cat or puppy. The licking and purring ... Dragons purr? I had no idea. It is wonderful to all be safe in a new place of beginning.

We have quite a bit of cleanup to do on the location so that the building can be pulled ashore a little further. Then we can get on with our journey.

Of course, this is all part of it. The shifting that is being done while we help others and learn is priceless.

See you tomorrow!

MONTH NINE – DAY SEVEN

Thank you for all the wonderful help in getting the main building pulled onto a flat, dry spot. It was a lot of work, but well worth it. I got to see how easily the job was made while utilizing the skill of our Avatars. They are amazing beings capable of helping us in more ways than we realize. Due to their sensitivities, they were able to get this aligned with the vortex which it sits on in the exact position for optimal creativity.

This new location is wonderful. It feels like it is just right for what we need at this time. We have more areas to explore in this location that carry new messages just for you to jump into your new Transformation as an Abundance Activator.

We are just in time for a tour of the area over your left and my right side of the main building. We get to ride our Avatars, so, of course, that makes me very happy! We are deeper into this Portal, and I am really excited to experience it in this new Dimension, so for me a tour is a marvelous way to get to know more about the area.

I see there is a very special lunch packed for us with beautiful tablecloths on top of the baskets. This is going to be so much fun. I wonder what is packed in those baskets?

First, we are learning about the botanicals of this Portal. I always find this information quite interesting and it helps keep me focused on the next method possible within this Transformational process. We never finish processing on some level. I learned how the botanicals directly reflect how we process and transform our lives. They actually release what we need according to our consciousness capabilities.

As we head out further, we are being guided to a large place where we can have lunch. We are next to a nice-sized lake I saw earlier. Yea! Toys have been brought for us to play with. We are being given mats to float on made from the woven grasses we just learned about. They really smell awesome.

I learned each of us have a mat exactly of the product that will help us in our healing and the processing of the work we have been doing so far. I must really be in tune with the mat I have been given as I am having a hard time staying awake. I can tell that, by being on this mat, I am starting to clear and process how the building tumbled into the water and was thrown around the river. That was a bit unsettling to me, and I can now feel an easier relaxation energy running through my muscles and brain. Exactly what I needed.

Floating on the pond is so soothing. It brings the water into our space in a calming manner instead of the raging torrent we experienced yesterday. The many aspects of water. Wow! I always need to remember and incorporate this space into my life.

This is interesting. A shower came over us and our mats suddenly turned into clear, floating balls with a bottom mat. The sprinkling sounds on the ball are like a musical instrument being played and creating a complete orchestra utilizing all of our spaces on this lake. The sound reverberates into the water and up through the mat creating a new level of healing activations for us.

The rain has stopped, and our mats returned to their normal forms! It is now time to unpack the lunch basket. I see we each have our own basket coming out of the larger one. They are filled with the exact meal that we need at this time. I love what is in mine. It tastes like it is exactly what my body and mind need, even if I have no idea what I am eating. I am learning to trust I will be given exactly what I need, even if I don't know or understand what it is.

I think I will take a little more time on my mat for some meditation, as I am now ready for another level of integrating the Abundance Codes from this Portal. I can now see how the clearing of some of my fears help me pursue my passions where manifestation will be easier. I just have to allow myself to recalibrate to the Now and let go of the old programs which were holding me in a stagnant state. This Portal has created the opportunity for me to do this, and now it is up to me to actually do it.

I see how the stream coming from this lake goes right to our Center. I am going to let my Avatar follow along as I float down the stream in a complete meditative state.

See you tomorrow!

MONTH NINE – DAY EIGHT

I am so relaxed today and ready for some big exploring, something to get my brain and body working again. "Ask and you shall receive!" We are going to need to be on our toes for this Autumnal Experience. I am on my wonderful Dragon Avatar and ready to ride into a new experience with the fall colors. Are you ready for an experiential day?

We are going to start by skimming the tops of the trees where the colors are still changing from brilliant green to radiating reds, yellows, oranges and all of the variances of color in-between. As we glide over the tops of these trees, I can actually feel the changes in the vibrational field as the colors shift. I realize that certain trees vibrate differently while others change to only certain colors. I just find it cool that, with all of the amazing shifting and clearing we have done, that the sensitivity level within me has shifted to this point. If you haven't experienced this yet, be prepared for it at any moment. You will love the new differentiations of the vibrational field of everything.

This is an important shift to help you recognize when you can or can't notice the changes within the vibrational fields of things. If you can feel these subtle changes, you will be able to recognize when something isn't quite right within your own business or various areas of your life.

Once you can recognize that you have gone into a state of fear, lack, or simply not receiving within yourself, you will notice that you need to make some changes to get back on track to be in the Flow of Abundance. That is exactly why we are going through these journeys and clearing so much stuff and then recalibrating within ourselves, so we can be in a state of Abundance, especially the money part.

After the tree skimming, we are scheduled to land in the orchards. It is also Harvest time for some of the plants. There is plenty of room at the farm for all of us to be within shouting distance of each other.

We will begin with the plants nearest the ground which are actually still green. You will be shown how to pick each item so as to not kill the main plant. If some plants are not harvested with a certain level of carefulness, the plant will be damaged and then die.

We are going to pick green beans. It doesn't matter if you like to eat them or not. Just pick a few, hold them in your hand, and feel the life frequency they emit. The plant will tell you what stage it is at. Is it at a state of being prime for eating, or is it going into the state of creating seeds for planting next season? There are people here that will take the produce from you when you are ready.

Now let's pick tomatoes. Notice the difference in not only the color frequency but also the life force of the entire tomato. Next to us are the zucchini bushes. They are a deeper green than the beans and have a completely different seed structure inside. Hold one to your heart and just feel it. What stage of life force is it in?

We will now move to the root vegetables. Pull a carrot or a beet and notice how they feel. The grounding aspect and color are quite noticeable. If you don't get it, you can take one of each item back to the Center to practice with.

Now, let's move to the fruits you may be the most familiar with. Pick an apple. There are many varieties to choose from. Each one will vibrate a little differently from the others, but they still have the apple vibe. Choose carefully. See if you can pick one that is perfectly ripe and ready to eat right now. You may be able to recognize what body part resonates the most with it. Ready?

Now try a stone fruit, like a peach, avocado, apricot, or some other one that is here. Notice how much different it is, yet how similar the subtle vibration is in how you can tell if it is ready for eating. Make some of your own choices and select another fruit with a different seed structure. Notice the difference in the zucchini and apple. Each has internal seeds. A pomegranate has seeds to eat.

We can now sit in a circle and let our bodies integrate these items. Let yourself feel when they are ripe and ready to harvest versus when they are still not ready. Take your time to really notice this, as it is the same with picking a person to work with. Will this person be able to pay my fees, or will they need a discount of some sort?

The same with a ripe versus not feeling. The ripeness feels full of life that is overflowing, ready to share. The same with a client or a co-worker that has been assigned to help with a project, hiring a person to work for you and your business. These skills are important to make your life easier and help you manifest the Abundance code you carry.

You can stay here as long as you want, or you can take some of these items back to the Center to practice with throughout the night.

See you tomorrow!

MONTH NINE – DAY NINE

I mentioned Abundance codes, didn't I? What I notice about the Abundance codes is there are actually many different ones. Many times, I have heard of classes about activating the Abundance codes. When a class or group gathers to do this, I wonder if they activate all of them or just the ones people are ready to activate as some may be blocked.

Actually, many may be blocked, because there are so many of them. Abundance is thought of to be about Money, Love, Gratitude, Family, Health, Lifestyle, and Good or Bad Luck. I could continue making this list for days, but we are here for learning about healing Benevolent Abundance Codes.

Many are in this Divine Portal of Abundance with the specific awareness of activating the Money codes within the Abundance. This is why we are given so many various types of activations to experience. Each of us carries the Money codes but they are often blocked from lifetimes and inherited experiences that have affected the DNA you carry.

So, when I take you over a cliff, for example, it is to awaken the blocks to clear that part of them. It also reminds you how to notice things like a frequency change helps your DNA to wake up sub-codes embedded within various codes. including the one for Money.

Now that you have some understanding of why and how this Portal experience helps you, let's go for a ride and see what else is out there for us.

My Dragon is being a little strange today. It is almost as if he is acting like he wants to buck. I didn't know that Dragons knew how to buck. Or, maybe he's just a little jumpy around having a new experience. I think he doesn't know if we are going forward or backward. We need a direction for this next adventure. How about right down the middle, specifically in the center of the Vortex, like in the middle of a tornado, but not with the harmful side effects.

This really feels good. It is like we are riding the wave of time travel. It is now looping back in time to find each block throughout this and other lifetimes where a specific area of the Money Code is stuck. As we fly back in time I see the darker ones turn off completely as others are turned on with a flash of light and brilliance. The darker ones were creating more blocks, as they were corrupt programs, just like on a computer.

The new ones are upgrades to be turned on in this lifetime. To me, it feels like how a video game shows a sparkling flash as someone gets a point. It is like a bigger breath of fresh air is rushed through my lungs at that exact moment. My heart beats faster with excitement as each one of these darker areas is turned off and another code is turned on with a flash of light.

How far back on this timeline are we going to go? I am told that each of us will have a slightly different experience. Some of us may be clearing ancestral-created blocks, as in how starvation or war affected the DNA of an ancestor. One was a very wealthy businessperson that was taken as a prisoner of war where there was a great deal of mental and physical torture. The DNA was horribly affected during this lifetime where codes of being wealthy or having anything ever again were turned off completely.

This is one example of how we create the Abundance Code of Money to be healed, turned back on, and upgraded.

We have reached the end of this timeline for the moment and it is time to turn around. As head back to the 21st century we will be gathering up the newly activated codes. When we enter the Center today, we will notice how the codes simply integrate into our physical, mental, emotional, and spiritual bodies. Take your time and breathe, as this can be quite a visceral experience. If you breathe and take your time you can experience this as a blissful integration.

Also know that, if you feel like you want to retrieve another level of the Money Codes, you can go back through the timeline and do it again with a focus of another level or aspect of the Money Code you carry. This can be done as many times as you feel it is necessary. Each time give yourself some space to allow for a complete integration before doing it again.

See you tomorrow!

MONTH NINE – DAY TEN

How do you feel after the Money Code changes in your body, mind, and spirit? I am feeling more connected than I did before having that experience. It seems to have shifted something and created an integration I was not aware I needed until it was completed. I can tell there has been some releasing of very old programs which were held within my being at some level. I know it isn't important to dwell on trying to figure out exactly what it is that changed. What is important is to recognize if it was helpful or not and move forward. I don't want to bring those old programs which kept me stuck back to life. I am ready for the New we are creating.

I am ready for another experience of the Divine Portal of Amazing Activations. Today is our next to the last day in this Fall Portal. I am scanning to see if there is some area of importance we need to follow through with.

To start out, let's get onto our Avatars and go for a fun ride to see what shows up. I find this is the best way to let go of expectations and receive what is next. Well, it seems the Avatars have it all figured out. Without telling them where to go, they just all started heading off toward the left. It isn't what I would have chosen, as there are some really dark clouds over there. I am certain our rain gear is packed. I would advise putting it on if it makes you feel better. I don't mind getting a little wet. It is refreshing and feels like the drops contain information that I need at this time. As they soak in, I can feel my skin releasing old stuff. Now, it would be good to just experience this moment.

Yep, the drops of rain are big but not too cold. I am okay with this. Oh, we seem to be weaving between the clouds. I would not have thought of them being separated in their formation like this. It is as if our Avatars know their way through the storm with the least resistance. It is as if they can sense the connection between where the clouds overlap. We are being taken right into the center of the storm. I am wet, but that is okay as this is an amazing experience.

In the center of this storm we can watch how lightning can form and radiate out from the center like an old wagon wheel. It is a great way to watch what is going on around us. In the center, we are not getting the effects of the wind or rain. It is nice to be in a calm area like this and just be able to notice all of the chaos going on around us.

We can absorb this awareness into ourselves as a place to go when life is crazy. The center of the storm is the place to be. It is neutral! You can tell yourself to just download this capability of going into the center of a situation where all is neutral. The point of being able to see all angles of a situation without being pulled into any of them. From this vantage point, you can make the best decisions.

We can now go to an event happening below us. It is sort of a horse race, except they are what a horse is like here in this Portal. We get to practice what we just learned. Activate your downloaded neutrality center. Hold it within you and notice how you feel. Hold it as you enter this loud stadium. Ask your inner Self what horse is going to win this race. Your inner Self may tell you it is that old big one and your brain may tell you that's crazy! He is too big to fly down the track and beat all of the young, energetic horses. Which voice are you going to listen to? I am betting on the big old horse! I know my inner Self knows things I don't.

It is time for the race to start. My horse is slow getting out the gate but is steadily gaining on the others. He is holding up well on the muddy track. The younger horses are struggling with the deep mud and how it clings to their hooves. The old one that I bet on is doing just fine. He has been in these situations before and knows it's best to just continue on. He is not getting tired – he has a lot more strength and muscles. Yeah! We won! And we won big because others thought that one was too old. See what staying neutral and listening to your inner self can get you?

Activate that download of neutrality. It will be your best friend in the days that are coming. Now, do you want to try it again? There are more horses and the track is starting to dry up. This is a good way to practice what level of neutrality it takes to make Money.

See you tomorrow for our last ride in this Portal!

MONTH NINE – DAY ELEVEN

Today is our last day together within this Divine Portal. We have had some experiences that are as transforming as we are ready to incorporate them into our lives and our physical beings. Since it is a free will Planet, we get to pick and choose what we want to be ready and willing to change what is around and within us. Sometimes it takes a while to open the door to the level of using the heart and head together to manifest the passion we desire to create for this lifetime. These journeys within the Divine Portal are a part of assisting us in that opening as we allow the Activations to help us shift out of old programs we carry.

We have time for one last journey as we venture toward the Portal exit. I am ready to view the Portal with different eyes than when I entered it. Let's fly with our Avatars through that veil in the center and just notice how it feels this time.

I notice a deep, electrical, finer tuned vibration move through me as I fly into the white and sparkly veil. It's as if each sparkle in it activates a method of cleaning and resetting my body's nerves. Sometimes I think our nerves get stuck in a state of when something happened. It could be anything from falling off of my bicycle, cutting myself while chopping carrots, hitting my head in a car accident, or anything where a trauma sets a point of stagnation or a stickiness between the nerve relays and the rest of the body, mind, emotions, and all it takes to experience greatness again.

As I move through this veil I can feel an opening of areas of my body as these points are cleared of the traumas. I feel this will help me to experience what I do next in here and on the outside.

My Dragon has informed me that we are to fly through that canyon, as it is a shortcut. It is beautiful with the river running at the bottom and the many colors along the sides in the rock. The trees and bushes are beautiful with all of their fall changes. As we move lower in the canyon the greener there is. As we go up in altitude, we have more of the fall colors. It is hard to decide which level I want to fly. The energy they are emitting is a little overwhelming. When I first came into this Portal I would not have noticed this, but now I do. I am finding it quite interesting.

The river emits bursts of light that are like a bubble to fly into. The bubble is completely surrounding my dragon and me. It is like being inside of a bouncing ball. It can float on the river or just be a part of us as we fly along the canyon. Now I am experiencing what the bubble is all about. It is shrinking around my Dragon and me as a level of protection from the elements we are going back to in Earth's environment. We have been in a clean environment within the Portal, and going back out into the chemically-polluted atmosphere can be shocking.

I already find it helpful. As I fly past all of these colors, just as I did a little bit ago, I can now observe them in more of a neutral state instead of being overwhelmed with the energy from them. I also notice how I can breathe easier without being overwhelmed by so much input. This bubble not only assists in protection from the elements but also the energetic protection I need.

Of course, you don't have to have the bubble around you unless you want it. You may also receive something else which is more of what you need. I did see an ancient sword and shield fly out of the river into someone's hands. There was also a beautiful bottle of an elixir to drink that had Immune System written on the label. Someone also got a bag of gold coins.

WOW! You are all getting what you are asking for! It is most certainly what you ask for you shall receive. A great way to experience what we can continue to practice when we get home.

What we activate within a field of energy can be manifested into the physical. We live in a world of unlimited possibilities. Each time we do a clearing of the blockages within the Money Code, which is within the Abundance Code, it makes it easier to receive.

I nearly forgot about the stone necklace we were given near the beginning of our journey. I think I will wear mine as I enter back into the new World.

I see the exit ahead of us. We can land on that giant leaf. There are Avatar handlers waiting for us and ready to take care of our wonderful companions. This is the hardest, yet most rewarding, part of this journey each month … Saying goodbye to everyone. We will meet again – either on the next journey, in our multi-Dimensional dreams, or both.

I will see you next month!

See you soon with Truth, Love, and Gratitude

Pat, The Cosmic Cowgirl

Journal Your Neutrality and How You Are Asking and Receiving

CHAPTER TEN: PIRATES & VIKINGS

MONTH TEN – DAY ONE

Welcome aboard! We are going to have a little fun in the Portal with the Pirates and Vikings. The masters of the waves over the open sea of Potential and Opportunity may be our companions on this journey. Of course, it is still a Portal of Divine Money Activations.

Just look at that, would you? The entrance resembles a huge Viking ship with the strength and stamina of those that can handle any rough waters ahead inside of this journey. The masts are of the sturdiest wood I have ever seen, and the bow and stern are of beautifully carved Dragons which the Vikings are so well known for. There is much pride and love of life in the crew that will be assisting us within this Portal. They are a rowdy bunch that can be trusted with your life. Yes, they were quite ruthless in their time on Earth but do have things to teach us on this journey.

Perhaps we should take it slow to start with and get our sea legs under us. Of course, the Portal will have its own ideas of what each day will be. To start with, the seas appear to be calm as we climb aboard. I am impressed with the durable ruggedness of this ship. The wood is clean and polished to a beautiful sheen. My feet glide easily on the deck. I notice the rolled-up piles of rope in various areas, I am not sure of their purpose, but I am thankful that the crew does. There are places for all kinds of warfare on here. The cannon holes in the sides are covered but ready to be opened as needed. Hopefully not.

Take a good look at this fun-loving crew. They seem like they could have stepped out of a movie where they combined Vikings and Pirates in one huge event.

Jack Sparrow and his crew are a great example that we all know as well as the son and daughter of Eric the Red. Jack Sparrow is, of course, well known from the movies, but does anyone know who Eric the Red is? He was quite a ruthless Viking & known for his red hair as well as the level of NO Fear and, from what I have read, NO mercy. His daughter Freydis was also known for her ability to stand for what she needed and wanted no matter what.

Then there was his son, Leif Ericsson, known for beating Columbus to the New World by 500 years. He began the delivery of timber to Greenland from North America. All of the Vikings appear to be quite intimidating in their size and the incredible clothing they wear. But how bad can they be if they carve their ships to look like Dragons!

I am sure we will all have something to learn from each other. I am told for us to make ourselves comfortable. We can go into the bottom of the ship, if you feel safer there, as we enter the Portal. Or, stay on top and experience the wind and waves swirling us into the Portal. This one seems to be like entering a Star Gate.

The fun begins. We are given swords and armor. Great for stabbing the food we want to eat from the large table at the bottom of the stairs. The shield makes a great tray to place the food onto. There are kegs and stools to balance on while we eat. I find this food to be quite interesting. It's a whole new way to look at what we would call healthy nutritional meals. So far, my stomach is okay, even with the seas getting rougher.

I see we are being presented with choices. Are we to join with these raiders to learn how to receive what is rightfully ours?

How do we maintain our personal integrity and boundaries or, in this world, are they considered self-righteous? Perhaps we have become so politically correct that we have given up our own sense of standing in our rightful power of being in Truth.

Our first lesson on the seas is being taught on the top deck. The use of a sword is much more difficult that I thought it would be. First, I need to develop more upper body strength. These are heavy! It takes a lot of control to stop the momentum of the direction a sword is going, especially if you are the one that puts it in motion. In other words, I was swinging my sword as if to cut off a person's hand, but didn't really want to actually cut off the hand, just touch it as in playing tag. Perhaps there is no such thing as tag in this world. The person's hand fell off! I am so sorry!! There is so much to learn here. I think I am more traumatized than the pirate.

Thankfully, I know how to help him grow it back. He will only have to wear a hook for a few days. I guess we are teaching each other in this Portal.

We are being prepared to defend ourselves as needed and to take and receive what is rightfully ours. This is the picture I'm given. Too often I loan an object, like a movie or book, to someone and then don't ask for it back, thinking they will give it to me when they are finished. What has happened so many times is that they forget they have it and move away. Then I am left to buy another, as it most often is a valued piece of resource material. I can see that we have many lessons to learn on this journey.

See you tomorrow!

MONTH TEN – DAY TWO

I hope you had a great night's sleep with the waves rocking you all night long. I was really thankful it wasn't a stormy night. I was reliving the activities of yesterday and felt the ease in how we fit into the flow of the ship. That sword-handling lesson seemed to be quite beneficial. So much to learn in how to handle our own movements and then adding an extension to our hand is quite a powerful way to utilize our capabilities. This is a whole new way of utilizing your 'gut' instinct with your mental, emotional and physical as one moving person.

Our lesson today is a treasure hunt right here on the boat. We will be given a map with things to find and bring back to the top deck. We can team up or go solo. I think our best learning experience would be if we teamed up with one of the crew members. I don't see any rules listed on the map. Of course, why would there be any rules to a game or lesson from Pirates and Vikings, the greatest rule-breakers of all times. I wonder what happens if we win or, worse, if we lose. Do they make you walk the plank?

I chose to do this exercise with Freydis. I want to learn all I can for holding my boundaries and standing up for myself. Great qualities I do admire in her. I see most of you are pairing up with various crew members. Those that are going it alone, I wish you well.

Freydis was a perfect partner to work with. She told me how, in the days of her youth, it was a huge battle to be a woman. The men got all the fun and cool stuff. They came home to everything taken care of while they were out exploring. She would have none of it. She wanted to explore and help her family be better in different ways than just staying at the village. I let her know that we were still undergoing a similar battle of sorts in the 21st century. She could hardly believe it was still that way. She is a great teammate, plus she knows every inch of this vessel.

It made it even easier when we would look at our list and, by using our instincts, we would know the direction we needed to go. With her knowledge of the ship, she would know what is ahead of us. Sometimes, she also knew where things were before I could interpret the map.

We were teaching each other how to use our intuitive skills in a manner to find the treasures. This is exactly what we need to practice – letting our intuition kick in beyond survival mode. Learning to utilize our consciousness in these basic skills is what we have missed. Sometimes you just have to go back to the beginning to pick up some lessons that have been skipped along the journey. These are lessons in relearning it's okay to use our intuition to produce the Money we are destined to have.

How did you do? We came in fourth. My sides still hurt from all of the deep laughter and excitement. It was fun getting to know the layout of this huge vessel. I had no idea it had so many small, secret hiding spots. We most certainly used many of our combined skills to reach some treasures.

Tonight, we need to get some rest as I have no idea what tomorrow will bring.

See you tomorrow!

MONTH TEN – DAY THREE

Wow! Smell that sea air! It is so cleansing and invigorating. It is a little rougher than when we started out. The Portal's spinning movement, combined with the waves, make it very hard to know what direction we were going to be moving. I am thankful that my hammock sort of helped keep some form of a gravitational balance for me to stay in the flow of where we are going.

I have been thinking about how much different it felt yesterday when we were on the treasure hunt. Finding items that were placed around for us had a whole different feel from the terms we are used to using like hunting for work, or receiving a gift of cash. Also, being given a paycheck with a raise is exciting but still gives for many a sense of "Did I earn all of this?" or, "I worked so hard for this little bit of acknowledgement?" The idea of having to work and earn the money we use feels different from finding it in a treasure chest. It is as if the treasure chest is for anyone that finds it, and no one owns it, as if there are no strings attached to it. There is a different excitement around the treasure hunt.

Let's see what we can do to help ourselves to become clearer with this relationship to Money. The easiest way to clear these types of blocks is by having adventures with Fun and Magic. Also, where quantum physics is involved.

Today, we are going to be climbing the poles that hold the sails. We may also be climbing the center mast lookout. I know I am not using correct sea terms, but I don't want to offend the Pirates, Vikings, or those who actually study ocean travel. It's just so we know what I am referring to. We have a lot of help teaching us how to use the ropes and nets in this exercise.

We are being divided into two groups, not for a competition but to help us spread out more so we get additional practice. I can see where this is going to turn into a lot of fun. The directions I understood are: we climb the first pole, grab a rope, and swing to the second one, reach out and grab a ring before we grab the next rope.

Take your time to get a good hold onto it, then, with just the right push we can reach the net to climb higher. Once we make it to the top, we place the ring into a tube that gives a signal that we are ready. It is now our turn to jump out and free float down to the big net near the bottom.

Okay, I think I am ready to do this. It is not nearly as hard as it looks. Of course, we are in the Portal. Wow! It is actually fun. Now I am ready to jump out and fall into the net. As I get closer to the bottom, I see many bubbles of a clear liquid have been placed in the net. As I fall into them, and they create a softer safe landing. Also, I feel the ones I broke start to meld into my skin. It feels really nice and helps my head to be clearer.

I am ready for another turn. This time, when I land in the bubbles, they are completely different. They start jumping onto me and melding into areas where I have been sore. They soak into areas of my body which have experienced trauma to clear me, so my children and grandchildren won't carry old patterns and ideas ingrained in me. This is great, as I had wondered about them taking on something I shifted within my own DNA from many old accidents I had from riding horses.

I don't want them to be afraid of horses, think they are terrible, or have the same aches I have related to my horse experiences. I can feel the changes helping me in this Portal.

The final time, I get to go up the masts and fall into the bubble pit. I notice that I am being cleared of so many fears I have had to push through. Pushing through doesn't clear anything, it just buries it deeper. A specific clearing needs to be done. This does not mean you have to spend endless hours in a therapist's office. By using Consciousness Technologies, which is what you have experienced throughout these journeys, change can happen in moments. When you are having fun, your mind is taken off of the wait for change. It just happens. I love having it be that easy.

How are you feeling with free-falling and landing in the bubble pit? You can continue with this fun as many times as you want. There is no limit to what you can become.

This was a lot of shifting for us and the crew who got to see this change. Now the crew wants a turn. Let's show them how it's done! As we change the Now, we can create change in the Past and Future within our DNA. This crew is really excited about that part as well.

It is time for all of us to take a few moments to allow a little recalibration to take place within all of our bodies.

See you tomorrow!

MONTH TEN – DAY FOUR

We have been experiencing what it is like to ride the seas in this Portal on a pirate ship. Today it is going to flip into a Viking ship. For those that watched the *Harry Potter* movies you know exactly how this is created. One moment, it is Pirates. The next, it is Vikings!

Notice the differences in how the layout of this vessel is. It is deeper on the top deck and does not rock side-to-side as much. It is built to work with the heavy North Seas. To me, it just feels more rugged and sturdy. Of course, it is awesome with the Dragon carving at the front. Yes, I am missing my Dragon. Maybe we will get to bring our Avatars into this Portal soon.

This ship does have a lot of the same things as our previous one, but it seems to be missing the cannon holes. That is okay, as we don't really need them for this journey. There are still the sails, oars, and a place to eat and sleep. Just what we need as we go into deeper, more mystical waters. After all,

Vikings were from the Northern lands and traveled to locations with a good deal of magical and mystical lore associated with the times of Avalon.

I see we are landing for a little while on an island within this Portal. Our Viking crew will be with us as we explore this new terrain. They are quite familiar with Northern Island lifestyle and many of the magical aspects that are a part of the everyday walk.

I think most of us are familiar with the mist and many of its properties. As we follow the path along the shore of this island we will walk through the mist of this Divine Money Portal to get to the next level of learning about Money Codes. Vikings don't seem to have a problem with these codes, so they get to take the lead. It takes having a certain amount of them to open the mists in the Divine Money Portal. They will open it for us, so we can walk in as their guests.

As we enter the mists, I notice that, if we didn't have the codes activated enough to open it, they are being turned on and balanced as we glide through this area. I can feel their pulsing harmonizing within my auric field and triggering a different vibrational frequency within my body. It is so relaxing and easy, it makes me feel like I am gliding with my feet barely touching the ground.

This is really a nice and gentle way to move us to a new level. It feels like a more solid activation than I have previously experienced. I hope it is the same for you. You may want to journal about this when you have time.

I see a campfire up ahead ready for us. There's a breeze off the water, and the mist is damp and chilly. Oh, yes, this feels wonderful. There is nothing like a campfire to warm us all the way to the core. The table is loaded with food to eat as your stomach is ready for it, and blankets to wrap up in as we walk around to download the changes occurring within and without. Take your time, there is no hurry as each person processes these changes differently. I feel like I am here, then not here, then here again. Also, one moment I am freezing cold, and the next there's power surge going right through me. We have been preparing for this. Allow yourself to receive this shift.

There is a stone building just down the path with lots of rooms for us to spend the night. It will be warm and comfortable. Before we leave this fire, let's gather around it in a circle, hold hands, and just breathe for a few moments. You may stay here as long as you like. I am ready to find my hot bath and comfortable bed.

See you tomorrow!

MONTH TEN – DAY FIVE

I find myself still slightly floating above the ground as I walk. That mist was really powerful. I notice a different vibrational field around each of you as well. Let's gather at the table to find out what our plans are for this day as we enjoy what has been prepared for us.

It truly is a magical table. I was hoping for some really hot tea, and there it is! A huge comforting mug sitting on the table just for me. Make your wish, and I am certain it will be delivered to you within reason. I have been told it has become quite chilly overnight, and that there are plenty of warm clothes and furs for us to choose from near the door. We will be hiking up a mountain to an ancient area similar to what Merlin was familiar with.

We will leave when everyone is ready. This is going to be an exciting adventure. Even though it is freezing outside, it is still beautiful. The green plants are of a color I have never experienced, or perhaps the mist has enhanced my ability to sense color.

I have had that happen before with other activations. Either way, the colors seem to dance in the sunlight.

The clothing I get to wear appears to be real fur. It has the texture and smell of what I would think real fur would be like. The coat and leg warmers are wonderful. They are amazing at stopping the wind from going all the way through, and they hold in body heat so nicely.

I think we are all gathered and ready to begin our climb. I have an amazing walking stick. It is very similar to what I would imagine Merlin or the Lady of the Lake would be using on a hike like this. So far it is steep, but, with the back-and- forth movement of this trail, it isn't too hard. Also, notice how this movement hypnotizes our cells as we ascend up this mountain. Great symbolism.

We are nearing a cave where there is a fire and refreshments for everyone. Take a little time to enjoy the break and notice how you feel at this altitude. Are you out of breath, or a little tired? Make sure you drink lots of water. It is easy to get dehydrated at higher elevations and not even know it.

I am being told we aren't moving on higher up the mountain. We will be going one by one to a location in order to view what is inside of it. As you are ready, get in line for your turn.

I will take my turn now. I have no idea what this well is, and my curiosity has me pulsating with excitement. As I get nearer to it, I hear a tone vibrate through every cell. I am not sure if I hear it with my ears or if it is a spiritual tone. I notice a person standing there to help me. First, I am asked to look into the deep water and notice if I see anything. I do. I see a sort of movie playing out in front of my eyes. I am not to speak of it yet.

Then, I turn a handle that rolls up a rope to pull the bucket from the bottom of the well. It is heavy. The bucket finally gets to the top. I am to reach inside and pull out whatever is in there. I am a little hesitant, as I can't see the bottom of it. It is a stone with a symbol on it. I don't know what it means, but I was told it is a rune. I will have to look it up later. I can't wait to hear about your experiences.

Everyone has arrived back at the cave and is so quiet. The sacred level is felt within each of us. Let's take a moment and journal about our experience so we don't forget a single part of it. Once we are finished, we will go down the trail to the stone house. I am sure they will be expecting us to stay one more night.

Going downhill was a lot faster and easier than going up. The stone house is so lovely. It looks like a picture in an old book I read a long time ago. The Ancient Ones have taken great care of it as it is the gatekeeper of the well.

As we gather around the table and fire, I hear the Vikings telling stories of their own about how they traveled from one country to another. They also say some of the battles listed in literature are exaggerated to make them seem to be like vigilantes. They say that they did not raid unless they had been raided upon first. It was more of taking back what was rightfully theirs in the first place.

The one thing we are to learn in this Portal is to receive what is rightfully ours. I am not sure about the taking or how we are to take it. One thing I am certain of is that we are to not kill in order to take back what is ours.

There must be a method of boundaries and a certain air of power within that creates us getting what is rightfully ours. This also pertains to how we run our businesses and manage our time.

You are welcome to stay up as long as you like, but I am going off to bed.

See you tomorrow!

MONTH TEN – DAY SIX

The sun is shining, and the wind has stopped blowing so hard. This is going to be a marvelous day. I had my tea outside on the grass, with the animals around me, and the peace of knowing we are on the right path in this Portal. The Vikings and Pirates are taking us on some interesting journeys through this spinning vortex where we get to find what we are missing in our Abundance Portfolio. Then, we are presented with the opportunity to retrieve what we need next.

I still do not know what the rune I retrieved from the well is all about. It just feels right to carry it in my pocket for now. Did you get any information about yours? Perhaps you didn't get a rune from the well. You got something entirely different. I am certain it is very important to your next adventure in the real world.

We will be gathering up all of our things to leave this magical island as soon as everyone is available. From the looks of how slow some of you are moving, you must have stayed up late listening to some amazing stories from our wonderful family.

The Viking ship will be sailing with the tide of the Portal within the hour. You can sleep more once on board if you find that you need to.

Oh, that fresh sea air is quite a waker-upper. I don't think I will be going back to sleep. Do you see that school of whales around us? They are staying right along with our speed, sending messages back and forth with their beautiful songs. I can feel their tones echoing within my cells. It is as if I can understand everything they are saying.

They are sending messages to help us to remember who we are and where we came from. The memories are about our ancestors that helped create this Planet. The information is about how they built the cities and the temples to hold the information encoded within the energies we are being downloaded with during this Divine Portal journey. The whales remember everything and are giving us the information as we are ready to receive it. It must be time for us to receive, as there are so many whales sending these messages.

As we listen closer we receive messages specific to each one of us giving directions to our purpose on this Planet. These tones seem to awaken within each of us DNA information that has been stored for many generations. An example of this might be new healing techniques, or how to build the free energy machines. Perhaps new ways to teach in our schools or create new school systems. We are the ones that have been chosen to assist this new awakening on the Planet to move forward.

While you are listening to the whale songs, you might want to have a paper and pencil handy to take notes as it pulls you into a deeper meditative state where the memories can be accessed. As a word or message comes through just put down a word or two to jog your memory later.

You don't need to be concerned about the ship nor the direction it is going. Our amazing Viking family is leading us along this path. Actually, they are letting the whales lead and they are just manning the ship. They too are being reminded of their purpose.

It will take several hours for us to get to the main island within the Portal. We have a lot of time to awaken our memories and translate them within our own mind. No need to hurry. Just relax and allow the whale tones to fill you with exactly what you need. Let yourself receive and be open to the new memories of why you are here and what your job is. As the information comes in, ask for the financing to be there for your new projects. Don't try to figure out how it will happen, just put it in the mix of what is happening next in your world.

We are now at the center of the Portal with the main island. We can either stay on the ship or go inside to a room that has been prepared for you. I am staying on the ship this time as I am still getting information from the whales.

See you tomorrow!

MONTH TEN – DAY SEVEN

That was some amazing shifting we were offered the opportunity to participate in the last few days. The rune I received from the well is the symbol for Prosperity, Wealth, and Overcoming Opposition. When I looked up the symbol that came to me, I was shocked as it is exactly what we are participating within each of the Portals. I think I will continue to carry it with me.

The whale songs are still echoing within me. I can feel information about new healing technologies being fed inside of me. I know that soon I will be able to practice them on my wonderful clients and friends. As for now I will continue to make little notes as I get pieces of it. I can't wait to hear what new and exciting journeys your lives will bring to the Planet. We are being given an opportunity to make the changes we have been dreaming about.

As for today, I feel like it's time to assist our new family of what we call Pirates and Vikings in the experience of choosing an Avatar to ride. For those who are ready, go into your heart and focus on an amazing being that can assist you in getting from here to the mountain top in a short period. One that you can sit on and follow the commands you give. Yes, I have my Purple Dragon again this time, as we are quite a team.

Once you have created or summoned the being you are to bond with for a few days, allow it to be beside you with riding gear ready to go. Take a few moments to bond and examine the being you have chosen. Run your hands over its neck if it has one, across the back, down the legs, tail, and wings.

As you are doing this, focus on love from the heart. Let go of fear or even questions of how is this going to work.

I have never done this before. Can this being save me if I fall off? I did hear a pirate or two's thoughts about meeting me back at his ship, because there is no way they will ride a beast into the sky. That is just fine; you don't have to if you don't want to. We each have our own comfort zones. Perhaps, once you see us having so much fun, you will change your mind.

Take your time to get into the riding gear. Each being is a little different. There are assistants ready to help you if you need it. Once I see everyone on their Avatars we can take a short ride. I will check in to see if we can venture inland a little further.

You are all doing great! Let's do some other exploring. I see a mountain not too far off that we can quickly get to. Follow me.

Look I have a treasure map! Oh, now you're excited about this adventure. I should have known that it would be exactly what a pirate needed to see to participate. I am not sure if I can read it correctly, but I do think it shows that X marks the spot right over on that mountain.

Not far now. I see a place where we can land not far from the huge X on the ground. It must be the right place. I am being laughed at, but let's just wait and see.

Sometimes those that create treasure hunts actually make them appear easier than they really are. Yes, there is a huge X, but it is not exactly flat on the ground. It is raised and is a puzzle that we must solve to get the next message of where to go.

We can do this. Puzzles are a lot of fun when we all work together. It is a puzzle of pictures, not words. I think we got it.

It shows a cave up the side of the mountain. Yes, I can see many caves up there. Now which one is it? Walk around this large X puzzle and see if there are any other clues stashed in a crevice or under something. Yes, you found it just before your Avatar started to eat it. Great save.

It tells us to ride to the cave second from the far left and see what awaits us. We can get there easily. It also looks like a storm is coming, so it will be nice to be in a cave for a while.

The cave is really a nice size. All of our Avatars fit in here with us, and someone got here first. There is a nice fire to keep us warm, bedrolls, and food for us and our Avatars. It looks like we will be spending the night. This will be fun. Maybe we will get to hear more stories about the sea.

I also think there should be another clue somewhere in here. Each clue leads us to just one more place instead of giving us the whole picture. In my head, I hear patience. I know that I tend to have a problem with wanting to know the big picture before I begin. However, there must be some reason we are in here for a whole night, beyond to just stay dry.

The Divine Portal always has messages for us in these types of places. Keep your awareness up as we tend to our Avatars and our own needs.

Yes, just as I expected. There is a new map in the feed bin. Let's gather around the fire and work on solving this one together. It looks to be rather complicated for my tired brain. Since this is going to take a different type of thinking, it might be beneficial to form smaller groups to talk it out.

If you come up with a plan come find me. I am going to go into a little journey in my head about it.

See you tomorrow!

MONTH TEN - -DAY EIGHT

Look who arrived during the night! I am so excited to see how much the Vikings and Pirates who decided to stay at camp with their ships learned in just a few days. They were able to get their ships to fly. They were not comfortable with the incredible beasts we work with, but they learned how to set their sails just right and, with the command of their focused intent, they activated their ships into flying and finding us!

Now we can show the Map Masters our problem. Of course, it only took them seconds to know the answer. I think I will let them lead today's journey. Are we all ready? Let's get on our Avatars and follow the flying ships to the treasure where we can all collect our bounty.

Of course, there are a few challenges along the way. One is that not everyone here has the capability to hold a frequency of receiving a bounty of this magnitude. We each have shifted our frequency a lot since we started, but being able to receive money or a treasure is a big one.

I see the first experience we get to do is board the ship with our Avatars. Then we let them fly around us as we walk the plank. Yes, we are going to walk the plank and trust that our Avatar is right there for us to land on. Who volunteers to go first? No one?

Okay, I will go. Step one is to connect telepathically with your Avatar. In this case, me to my Dragon with a picture in my head and heart of what is happening. The picture I sent is of me walking on a board out over the emptiness beyond the ship and stepping off. My Dragon's part is to come up under the ship, so I can land right on his back.

I am focusing that I am ready to step out and receive what is rightfully mine. One of those is being ready to receive the Help and Rewards as I take the first step toward Manifestation. Watch how this is done! See, that was easy. Now it is your turn. It is all about taking that first step into nothingness.

Each of you did awesome! On to the next part – clearing our ability to receive. We will not be able to lay hands on that bountiful treasure until we are ready to receive it.

Do you see that huge waterfall? It looks like we are going right into it. What if we crash into the rock wall behind it? Okay, I just have to trust we are being led on a safe journey. Yes, right into the center of the waterfall. It is a cold one, but it is also magical as we allow ourselves to enter into the very center and, in slow motion, glide through a webbed multidimensional curtain which clears out the old fears of Not Enough, Not Good Enough, and Not Worthy.

Then, in the next second, it activates the codes around us related to being in our own power and taking what is rightfully ours with Love and Gratitude. These are new codes to us and feel completely different from the ones we have activated in the other Portals.

There is still a part of me that feels like it is being selfish to stand in that level of Power. I think I will fly out and back in again to see if I can clear another level of this missing piece for me. You can do the same if you feel like you need to.

We entered a cave behind the waterfall. There is a ledge with a treasure chest sitting right in the middle. It is open, and strings of pearls hang over the edge of it. There are precious gems glittering on the top of a stack of gold coins. Are you ready to divide it up, or do you think it belongs to the Portal and should be left alone?

Well, it doesn't matter what we think. The Vikings and Pirates know that it is to be put onto the ship and taken back to the main island. Perhaps we can divide it up once we discover if it's really Finders' Keepers. We did sign up for this journey with the idea of getting to keep our bounty, right?

I notice that some in the group are not okay with this idea. They think it should be left right there on that ledge as it probably belongs to someone in the Portal. Yet, we were given the map to find it.

I guess we will go back to the main island and let the committee decide. While we are sleeping, we can come to a decision on if you'll take your share if it is offered or will you fight for your share since you found it.

See you tomorrow!

MONTH TEN – DAY NINE

Hello, everyone. This is going to be an amazing day.

Remember that treasure we found? The island committee will be reviewing the treasure chest dilemma on if it is ours to divide up or if it is just part of a game we're all participating players in. It was quite exciting to get cleared and find a chest full of what may be pirate booty.

While we are waiting, let's go for a walk. To sit around waiting for a decision is a nerve-wracking event in itself. There is a stream close by. We can easily get there and back rapidly once the decision is given. We can wade in it or just sit on the bank and put our feet in.

Yes, that feels so wonderful. It must be a magical healing stream. I feel like it is realigning me so that I can think clearer. I hope it helps you as well. I can feel the realignment of my Abundance Codes of Money to include a Truth Frequency.

I remind you that this is also a magical island in the center of the Vikings' and Pirates' Divine Money Portal. I have been thinking about the Viking and pirate time periods and how Manifestations worked back then. They did it a little differently than what we do now. They knew what they wanted, what was theirs, what they were entitled to, and how to get it. We seem to have lost that drive. Even with the Law of Attraction as we have been taught by so many professional people, it doesn't work for everyone, nor in the same way for each individual.

One thing for certain is to get clear about what you want, and own the energy of it as if it is already yours. I know that some people say to picture what you want and to feel like you already have it. My teams have told me that one must also hold their own Energy of Power. If you don't, what happens the energy starts drifting into a Victim level. Your brain gets in the way saying things like, "How can I say or feel like I have it when I really don't," and, "At this time, I don't see a way of getting it." It feels like a stagnant, false energy. We are not supposed to be going backwards, only forward, as you can't find your stash of cash in the past. The big clue here is to own the energy of it as if it is already yours.

I have also found that many people that are on this journey of becoming a Lightworker tend to focus mostly on the upper chakras. We are to actually work with all of our chakras to completely balance them to work together. The lower chakras have been the manifesting ones.

If you stand up and take a motorcycle rider's stance, or a pirate/Viking sword-wielding stance, you are in a different state of inner power. Take a deep breath and notice how you can ground better. This is the world that the beings of this Portal lived in, and many still do on this Planet. Once you start focusing on the upper chakras and forget about the lower ones you become out of balance.

Take a moment and ask for all of your energy centers to activate, balance with each other, and harmonize. Notice how you feel now! Standing in your own Power, yet aligned with the Creator at the same time. This is how we are to use our Manifesting Money Codes of Abundance.

For some this is a new concept. It is also a new concept for the Planet to work with. It takes a while for many of us to remember to use this alignment for our code activations to be utilized. This takes practice, even when you are back on Earth. Let's go back to the main building and see what has been decided about the treasure chest.

Yes, that was a game where we were to learn how to follow the map placed before us, how to use our abilities to find and sort out what is put before us, and, also, how to maintain the integrity within ourselves when the opportunity presents itself. Or, do we take the whole booty and run without knowing all the details. It is a huge opportunity to learn about integrity and how to stand in our Power in Truth.

The Truth of the booty in that chest is also now clear. It had a Magical Glamour put on it to give the impression that everything we saw were extremely valuable items. It was actually costume jewelry and candy. It is also something for us to be aware of out there in the real world. The saying 'All that glitters is not gold.' is something we need to be aware of.

Learning to read energy is very important at this stage of the game. It is the same ability as determining truth from falsity. There is no need to waste time on the falseness that is around. Keep your focus on the prize, the bounty that is yours for the taking.

I can hear our new family cheering us on. We are asked to line up to receive a very special token for passing this test – a gold coin from the pirate booty bag. It is up us to decide if it is a real gold coin or one gold-wrapped chocolate coin. What are you ready to receive? There is a lot to learn about the Money Game and how to play it with integrity.

Tonight, we get to board the ships again and spend some time on them as the Portal goes through another shift while this magical island is swept on down the swirling vortex to the end point. All of your items have been moved for you, and a comfortable space has been prepared for your Avatar.

Time to practice Manifestation from all the energy centers we have available to us, and meditate with the gold coin to find out if it is real gold or a chocolate. What are you ready to receive?

See you tomorrow!

MONTH TEN – DAY TEN

Gliding along in this amazing ship was the most relaxing time I have experienced throughout this entire Portal. The silence as we moved beneath the stars was comforting and hypnotizing to help me go deeper into a meditation about the gold coins we received. It was quite an opening of information. It reminded me of a movie I saw when I was on the other island looking into the well. I know we each saw something different and specific to our own path. This reminder I had was for all of us.

We are each to do our own work, like with my clients that come to me for help, or me going to my own therapists. The therapist is the catalyst to help you or me move to our next level of knowledge or vibration of power within. We must take the time to do our own meditations and journaling. No one else can do it for us.

Also, the one thing that I really don't like for myself is that no one else can give us certain answers. We have to do it ourselves for ourselves. This is one area I struggle with, as I get so involved with doing for others,

I don't take the time to do for me. We must do our self-care. This is where I find that mini meditations are extremely helpful for me. You may need something else.

I wonder what we are going to be doing for our adventure today. I see there is a huge drum in the center of the upper deck. Someone is beginning to pound on it in a rhythmic manner. It is very soothing on one level, yet stimulating to my muscles on another. It seems to help stabilize the ship. I am not sure how, but I can see why.

A storm cloud is coming at us really fast. I think we should hang on to something. The wind is getting stronger and it's getting rougher. I didn't think that the airwaves could be as rough as those in the water. Maybe it was just wishful thinking. The activation of our muscles by the drums helped all of us stabilize ourselves and the ship simultaneously.

Wow, that was intense. I hear we are ready for a new adventure on our Avatars. Okay, I am ready for this one. It only takes a thought, and our Avatars are right there for us. We are heading off to the left to that very small island rolling with the waves of the Portal. It looks so small from up here, but, as we get closer, I can see it is actually a nice size for us to land with our Avatars and have some room to explore.

I didn't know until now that this Portal was inhabited with others not a part of our journey. I hear a person crying over in that meadow. Let's see if we can help. I understand this person is lost and once lived in a village on this island, but the storm that went through pulled her away from her home. She seems to be about six or seven. I told her that we will help her find her way home.

I have her on my Avatar with me as we fly over the island looking for her village. I see one place I think a village once was, but now everything is blown to the ground. Let's go down and take a look.

Yes, this was her village, but everyone is gone. Perhaps they took shelter in one of those caves up on the hillside.

I think we could have this rebuilt for all of them in a couple of hours. With the help of our Avatars to move the debris quickly and carry the building materials that we need, we can do this in record time. Let's do it before they come back. That would be a great surprise for all of them.

Yes, we are an amazing team. Since no one has shown up, let's go up into those caves and see if they are there. Of course, they are, but they're very afraid of coming back to their old location. They never experienced anything like that before. We told them their village is back to normal and a team is there preparing food for them.

We helped them understand that what happened is a one-time event, and they shouldn't worry about it happening again. They are now ready to return and want to repay us. Of course, I say we don't need pay, but they insist. They have nothing that I can see to use for payment.

They told me they have one of the most brilliant healers within this Portal. We are to gather in a circle in the meadow and she will meet us there shortly. We are to have our Avatars sit right behind us. We are not to hold hands, as we are to maintain our individuality.

As she starts her prayers, I feel and see an energy of a light mist surround our group. It is as if we are being separated from the rest of the world. To be within this sacred space is so heart opening. I see each of you receiving this healing. At times, we don't think we need a healing, but I have found that some healings encompass areas that we are not familiar with, even within our own being. Once the healing is complete, the mist lifts. We give a thank you to her as she moves to each one of us and places a sacred stone in our hands.

This has been a great deed we participated in today. We saved a village from horrific trials of rebuilding and coming back together. This is as much for us as it was for them.

Let's ride back to that huge ship in the sky and enjoy a relaxing evening. You might want to go further into that gold coin or just put it in your pocket for later.

See you tomorrow for our last ride in the Portal!

MONTH TEN – DAY ELEVEN

This is our last day together in this Divine Money Portal with the Vikings and Pirates and experiences with how they attract and receive their treasure chests filled with gold. It is sort of sad, but it is hard to be sad with these amazing people that have taken us on this journey. They have been extremely gracious with the use of their ships and guiding us throughout this Portal. I know that I have learned a lot about their history and the ancestral part they played in my family. Also, why my family changed their ability to Manifest on the same level.

I am now ready for us to find out what is in store. I hear that we are to mount up on our Avatars and begin flying in the direction the Portal is spinning. I really hope we don't do the spinning part. That is sort of fun, but I do not want to take the chance on losing any of you into the deep beneath us. The ship will follow along behind this time – all by itself – as our new friends decided they would also like to ride on a huge beast for a while with us. I can see that we have all learned a little from each other.

Do you see that rainbow up ahead? We can fly through it. Oh, yes, as we fly through each color we get a new awareness downloaded into our Money Codes. The changes within our energetic body are subtle, but very deep for most of us.

Some of you may notice an extreme feeling if you have not done work in this area before. The colors' vibrational pull is great to help those Money Codes come alive all around you for easier access. This is one of those Activations that may be easy on you now but, when you go to bed, they will do more work with your energy body. That way, you can stay on your Avatar without too much of an equilibrium shift. Once that awareness was brought forward, I can see how each of you have been able to receive on a deeper level. This will really help your Money Attraction and Activation of Receiving.

Now, as the Portal does a bigger shift within its counter-rotating field, it feels like my stomach did the same thing. It's like the outer layer rotates one direction while the inner-lining rotates another. It must be digesting all of the stuff we leave behind as we clear. It is very interesting to see this happen.

I can see up ahead the center island which was rapidly washed down through the Portal. It looks like there were some building upgrades since we stayed. There were also some huge repairs from that last storm. I notice a protective mist around the entire island.

We are being told that is due to the beings that live here in the Portal who have had some rather traumatic experiences with the recent storm. They are trying to keep the island in a higher frequency, because it's the best way to be of service to all in need.

Those that want to come onto the island have to pass through this mist that will help them clear a lot of the old energy other than the most recent trauma. It will create an amazing uplift for the whole Portal.

Getting all the old energy cleared out is as great as receiving a raise. This is a raising of the frequency and the lifestyle of the entire Portal. Sometimes we only see the damage done by a storm. Yet, sometimes those storms help us clear out the Old in order to receive the New.

We too must fly through this mist. Sometimes it may take more than once to be admitted onto the island. Our Avatars will also be cleared as we fly them through the mist. I see there are several different mists for us to proceed through. One is for the physical body, one the mental body, one the emotional body, and one for the Spirit.

We are to be cleared and balanced before moving forward. Some of the activities we participated in, worked with only certain aspects of ourselves. Before we can enter the center island, we must be balanced in all aspects. I see the ship is also going through the various mists. Of course, it is, as everything in here is a living being, including the ship.

Now we can land and enter the new Center. It is a going away party Viking/pirate style. You are given a drink and lots of food. You can choose the drink you want. It will be flavored as to what you want it to be, but it will be non-alcoholic, as we don't mix Spirit and spirits. That may be a new concept for some of you. It is something I was shown many years ago about how the spiritual level works.

There is plenty of food to try based on old recipes. There is also a bell to ring to get everyone's attention for you to give a toast or say something important on this journey. Perhaps how you experienced being with all of us. Maybe you can include what you liked or didn't like.

I do have a reminder to all of you that the changes you experienced within the Portal will continue working with you for a few more weeks. Take your time to drink lots of blessed water and get plenty of rest. You will continue to recalibrate with the new You. I have thoroughly enjoyed sharing this time and space with all of you.

See you next month!

See you soon with Truth, Love, and Gratitude

Pat, The Cosmic Cowgirl

Journal Changes in Your Mind, Body, and Spirit and How the Pirates & Vikings Helped

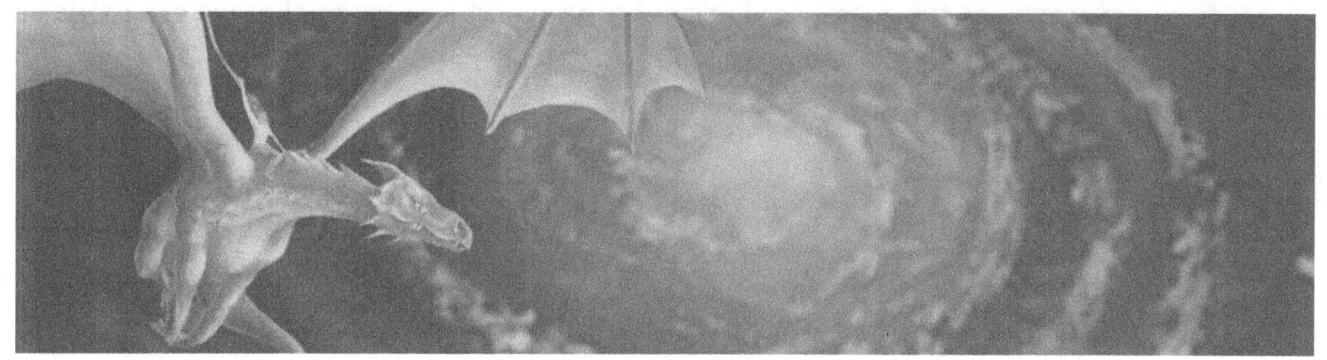

CHAPTER ELEVEN: THANKSGIVING, THE CORNUCOPIA OF ABUNDANCE & GRATITUDE

MONTH ELEVEN – DAY ONE

Welcome to the Divine Portal of Abundance and Gratitude. I notice most of you arrived on your Avatars. If you don't have one, look around your consciousness and notice what you would like for an Avatar. Call it to you. Mine, of course, is the amazing, multidimensional, Purple Dragon. We have worked together for a very long time. So long, that we know what each other thinks before it is put into action. It would be nice if you could find yourself an Avatar that you can develop a connection with of that sort. If you don't have it at first, by the time we are finished with these eleven days, you will.

This Portal is in the shape of a Cornucopia, just like you would see as a Thanksgiving center piece. I notice how it spins within itself and how it is changes shapes as we get closer. The exterior color is a mixture of brown and orange, and a little red in some areas. I can feel the energy of it as it gets ready to open for us to enter.

I see a platform at the entrance. Let's get to the landing spot so that we are ready as the larger door opens. Just in time. We made it in.

This entrance is filled with a white, gauze-like substance that we are to walk through. Yes, your Avatars can also go through. There are several layers to flow through. This is a clearing area to prepare us to be able to enter the sacred space of this Portal.

We are to begin with the one that has a letter E woven into the fabric. This represents East. We are to begin with clearing off the old patterns we are so attached to. As you walk through this fabric, take time to breathe in & release the Old to prepare for the New beginnings.

The next layer has an S woven into it. South clearing is to prepare us for fun. It activates our curiosity into play and fun. Just like the old coyote, the Trickster, life is to be lived, so enjoy it. Breathe in this allowance as you walk through it.

The next layer has a W woven into it. West is for letting go of limited belief systems, fears, stale patterns and readying us to be reborn into our true Selves. Breathe and release the Old and prepare for the New.

The next one has an N woven into it. The North is a reminder of the reverence of life. Take a moment to reflect on the wise silence of the North. Take a deep breath and allow yourself to be in a space to receive. This is a place where you will be given the opportunity to receive the gifts that have been waiting for you. It's a preparation for you to expect the miracles available every day.

It's interesting how this fabric moved through every cell. This is quite an interesting way of entering the Portal. We were also decontaminated to bring us to a level of vibration where we can work within this Portal's rulesets. I think we are now ready to move ahead.

We will begin by riding our Avatars over to that ledge on the right. It sticks out of the wall just the right amount for us to fit. I see vines and pumpkins everywhere. Notice which one stands out to you the most. Pick it up and notice its color and feel. Is it ripe enough to pick? Ask it. If it isn't, get another one. Once you find one that tells you it is ready, pick it and carry it with you.

The light is changing. It is time for us to find the Center where we are to stay. Bring your pumpkin with you. If it is too big to carry, talk to it and it will shrink down to a size where you can handle it while riding your Avatar.

The Center where we are staying in has a large meeting room with cabins or tents set aside for each of us. Bring your pumpkin inside, as we have a game to play with it. Don't worry about your Avatar, the people that work here have had a lot of practice with just about any type of magical critter around.

There is a huge table in the middle where we get to open our pumpkin and remove its seeds. Can you do this? After all, you just talked to it, and it talked back to you. You get to experience a new way of doing this. There is a knife available if you want it. How are you going to retrieve the seeds from this pumpkin without hurting it?

I will start. I thank this pumpkin for being a part of this moment for me, and I ask if it is ready to give up its seeds for the good of what is to come. It says, "Of course, I am." It knows it's purpose. It also knows that, after this fun game, it will become a part of the meal for later. I am still not comfortable with cutting into it with a knife though it keeps telling me it's okay. I ask if there is a different way for it to give me its seeds.

It shows me a small space between the cells of the wall where the seeds can just flow out. Of course, it can. Each of the Portals are filled with a level of Magical Energy of 'Ask and you shall receive."

The seeds are just flowing out of this little crevice. I had no idea this tiny pumpkin could hold so many seeds. I am told that it will continue to make seeds as long as I need or want them.

It was endless. I finally had to say, "I think this is enough seeds for everyone." By this time, the pile of seeds was more than double the size of the pumpkin itself.

How is your process going with the seed retrieval from your pumpkin? Remember to be respectful to it, I just saw one jump off the table and roll out the door. I presume it was not properly prepared for the next step that it was to undergo. Keep experimenting with this process in seed removal and the preparation for your pumpkin to be a part of the food source we will experience soon. Take your time to develop a conversation first before using the knife. You can still use the knife if that is what shows up for you to do. It is all your choice. There is not one way better than another, it is just a learning experience. The kitchen staff has arrived to take all the seeds to be roasted and the pumpkins to make food for us.

This has been a glorious way to begin our journey into this Cornucopia Portal. When you are ready, you will be shown to your rooms. There will be some calibrations within you, as you rest from the fabrics we moved through.

See you tomorrow!

MONTH ELEVEN – DAY TWO

I am so excited for this new day. I wonder what type of Abundance and Gratitude we will be shown?

To start with, I see our Avatars are being brought to us along with a backpack. Let's put the pack on. Mine is already heavy, and it has a funny shape inside of it! I don't have time to look inside to see what it is. I just trust it is something needed sometime today. We are also given a map. That is good, now we have some direction.

Take a deep breath and prepare for the unknown. It looks like we will be flying right down the center of the Portal until we get to that very large mountain, then we turn to the left. Let's see what is next once we get there. We don't have to hurry, but I tend to as I get excited for what is next along the way. I know, I tend to get impatient. That is probably one of those lessons I will learn about someday, or maybe not.

Turning left, just as the Portal itself takes a little swirly move. Every time that happens, my stomach does a little flip-flop.

WOW! We just found the Orchards that are being harvested. They are beautiful.

Usually on Earth, ripening is done in stages. For example, tree fruits like cherry, apple, and oranges, are not all ready at the same time. Here, it looks like there is continual ripening and harvesting. The seasons here work for that to happen. This creates a great abundance for everyone all the time. Fresh produce all year long! That would be wonderful.

We are being motioned to come over. It looks like they need us to help them with something. Their harvesting equipment cannot keep up with what is needed done today. We can have some fun with helping them as our Avatars can carry big baskets to the trucks and easily lift a lot of workers to the treetops This will be so fun. I haven't helped with picking fruit like this in a long time.

Oh! Did you notice, this isn't just any fruit. This is as sort of Magic. How we readily give of ourselves in this journey, we get back in multifold what we put out. As I touch an orange, I feel golden coins going into my backpack and then depositing into my bank account. This is fun. Sort of like feeding a piggy bank. I pick a basket of lemons & take them to the truck to have my backpack filled with a variety of coins of a size I have never seen. They just flow right into my account!

I can hear them clinking they swirl around the thing in my backpack then go through some Dimensional jump into my bank account. There is a lot of laughter each time it happens. I have no idea how much money went through this strange process, but I trust it will be awesome. I guess it doesn't matter. It was all a part of fun in Love and Gratitude.

I also love how everyone here is singing as they all work together. It makes the moment of being a part of the harvest so much fun. It is good to have a job that you love combined with people that are Loving and live in a state of Gratitude. Everyone here plays an important part in keeping this Portal working smoothly. It has been an honor to get invited to participate with these loving people.

We complete this day's work in record time and have been invited to a celebration for the evening. You can stay or go back to the Center. I think I will stay. It reminds me of an old-fashioned farm gathering, maybe even a barn dance. People are arriving with covered dishes of great smelling foods and a band is setting up at the other end of the building.

I am amazed how many different types of people are here to participate in this party. There is every age here and something for each of them to do. They even brought their pets. Dogs, cats, and what we would consider wild animals like bears and wolves. My Dragon fits in just fine. He was able to shrink himself a little to get into the building.

I did get another huge surprise within this experience. As we are dancing and singing, the more we laugh and give of ourselves to those around us, the more coins flow into my backpack as well as each other person that was wearing one. Abundance of Money comes with Love and Gratitude. I think laughter helps too. That is a great concept for me to remember.

See you tomorrow!

MONTH ELEVEN – DAY THREE

I am still in a state of Love and Gratitude after the wonderful experience with being a part of the community in this Portal. Getting invited to participate in the local activities is quite an honor of acceptance. I have a feeling that today is going to be something entirely different.

Our Avatars are waiting for us in the stable area. The little walk to get there is good for us to stretch our legs. The cool air is invigorating and waking my intuitive senses on a new level. We are handed a map for the day, and I feel like I already know what it's going to say before I open it. Yes, we are going to the area of the waterfalls.

It is almost the same distance as the orchards but in a different direction. As the Portal turns and swirls within its own vortex, the directions to a specific area are no longer the ones on the compass. They are designated by signs which don't move, like the largest mountain. I want you to know that you are not losing it if you can't figure out what direction you are going. Some people are in tune with the need to know the direction they travel. I think this has something to do with the deprogramming of what we have become accustomed to. Each of us has our areas we will shift in and out of throughout this journey.

Are you ready? I can see where we are going. It isn't too far, and I can hear them. Waterfalls have a distinct sound. Perhaps I am keenly aware of them as I usually don't like anything with water events. And this is why I have to work with them. I have much shifting to do in this area to get this water thing clear. Maybe this time will do it.

I love flying high enough to see the beauty from an overall view. The land is so green in some areas while the leaves in others are turning brilliant oranges, reds, yellows, and many shades in-between. The smells are sharp with a chill bringing them directly to my awareness. I notice the aromas of various pines and spruce.

Being from Colorado, I didn't know there were so many distinct smells of each type. They wake me up. There's something in the pineal gland and how it responds to a specific scent. It really creates a great opening for us to Receive.

The waterfalls are huge. I can see some that are very deep with a spray boiling up from the bottom. Others are so intense the bottom really isn't visible. I can feel the power they create. Then there are some that are tiered. They have short drops, and fall all the way down into a lovely valley. Any ideas what we are to learn here? Which one do you want to explore?

I am ready to explore the multi-tiered one. I see a place to land right after the first tier. There are many shrubs with amazing colors around this area. My Dragon is a little hypersensitive for some strange reason. Maybe there is something in this area to just be aware of. I really want to put my feet into the water for a little bit and enjoy the cool water flowing through my toes.

Oh, I didn't expect this at all. As sit on the bank, there is a fish that swims right up to me and raises itself out of the water so only its fin touches the surface. And, it talks.

It takes me a moment to understand it. I didn't realize that I could. It must be the extra opening in the pineal gland helping with this form of telepathy.

The fish tells me this Cornucopia Portal is ready to give to us what we are ready to receive No more, no less. It is up to us with what we do with our journey here.

As the fish goes back into the water, a very large brown bear comes over to my side and sits down. It starts singing the song from the *Jungle Book*! I recognize the tune right away but had to think about the words. "Just the bare necessities. The simple bare necessities. Forget about your worries and your strife."

It goes on to mention how to be aware of what are picking for your life, or working too hard like the bees, or spending time looking around for something that can't be found. Relax, and let the bare necessities come to you, plus a lot more.

It makes sense as to how we struggle with our worries so much it creates more strife in our life. When we just allow the necessities to come to us ... Well, we do search them out a little, ... we reach out and take them as we notice their availability.

We are to be ready to receive when they float within our grasp, and we don't turn them away saying, "I am not sure if I am ready for that, maybe later." This is sometimes too late. We have the opportunity and the responsibility to take it as presented at that exact moment. We are to then utilize it fully.

That bear and fish had quite a lesson to teach me. I had no idea that Baloo was singing such an important song to Mowgli in *The Jungle Book*. The balance of life can be much easier than what I have made. I have a lot to journal about with this information.

I am ready to ride my wonderful Dragon back to the Center and find my journal before I forget this amazing day.

See you tomorrow!

MONTH ELEVEN – DAY FOUR

I have been told we're going back to the waterfalls. We didn't get to interact on any level with the big one, and it wants us back. The fact that a waterfall wants us to come back is a little odd for me. I have to remember that these Portals are very Magical, and anything can happen.

We have a little notice to bring along swimwear this time. Get it if you want it. Since the air is cooler, it might be nice to wear a wetsuit for that purpose, and bring a towel. Here I am being a mom again. I know you can think for yourself in all of these areas. I just get pulled into that realm sometimes.

We just missed a rain storm over by the falls. Look at that rainbow! It is totally ... well maybe not totally ... different, but very cool colors for a rainbow. I have never seen those shades of purple, orange, red, and blues all mixed together in a very non-logical order. It's odd. Yes, what is so amazing about it is it isn't in the order that we normally see on Earth. It also seems to arch over the whole waterfall area.

Hurry, we need to get there while we can still see this once is a lifetime experience. As the rainbow eliminates the beautiful array of sparkly iridescent colors, it makes changes in the frequencies of each color. For example, if you feel the frequency of red, it has a certain touch to it. If you feel sparkly iridescent red, it has a hint of the normal red but magnified to a whole new level of expansive energy.

As we get closer I can feel an energy coming from it like a tractor beam pulling us in. Due to my experience, I stop for a moment to see if this is a safe thing for us to participate in. Not to be in fear, but to be in a state of curiosity about safety.

I look at it closely to notice the reality of the situation. Are we going to be pulled into the flow down the waterfall and the speed of which it is happening, and is it going to be worth it? As you know by now, going down a waterfall creates a huge energy of caution in me.

Let's get a little closer and take a moment to think about it. Too late. There is no turning back now. So far, okay. I'm still breathing normal. Well, maybe a little excited, but mostly normal. I can feel the magnified effect of the rainbow already. My Dragon also notices it. I can feel the tingling in his skin and see that his teeth are becoming shiny. If that is happening to this big guy, I know something is happening to me.

I can feel us circling around and through each color, then into another one, and back and forth in some areas. I can also feel many of the old energies that held me back in a state of fear are shrinking within me. I can feel my skin sparkle and glow. Not just that little getting married or the having a baby glow. I mean a real sparkly, iridescent glow. Yes, as I look around, I notice others in this space are also starting to glow.

Sometimes it looks really strange as to what the purity of each color can do to you. The sparkly, yellowish-green face I saw on a person next to me was a little creepy at first. I know, I am not used to it being a normal color for a human.

We are going down the waterfall between it and the rainbow. I am glad I have a wetsuit on as that spray is a little chilly. Combining it with the frequency shift from the changing colors often chills me to the bone. This is more intense than I have experienced in a long time. So far, so good.

About midway down, I feel a swirling start to happen and pull me from the rainbow into the waterfall, then back into the rainbow, then back into the waterfall. This is intense. Sort of like repeatedly heating up, then cooling off. It reminds me of how metal workers temper the material they work with. Heat up, do some shifting, then cool down to do it all over and over again until perfect.

I think this is what we are doing here. We are being fine-tuned to be able to do our best in our purpose based on what we are to Be and Do on the Planet. Just like a metalsmith will work with creating a horseshoe so it's perfect in shape, size, and exact form for the horse's foot. And each foot looks alike, but it isn't where most would notice. However only the metal worker himself knows when it is ready. Our fine tuning is that important to us. It is an intense shift for us, but we will be so much better at what are going to be doing that it's worth it.

I notice my Dragon is changing. I am thankful that is happening now as it is difficult when only one changes. The feeling of leaving one behind or being the one that is left behind is very hard for everyone involved. To work together as a team, we need to evolve as a team.

I am ready to head back to the Center. I have much to journal about as I recalibrate.

See you tomorrow!

MONTH ELEVEN – DAY FIVE

WOW! You are glowing even more than when we left the waterfall yesterday. It is a healthier glow, not the weird, iridescent, sparkly glow. Much better. I think we will all have a lot more fun now that we are becoming healthier and more aligned with what our purpose is to be on this Planet.

Today is a good day to go for a ride for fun and see if something important shows up for us to participate in. Our Avatars are ready and seem to be excited about something. Maybe they know something we don't. Critters do tend to have a way with knowing things before we do.

Let's see what's on the other side of the Portal. I think there has been some sort of mining on this wall of the Portal. Let's see what they were looking for. Mines can be a very interesting place to explore as long as we follow the safety rules. There is a place where we can land. I see there are people here to help take care of our wonderful Avatars. They have baskets of food and water for them.

There are two narrow, partially-hidden trails, but I think we can follow one without a problem. It starts to get steep real fast in this area. Let's take the winding, back-and-forth one to make it easier. In order to get to that ledge, we will have to crawl up the last little bit.

Now that we are all dirty, let's see what is inside of that hollowed-out cave. Maybe there is a tunnel that goes further so we can see what they were mining.

This is truly a surprise. There must be a better way to get up here than what we used as everyone here is clean & has been waiting for us. I can see several rooms that go back into the cave, each one decorated with a different theme.

This first one is all about a jungle. It has vines, streams, and a rain-forest feeling. Let's explore it first. We are given a shovel and told to take off our shoes. That is very strange, as I usually wear my sturdiest boots when I use a shovel, but okay, I will follow the rules of the journey.

We are being led to a small stream & asked to walk out into it with our shovel. We can dig anywhere we want. First, I want to know what we are looking for, and do we get to keep it if we find it? Yes, we get to keep what we find. Now they are hesitating to tell me what it is we're digging for. They must be picking up a vibe about me that I may not be too happy with this.

I think I know. It reminds me of a movie I left with a shocked feeling, swearing an oath that I would never buy another one again. Diamonds. I guess it is time for me to get over my feeling about the stone based on the movie.

Start digging when you are ready. You can use your shovel or your toes. Just notice what you find. I see many people finding some amazingly-sized stones. These are already cut and ready to utilize.

Oh, my goodness, I just felt something under my toes. I can feel how it is already sending a current of energy through me to clear my negative attitudes toward diamonds. Of course, the stone is not the cause of my prejudice, it was the people in the movie *Blood Diamonds* and how they mutilated the people who mined and their families. It was their greed that turned me away from this beautiful stone. I had developed a complete repulsion of diamonds since watching the movie. I guess now is the time for me to start some understanding and clear this energy I put this on myself based on an emotion that didn't belong to the stone.

I now feel an amazing energy coming off it. I am beginning to get an affinity for this stone. I feel the energy of the numerous diamonds within this stream. We are to each take as many as we can carry.

I am shocked at that, as I was totally thrilled to have an affinity for only one. Of course, I don't want to be greedy either. Perhaps that is another emotion which interferes with Receiving – not wanting to be one that wants money to cause greediness. That is another way of pushing wealth away, another way of not being able to Receive. Oh, the lessons we learn in these Portals.

I finally realize I can be good with taking more than one stone. It's a huge lesson for me to accept what is given to me. I am not comfortable with filling my pack up to the top, but two-thirds is good.

I love the vibration they give off as they are on my back. It is like the diamond is healing a part of me that has held me back. How do you feel with these stones? Can you feel the vibration of them, or do you recognize them for a different value? This is a great Moncy Code Clearing for me.

Once I have my backpack on, I am escorted out to the front of the cave. Maybe I can tour the other caves at another time. I am shown not to climb back down the way we came. There is an easier way for us to get back down so we can return to the Center.

As I stand at the cave opening, I call to my Dragon. He is right there, hovering, ready for me to climb on. This is so much easier than climbing around in the dirt.

I am ready to go back to the Center, are you? I am excited to dump out my pack to see if I can learn more about these diamonds. It will be great to journal about this very large experience.

The clearing of my dislike of the diamond shifted. I now totally accept its healing energy. Perhaps I need to journal on this to not forget where I once was to where I am now.

See you tomorrow!

MONTH ELEVEN – DAY SIX

I must say that yesterday was quite intense for me. I had no idea I carried so much energy related to how *Blood Diamonds* had affected me many years ago. I am thankful for the experience of healing I had with a specific diamond. It will be a stone that I will cherish forever.

I am also surprised how the reverse energy of Not Having, in relation to Not Wanting to be Greedy, still resided within myself as well as others I know. That was a great experience in the process of me being able to receive Abundance in the form of diamonds and not feel guilty. It also helped for me to journal and meditate on it for a while. I feel like a new person, ready to take on another adventure.

We are halfway through our time in the Cornucopia of Abundance Portal. I am amazed how much has already happened with this journey. Are you ready for some more shamanic adventures? Let's see what is in store for us today.

My silly Dragon is ready to go. I can hardly hold him back. This is not like him at all. I see your Avatars are also ready to go. I think we really need to hang on for a while and let them get their energy out. We need to try to stay together in some sort of a group, at least maintain contact with our headsets. You did bring yours, didn't you? I think it was one of the main things that comes with the backpacks we were issued. Good. Now I feel better since we are all within contact range this way.

I'm surprised that we are all headed the exact same direction. I am not sure what is over there, but our magical beasts seem to know. It looks like some sort of farming area. As we get closer I can see grapes.

Of course, grapes are usually one of the items in all of the pictures of Cornucopias that I have seen. These are not just grown for wine purposes. They are ones you eat. The arbors are quite different than what I have seen before. They are enormous. We can fly through their arches, but we shouldn't, so as not to destroy them.

There is a very magical set that we are to participate within. It is just off to the side at the farm next door. The arbors there are made for our magical critters to fly through. The grapes hanging down are also a variety of colors, similar to what we have in our Earth stores. Yet, something is different. Let's take a closer look. For one thing, they are like see-through bubbles with little words inside of them.

They have specific qualities for those that have a certain need. They are of various sizes, shapes, and flavors. I hope they are seedless … Just one of my little quirky things. As you fly through the arbors, take your time and pick the ones you feel you need. Gather several bunches you are attracted to. We can sit at those tables under that large tree to taste them.

I have three bunches, and I'm very curious how they will taste. I grow grapes in my backyard, and if they are not perfectly ripe, they aren't very good. Some of the skins can be really tart. Since I have tasted some truly nasty ones, I am a little hesitant about trying these. You don't have to wait for me. Go ahead and eat what you gathered. Well, here goes.

Oh, they are amazing. The words inside of them are good as well, just a little chewy like a candy my kids used to beg for. I think they were called gummy worms. Can you tell what the words are in yours? I am not sure what language mine are, but I trust them to be what my body needs.

I have eaten one of my three bunches and am feeling the energy from the words. I notice my stomach is nice and calm. It seems to be really liking whatever they consist of. I feel this second bunch is for my Dragon. They are quite a bit larger than the others, just the right size for a Dragon to munch on. Yep, he loved them. However, they put him to sleep. Maybe it will be a short nap.

The third bunch I picked is now calling to me that it is their turn. I can actually read the words inside of some of them. Love, Gratitude, *Ho'oponopono*, Thank You, and Abundance. Other words attached to it like Money, Health, Freedom, and Time. There are so many that I can't read them all. They just keep repeating these words throughout the entire bunch. Yes, they taste just as awesome as those words are. They make my entire body tingle with a nice, relaxed feeling. How are yours?

My Dragon finally woke up. We have a choice to fly through the arbors again and pick more if you feel like you need them, and then head back to the Center as you are ready. Or, we can just take our time flying back.

Remember to thank the person that created this amazing place for us and the bounty that we were able to consume.

See you tomorrow!

MONTH ELEVEN – DAY SEVEN

It is time for us to prepare to move deeper into this Cornucopia of Abundance Portal. Due to the structure of the Portal, it continually moves in a vortex like a tornado, but slower, and we are in the middle of it as it moves through the Universe. We entered the larger end where it was easy to get into. We will exit the smaller part. It is like we get scrubbed up, wrung out and put out the other end all clean and ready to move in a better direction than when we started.

As we move through it, we get a place to stay. This time it was the very nice Center, but this was at the beginning of the Portal. Now that we are moving the other direction rather rapidly, we must relocate ourselves for the last half of this journey. The Center will be sort of closing itself up and lifting off to go on down further toward the other end. It is like a spacecraft had landed which we utilized for the past several days. It is going to lift off and go down into the Portal near the other end. We will leave from here today, but meet up with this Center in the evening in a little different environment.

I really should have explained all of that to you at the beginning. I guess I didn't think of it until today. It will be quite an easy transfer. Your belongings will be exactly where you left them within the building.

If you are ready, we can leave in a few minutes for a new adventure. The Portal is quite active today with all of the moving taking place, so I have been advised to not go as high as we usually do. This is fine, because we can actually see what is going on below us easier if we fly lower. Let's get in the air and see what adventure awaits us today.

WOW! It is very interesting that, from this height, this Portal actually does look like a Cornucopia. There is a twisting of the sides from the inside. It is cool to see how the pumpkin and squash areas looks like twisting vines from deep inside. The corn is off to one side, the grapes are off to another. Oh, we have an area of where cabbage and cauliflower-type plants are grown. Then there are the apples and oranges, actually, the various orchards, plus other things that are grown in trees to eat. The layout is beautiful.

As we go deeper into this Portal it is getting darker, just like when fall moves into winter. We are able to see different lights flashing in the sky and creating some great visual effects. They also generate an electric current in the air that shifts the vibrational field of the water molecules. Oh, wait, that is us, as we are also made up of so much water. It is strange how I can breathe easier right after each one of the flashings occur. Can you tell a difference within yourself in an area? Some say that their aches and pains are less during this time while others claim to have more pain and are more tired. I find them fascinating. I heard amazing stories about them but never actually saw them for myself.

We are getting close to the fields where the potatoes and carrots are grown, the root plants. Let's see what these fields have for us in the way of why are we here. I am shown how they are planted in the ground. The growth above is what we see while the harvestable part below growing in ways we never know until we dig them up. In order to know when it is time to dig, the part above ground often starts to die back a little telling us that it is time to prepare to harvest.

Perhaps the best way to learn about this is to participate. We are given a shovel and a basket. Start digging with great care as we don't want to damage the produce. A quick shovel jabbing into the ground can cut a potato in half or slice through a carrot or onion. It may not destroy the plant immediately, and it can be cleaned and eaten if done so very soon.

However, the damage gives room for germs and rot to set in. So, it won't do well being kept in the bin with the other produce. Once one starts to rot, so does the rest. There is also the possibility of it not being cleaned properly, it will heal back without rotting but the damaged area is still there in an active mode.

Interesting how this relates to our lives and relationships with family and those around us. The little jabs with words can fester for many years destroying what was once planted. Sometimes there can be a healing around it if the desire is there. Taking care to be Loving with those around us can heal those wounds and, better yet, not even have them.

This is creating a lot of things to think about as we travel to the Center. I am thankful that collars with beacons in them were placed on our Avatars before we left. We can find the Center in the dark as it will be soon.

See you tomorrow!

MONTH ELEVEN – DAY EIGHT

Welcome to this new day. Lots of journaling about this Portal journey, and I don't usually journal. I am usually one that just makes a new day from what shows up as I look at my calendar.

As we go through these experiences from within the Portals, notice if you feel differently, need more sleep, have more energy, or react differently from what you normally would to various triggers. Or, maybe there's nothing different. Each is important. The main thing is to notice is what if anything has changed from when we started.

Since we are over halfway through this Portal I started regretting that we hadn't gone back to the Diamond Cave, because there were other rooms I wanted to explore. This morning, I was told that it isn't in our best interest to go back there, with the emphasis on the word "back." I got it. We are to look forward to what is new and exciting each day. So, I asked my Team what are we to explore and learn today. I was shown a hologram of an area not too far from here. It is like … Well, I will show you once we get there.

I think this is the fastest I have ever seen you get ready to leave. I have been given a real cool tool that I didn't know existed. It can display a holographic map right in front of us that we can all see. Look at how it is a tunnel with various turns and an elevator going down several levels into this new area. Now we know exactly where we are going. It isn't too far. Once we get there, it looks like we are to fly into the tunnel. Okay, let's find it.

This is really nice. It is a huge tunnel, well-lit and big enough for us to continue flying through. We turn right at the next opening, then left at the first new opening. Now we are at an elevator. Amazing how we all fit as we go down. I feel a little uneasiness in the Avatars, or maybe it is just me. I get a little claustrophobic in underground places.

I think we went down five floors. It is still well lit down here. We can walk on that path. Our Avatars can stay in this area near the elevator.

The path is getting narrower, and I see a deep drop off. As I turn the corner, the path stops but there is a ramp to a sort of train. It doesn't have a top on it or very tall sides, but there are enough cars for us.

It zooms over an area as deep as the Grand Canyon, and it is starting to feel like a roller coaster with a lot of flips and turns, but not as jerky as most of those rides. It seems to have a directional purpose.

I still wonder why we are in here. I have to do some real deep breathing once in a while to not go into a claustrophobic panic.

Whoa, we are finally pulling up to a place to get out. There is a path with doors going both directions. We are each given a key and told to find the door just for us, then walk through it. Oh, but just before you walk through, have in your mind and heart what you want to do with your life. It doesn't matter if you know how to do it, just think of it and feel it.

As you walk through your door, notice there is a person to greet you that looks like you are doing exactly what you said you want to. Take a little walk with this person. Get to know them, have a cup of tea, and watch their mannerisms.

Is this really what you want to do and be? If it is, ask this person to merge with you. If you realize that it isn't what you want, just walk back out the door. I will be with you shortly.

To do this merge, just sit quietly. Have a little talk with the Creator to know this is all done in the highest of Truth, Love and Gratitude, and you will be completely safe in the process of becoming the new You.

Focus on your breath for several inhales and exhales. Don't rush it. As you feel your vibrations start to change, notice when it aligns with the You you're ready to become.

Keep breathing, stay calm. Feel this new You meld into you. Now, as you stand up, how do you feel? Take a moment to see if this is really a match for you. If it isn't, just shake it off. It is all about your intent. If it feels wonderful and right, take a moment to walk around and notice how your legs and feet are moving, then your arms and hands. See how your brain and heart feel. If you feel complete, walk to the door and step through.

WOW! That was incredible. I am ready to be the new Me! Not sure what that encompasses just yet, but it feels good.

I am not as claustrophobic as I was, but I am so ready to get back up to the ground floor. As I stand on this ledge waiting for the train to come back for us, I have another idea. Let's call our Avatars and see if they can find us. I see an opening directly above where we can fly out of here.

That was fast! I am always so surprised when my Dragon just has a way of showing up for me. Yours is here too! This is so wonderful. Now we can just take our time riding the air currents as we go all the way up and out, through that place where I can see outside light coming in. I am heading to the Center so I can really integrate and recalibrate all that just happened.

See you tomorrow!

MONTH ELEVEN – DAY NINE

Well, that was quite an experience! I didn't know it could be that easy to learn something new. I once heard of a plan to embrace your doppelgänger to find the real You. Maybe that is what it meant.

We are getting near the end of our journey within this Portal, and there is so much more in here I want to experience. What do we do first in this part of the Cornucopia? Of course, I want to travel by means of flying with my Dragon. It is hard enough to let him stay in the stables instead of my room, but I do realize a Dragon needs his own space. As we are discussing the day via telepathy, we have agreed to start with flying really high right down the center of this Portal.

Ready? Let's go! We are gaining altitude really fast so we can be in the upper wind currents. It makes flying and staying on easier for all of us. It is quite awesome to see the whole place from up here. You can't see the details but the colors and outlines of some of the areas are laid out beautifully.

It is nice to be floating along up here, I see what looks to be a circular sort of thing which seems to be a gateway. I don't really know what else to call it. It is like a huge metallic sort of energy that stays in a circle form with some angelic looking symbols along its edges. The energy flows back and forth and around the perimeter all at the same time. I am not at all sure what it is for or where it came from.

Let's get closer to have a better look. We could go around it, but with it right on our path in the clouds, we can just take a nice look at it. The thoughts that come to mind are scalar technology, but I don't really know for sure.

It is preparing to open just as we gather to look at it for our own wants. Of course, those that have also been praying for it are a key factor here. What sort of prayer creates a Star Gate? That is new to me. I do recognize the Angelic writing on the edges, and that is a good sign.

As it opens I hear music to assist us in clearing some old fear codes. The fears of the unknown. Just because we haven't heard of it or experienced it before does not make it bad or harmful. Take a moment and feel what you are experiencing inside. Get grounded, make certain of your connection to the Creator.

Now, evaluate the situation. This is an important lesson in how to work with your life, just like walking into an interview or a business meeting, a courtroom, or even a family gathering. It is all about the unknown and how to evaluate your-Self within the situation and how to know you are going to be okay with it.

I feel like I want to get closer and maybe go through it. Sometimes the best experiences are from the unknown. Yes, I am ready to fly into the center of it. Dragon is okay with this idea, too, so I am certain I will be safe.

It is a little cool to my skin as I enter into this Molecular Shifting energy. I can feel it going through me sort of like an MRI goes through a body taking multiple pictures of everything. This seems to be going through me and shifting every one of my cells into a cleaner, higher spectrum of function. My immune system feels free of the debris that was clogging it up in places. My heart and blood vessels feel clean and new. My bones feel stronger and aligned with themselves. My muscles are more flexible and strong. This is a very good Star Gate. It is sort of like the Regeneration machine I have heard about on some of the space stations on the Mother ships.

Now I understand how this was manifested. I had heard of some people praying or asking for a Regeneration tool. Yes, we have various energy classes to learn how to regenerate one's self, but, due to belief systems, sometimes they work and sometimes they don't. I can see this as being a tool that would work for those brave enough to walk through it.

Are you ready? Just fly right through the center. You will notice right away a different feeling within your cells. Sometimes, the first place I notice is in my eyes. They seem to be the most sensitive. Or, perhaps, it's what I notice first. Take time to breathe in the changes and allow your body to receive what it needs. If you need to do it again, just get back in line and go through with the intent of the outcome you are ready for.

I think I will send a hologram of this to my place on Earth. I want it in my healing room where it will be easy access to me and my clients. I may want to sleep in it. That is how good it helped me feel.

I am so glad we found this tool in here. Wow! I can feel myself growing a lot of new cells. I did ask my body to regenerate NEW stem cells instead of expecting the old ones to do a very difficult job for old cells. I can feel it happening.

Of course, it is all about intent. What do you want? Do you believe it is possible to have it? So much of our receiving change is done not from Belief but from Faith and Trust. If you are still in a state of belief, you are still waiting for it to happen. This is holding yourself in a stagnant space of waiting and believing that it will come about. The state of Faith and Trust is a state of Knowing. Perhaps that is one of the reasons you're on this journey, to obtain the process of regaining your Faith and Trust not only in the Creator but in yourself.

I am ready to get to the Center and let myself work on this recalibration, maybe while sitting in a warm, soothing bath.

See you tomorrow!

MONTH ELEVEN – DAY TEN

I can't believe we are already on day ten of this journey of the Cornucopia of Abundance and Gratitude. I have noticed how everywhere we have ventured within this Portal, we are given all that we could ever imagine. I have also noticed how we have had our hearts open with levels of Gratitude for the changes these experiences have created for us.

I do want to remind you that any time you need to experience one of the day's adventures to create a deeper shift within you, all you have to do is take yourself back to that experience. Take your time as each of these experiences can be very helpful if you are ready to receive what is offered. Also, some days may have been more in-tune with you than others, and, when you review a journey, perhaps a different day will resonate more. Every day is a new vibrational shift and need.

Today is an experience that just showed itself to me, and I will do my best to take you through it. We will be given a backpack with a variety of items that we may need throughout this day. One that was shown to me was a knife. It wasn't a basic knife used in the kitchen. It is a much stronger one with a black handle and a blade that is about six to eight inches long with a little curve at the tip. It's also very sharp. Take it out of your backpack. The sheath that it is in can be threaded through your belt. This way, it is easy access as required. I have no idea what it may be needed for right now.

The Portal is narrowing as we get closer to its end. The rotation is shorter and finer. It will not affect us or where we are going. However, the light can play tricks on us if we are not paying attention. It will be like a day and night will go by really fast and each one of our days may consist of two or three of these cycles.

We are going to be flying on our Avatars toward that mountain. It is actually quite large for this area. There is a place there with attendants for our Avatars. The cave we are going into is very big. There is a film over the entrance. I am not sure what it is made of. Perhaps my Dragon can burn through it. Yes, it was quite easy with his fire. Then he used his huge claws to drag it out of our way to finish burning it in a safer location.

I wonder what created it or why it is covering the entrance we were directed to enter. There is a fire going just inside with stools around it for us to sit upon. There is a pot of vegetable soup ready for us. It looks like they are using a lot of the vegetables found in traditional Cornucopias. It smells wonderful, even the cabbage-types of plants, onions, carrots, and many I am not familiar with. This gives us a little time to rest and get to know each other some more.

I see there is a person in charge of this cave who is also a teacher. This teacher is specialized in ancient beliefs of many civilizations throughout this Universe. She is explaining how the cave covering is similar to those that surround each of us. It is the entanglements that we carry around related to our families, our jobs, our friends, and all of their problems which get dumped on us.

Some of these entanglements have been carried over for generations of lifetimes. Right now, there are a lot of entanglements related to our belief systems and how they connect to what we want life to be and what it is turning out to be and how they don't match. Then there are even more entanglements in what is going on with what we see in the media. Some of it we can tune out, but sometimes it feels like the webs of entanglement just jump out of the technologies to pull us into their ideas. Perhaps we don't consciously believe all that is going on, but it still influences us.

As she talks I notice the entanglement strings on myself and many of us around this campfire. They are of various thicknesses. Some are so fine they looks like a fuzzy cloud encompassing a person. Some are a little thicker string-like micro filaments, and others are even thicker, like ropes of many variations of size and color.

So, what do we do with this now that we know about it? Of course, that is next in our lesson. We are being instructed to take out our very strong, sharp knife and bring it right to our heart area with the blade facing out or away from you. Now, we are to start cutting all of the entanglements away with the intent of them never coming back. As you get a pile of it, put it on the fire.

Cords are a huge form of energy stealing as well as power and control. The cords, even those from a chakra area to a loved one, are not appropriate to be there at all times. As we interact with each other, there is a stream of energy that flows between us. Once the interaction no longer happens, the cords should also be gone. Also, be mindful of your interacting cords so they are only of clear communication, not being used to sway a person into your belief system. I also need to clarify that this is not the same as a parent-child relationship with apron strings. That is another lesson.

Once you are clear of your cords and have all of them burned by the fire, put away your knife and know that, at any time you need to cut away cords, you can call upon it to be there.

It is now time for us to leave this teacher. I give her many thanks for her time and knowledge. I reach into my backpack and give her one of the diamonds still in there. Her knowledge is valued beyond what can be paid, but the diamond is the currency of here in this moment.

I am ready to ride to the Center and let myself recalibrate and perhaps do a little journaling about these many lessons.

See you tomorrow for our last ride in the Portal!

MONTH ELEVEN – DAY ELEVEN

This is our last day in this Cornucopia of Divine Abundance Portal. I feel like this has been an amazing journey of experiences that I would never have had the opportunity to participate in if it hadn't been for you going with me. Thank you for showing up!

Today is going to be awesome as well. Let's find our Avatars and go for one last ride within this Portal. My Dragon is always ready to get out there and see what we have the opportunity to experience before we have to leave.

As we fly over this lower area of the Portal, there is a pond calling to us. From the height of where we are, it looks just like an ordinary pond, but, once we are down here near it, I can see it has some surprises for us. To start with, I have never seen so many blooming lily pads with frogs and dragonflies on them. There are people along the edge of the pond, and they are directing us to land over to a side that has more room. It is very nice here.

I see there has been a picnic arranged for us. There is a table of food and a larger one set up with a Cornucopia in the middle, but without the normal harvest bounty that we would expect. Instead, it has a bounty of gifts displayed within it and pouring out onto the table for us.

We are starting a little Thank You ceremony where everyone is gathered around the large table holding hands. Each of us are being given the opportunity to voice what we are thankful for. It can be anything from before coming here or something that you have experienced within this adventure we have been on.

There is also the opportunity to not voice anything if you so choose. I am impressed with how loving everyone is as we go around the circle. The comments bring me to tears. This Portal is one that I will never forget.

I see some have brought musical instruments where we can sing along with the group. There is also a place for dancing if anyone wants to. Some have also brought along equipment for playing outside games like volleyball and soccer. There are even water balloons and bubbles for the little ones. This group is overflowing with an Abundance of Love and Support for each other.

It has been shared with us that, as you feel it is time for your turn, go to the large table and pick one of the gifts. I find it hard to choose as they are all wrapped so similarly. I won't be able to select based on the color of the wrapping paper or the type of ribbon. I will just have to pick one as it feels like it is for me. This is a whole new way of making a choice.

Now, this is a very interesting situation. As each person takes a gift, it is as if the Cornucopia creates another one. Each time, the table is again filled with an abundant supply of gifts. We are then told to take another turn as we are to really experience what it is like to have an overflowing of Abundance right before us to witness. We can continue with this process as many times as we want. I am amazed at just watching how this happens. It is an endless supply of Giving & Receiving.

When there is that much abundance, there is no need for Greed or Lack to be experienced. What you need is always there. Just reach out and receive it.

Your gifts are for you to open at the moment you wish. It can be done within the Portal or take them with you for later.

It is time to complete our ride to the exit of this Portal. There is a place to leave your Avatar for the next time, or you can shrink him and take him with you in your backpack. Mine is with me all the time, just in a different Dimension. It can be brought into my world at a moment's notice.

We are to go through the Center building as that is where the exit is located. It is a very small opening that, as you walk through the door, you are teleported back to your real world with all of the experiences you have processed to be a part of your life. You can incorporate the new You into your life as you wish. Thank you for being a part of this journey with me.

See you next month!

See you soon with Truth, Love, and Gratitude

Pat, The Cosmic Cowgirl

Journal the Changes Made in the Cornucopia of Abundance & Gratitude

CHAPTER TWELVE: WINTER INTROSPECTION & WHITE BUFFALO CALF WOMAN

MONTH TWELVE – DAY ONE

With this being the final session, month twelve of the Divine Money Portal, it is like going into the winter months. Winter is a time of going inside to rest, recalibrate, and take the time to find the part of Oneself that has been going into the caterpillar/chrysalis phase to finalize the metamorphosis for the renewal of Oneself. It means preparing for the New Year, or the new aspect of Oneself, and incorporating all of the changes we have been creating in order to access and receive the Divine Abundance that is here for us. Let's get started.

I can see the Divine Portal up ahead a short distance. It is spinning a whirling mass of white. It sort of looks like going into white out conditions at night with headlights in a blinding snow that is being blown all directions at once.

Are you ready? We are going to start on this journey already having our Avatars. We are prepared for this journey. If you don't have your Avatar ... remember it is a large magical critter that flies which you can ride ... just create one in your mind. Make it fun but not scary.

We can now enter this Portal right into the center of the spinning white. Just like the eye of a tornado. Wow! I am so glad it wasn't freezing cold like a real blizzard. This is beautiful in here, a magical and peaceful vibration, like drifting at a fast pace with everything spinning around us but not affecting us. Now it is leveling out as we are actually going into the Portal itself.

It was like we just flew right into a very high-end facility that we will stay in for a while. There are individual rooms already prepared for each of us. We don't have to share our sacred space. They also have a place created for our magical creatures. This is an amazing Center for us to receive and utilize as we need.

Many years ago, as I was walking through a bookstore wondering what I was in there for, a book called *White Buffalo Calf Woman*, actually fell off of a shelf and landed on my foot. Of course, I bought it, seeing it as a sign to pay attention. Since then, I have felt the White Buffalo Calf Woman around me as one of my guides. I am certain we will get some information directly from her throughout this series of messages. It is time for us to meet in the conference room. Right now, we will hear a little from her.

We are all here for a reason at this time on the Planet. We are very lucky to have the facilities we have to live in and the food so readily available. How often do we take that for granted? There was a time when the winters were so harsh that hunters could not go out to find anything for their tribes to eat. If we had not been taught to create storage large enough to weather out the storm, many would die. That seldom happens now. It is strange enough to experience on-going hunger, or freezing to the bone cold for days on end. In the times we live in now, we are gifted with a great ease with this part of our lives.

Now we are learning to receive on many other levels. Take a moment to think about how. As a person is at work all day to earn the money to pay for the things that the hunters would bring in, there is a constant complaint of the dislike for work or the aches and pains the physical body is undergoing. There are also traumas of dealing with an elderly parent or ill, unruly children. We have bills to pay, shopping to do before going home, and cleaning & maintaining the home. Of course, there is the hurrying from this point to that point to get there on time.

This and much more creates a level of stress within Oneself that is damaging to the physical body as well as the mind. In turn, this creates an energy that radiates out to all of those who are human and non-human. The entire Planet is being affected by this constant turmoil. This is also a part of Needy and Greedy energy around us, including the entitlement of "Mine. Now." Energy.

So, we went from the basic survival needs to a new way of what survival is and how to participate in it. This creates a different type of damage to ourselves. It is time to embrace what is wonderful with Loving Peace. We can now create within ourselves the moments we need to shift out of the grumblings of our day-to-day routine to Loving each moment. We can Love what we do, where we go, and those we interact with each day. It is a choice.

Take a moment to remember the work you are involved with. Visualize the people you are in contact with on a family level. Visualize those you interact with at work. You may not be able to see the exact person, but you will recognize the energy signatures of those that utilize your offerings. Let yourself breathe deeper. Go into your Heart Space and feel a Peace. Let it radiate out into an energy of Love. Visualize those that you work with also radiating this Love and Peace.

Notice how you feel. Breathe deeper into your lungs. Breathe out the frustration and trauma. Breathe into Yourself deeper, and breathe out Love and Peace. This will take some practice, but it is very important we do this.

The Winter of being with White Buffalo Calf Woman is a sacred journey. Take some time to prepare for our continuing trip! Breathe into the sacred space within you.

See you tomorrow!

MONTH TWELVE – DAY TWO

Welcome to our second day within this Divine Portal of Abundance with so many things to explore and create within our own Divine Space. We will continue to experience levels of Love and Peace within ourselves as we work with breathing out the frustration as we breathe in the Love and Peace.

We will be going for a walk within this Portal today. We will exit this Center on the north end. You will notice the main entrance and exit is on the north end because North is significant within the energy of ending of the Old and beginning Anew, just like as we move into the winter solstice where darkness starts the process of growing into the light again. Also, it is a time we associate with great joy. In the tribal times, there were ceremonies around this to chase away the darkness and call forth the sun.

As we exit through the north doorway, we will walk down the path on the right. It follows a stream on your left. There is evidence that Jack Frost visited here last night! For those that don't know, he is one of the many Fairy beings that help create the beautiful paintings at night of the ice crystals on the glass and outside plants when it is freezing.

Take a close look at the blades of grass or the branches on the trees. The delicate frost is beautiful from a distance! Now get a closer look.

You will see that each speck of frost on that blade of grass is made up of many specks, each unique unto themselves. This is a sample of going from the macro to the micro level of examining something. Each macro aspect is dependent on the makeup of the many micros. Each is perfect. If there is a change in the micro area it will create a change in the macro.

A change isn't a bad thing. It just creates a little different aspect of what the item is that we had pictured it to be in our minds. This is the same for the makeup of everything.

As we continue down this path, notice you don't have to be bundled up to stay warm. You will be the temperature that you want to be and remain comfortable as we change locations. That is the magic of being in this Portal. We are walking in the Fairy realm of the winter woods. They have prepared an area for us to explore ahead. The trail winds up this hill about halfway where it flattens out. There are rows and rows of caves with different doors on each one. We can enter one of the three caves open at this moment.

The first one radiates a golden orange color that I can see as I get closer. I think I will go inside to see what is causing this color to be so strong. I can feel the energy of it flow through me as I step across the invisible boundary. It is a specific energy of Compassion.

This is really strong as it moves through my body and is affecting my lower chakra systems to start with. I can feel a relaxation and expansion throughout my entire sacral area. There is a sort of awakening pulse clearing out old patterns of beliefs. Some are the Not Good Enough patterns related to being male or female. Some are related to having to only participate in certain activities, such as sports or jobs, due to being male or female. There is also a clearing about having to act a certain way due to what age you are. This includes what class you are in at school, or acting a certain way as a grandparent, or being expected to retire at a certain age.

The golden light energy is now continuing up my spine where it is interacting with the other chakra systems. As these energies clear I feel lighter and, the achiness in my hips and lower back seem to be lessening. My digestive system feels like it is lighter, so I can easily adjust to what I eat. My spine feels more flexible. It is getting easier to breathe and my neck has more range of motion. I can feel my brain shifting also. When you are ready, you may walk from that cave into the next one.

As I cross the threshold of the orange gold into the white gold, I can feel all my energy centers filling with Peace and Love. The emptied-out areas are filling with a Newness. It feels like my original Blueprint is being brought in and activated with new stem cells.

These stem cells are creating the healthy aspects of various parts of my body on the physical level. As the physical starts to feel more alive, there is a greater openness for the energy centers to pulse stronger and with a steady vibrancy. It is like the heartbeat of Me is being recreated. I actually feel myself vibrating higher and smoother, if that makes any sense at all. My brain is not able to take all of this in as it is so out of the normal realm of thinking. My guides tell me to remember that anything is possible.

I am now being led into a cave where I can just re adjust for the moment. I am given a refreshing glass of herbal tea to drink. It has been activated with the Life Force that we are to be using in all our food and drink. This is a great reminder that we would be healthier if we did that to everything we consumed. I am now capable of walking back to the Center and my room. I find that I do need a little time to recalibrate from all this amazing shifting.

See you tomorrow!

MONTH TWELVE – DAY THREE

We are still in the phase of winter. To some, it would be represented by the purity of the white snow, the cleansing crispness of the air, clearer thinking, a vibrant outlook of moving into a New World as the sun comes back out to shine on the sparkling, frozen water particles. To others, the white snow represents freezing cold, lack of food, a depressed and difficult time for survival. Where are you in this phase?

Neither one of these is representative of how much money is in your pocket. It is actually what is in your heart and mind that creates this reality that you live in. Of course, we have been conditioned to believe it is all about Money, and Money does make most things easier. Let's see where this Divine Money and Abundance Portal takes us today.

We will be venturing out the north door and taking the path next to the one we did before, except a little to the right. Our Avatars are awaiting us! We get to fly just low enough to keep the path in sight. Sometimes it is a little hard to see through the frosted, snow laden trees.

As we look at the way a path is seen from above, we can follow it. The trees may not be quite as close together in areas, and, once in a while, a speck of bare ground shows the path. You can see how it zigzags around in some areas from this vantage point. Since we are above it we don't have to follow the path step by step.

This also means we don't have to walk through the heavy snow or the frozen streams and tall grasses. We can fly over the switchbacks. Sort of ... how does the saying go? It is five miles as the crow flies, but walking it may be seven or 10 miles. Getting to our destination is so much easier this way.

I see a flattened out clearing up ahead. It feels like this is where we are to land. There is a frozen lake with a path leading up to a castle. Let's follow the path. I feel the excitement ahead. We are being greeted with a whole procession of people carrying flags and playing music. It is like they were expecting us, and we are right on time. We are being put into the middle of their parade of celebration. I asked one what the celebration of today was about. I was told it is the Celebration of life. Each day, we are given the opportunity to live life to its fullest, and this is another one of those days. What a great reminder! Every day is a Celebration of Life.

As we near the end of the parade route, we are escorted to another path leading directly into the castle. We are presented to the Queen of the North. I am surprised how much she looks like White Buffalo Calf Woman, just different clothing and, of course the amazing throne she sits upon. She also has on each side of her white Dragons instead of the white buffalo. Both are very much protectors of the Light.

She is so excited to see us. She had a feast prepared where there is anything to eat that we can imagine. The table we are being escorted to is as long as we imagine it to be. One moment, I saw it as a normal-sized table, then I saw that someone in the group thought "Huge, castle-sized table," and it became that with even more exquisite foods. Those from outside came and ate their fill. When they left, the table was as if it had not been touched. It was a never-ending bounty for everyone. When everyone was finished eating, it all went back to normal. Normal sized table with nice decorations in the middle.

At one end of the room I noticed a gift table. As each person finished eating, they were to take as many gifts as they wanted from it. Some people took an armful, while others just took one. This table also was never empty.

This reminded me of Bible story about feeding the multitudes with a few fish and loaves of bread. The baskets were never empty as everyone there ate their fill. I think the key here is to bless each aspect of our day as we move through life. Be happy and of great cheer. Love each moment and what is presented.

When our hearts are full of Love and Gratitude, there is a never-ending supply of what we need awaiting us. It is up to us to reach out and receive.

The Queen of the North is asking us to follow her into another room. She seems to know the dilemma we are dealing with. This new room is full of snowballs. I can see frequency codes within each of them. They are not readable, just symbols of energy that can help with what we need. There are so many of them with similar codes related to Fear and Victim states. She is demonstrating that, every once in a while, she has her people come in here and play with the snowballs to help them maintain their Loving vibrations.

To play with the snowballs we can pop them on top of our own heads, or eat them, or throw them at each other like a real snowball fight. I think we are to just breathe and consciously pick one at a time and put it on our body where we think we need it. They don't melt and become wet -- they meld into the body. For example, this one I am putting on my heart because it feels like it needs to be there. This other one feels like it needs to be on my knee that I thought had healed from an injury, but it still retained some fear of being hurt again. Yes, I can feel a difference.

This is a very important room to assist us in recognizing that we can receive anything we need. Take your time and consciously pick the snowball that you need and put it where it tells you. Breathe in the frequency of it into all of you – the physical, mental, emotional, and spiritual aspects. Once you are finished, take your time getting back to the Center. I am certain that your Avatar will be able to find the way back for you.

See you tomorrow!

MONTH TWELVE – DAY FOUR

Welcome to this glorious day! The sun is shining, and it is sparkly outside with its reflections coming off the snow and frost. This is the most wondrous time of the day in the dark of the year. The nights are still growing longer as the days grow shorter. Soon that will change, but, for now, I chose to enjoy each moment I can be in the sun.

Our Avatars are already waiting for us just outside the door as we will be flying to a very special event. We are given a map to follow. I present to my Dragon as he is better with maps than I am, and I trust him completely with following this type of direction. I am excited to see you are also ready for a new experience and prepared to receive what new and exciting event is coming our way.

Yes, we can fly as fast as we want to for a while. I am not sure how far this is but flying fast is always fun for me, however I still like to see the terrain we go over. Okay, we will fly fast at a higher elevation so I am not tempted to dive down to investigate. I should have guessed that, at this height, we would be going through the snow clouds. Oh, they are so sparkly inside. Slow down, I want to know more about this experience. As we know, we live in the moment of time where each experience is to be received for the moment it is delivered or made available to us.

As the sparkles get on my skin, they tingle and create an iridescent glow, like plants in the sun. Silly, but it reminds me of the *Twilight* movies and how the vampires' skin glowed when they were in the sun. It also feels like it's pulling and transmuting the toxins out of my body this way, sort of how a workout sweat rids the body of toxins. This is doing the same thing.

I am going to take off my jacket to expose my arms. Now, I am going to unzip the bottom part of my riding pants to create shorts and take off my boots so that my legs and feet can be a part of this experience. It is so cleansing. I can feel the toxins also being cleaned out of my hair. WOW! This is easier than a mud bath at a hot spring and feels even better. No messy clean up. Yes, I can balance on my Dragon as I zip my riding pants back together and pull on my boots. How are you doing with your experience on your Avatar? It is really amazing how they do all they can to help us balance and not fall off.

Now that we are out of the snow cloud and nearly to the destination indicated on the map. We can go lower, as I have a strange feeling that we need to be lower. Yes. From here I can see where we are to land. It is near that pond with the campfire.

They have ice-skating, hot chocolate and s'mores for those that want to participate in this event. I feel a little exhilarated from that sparkling clearing I just went through. Ice-skating would be great to burn off some of this new energy right after I have a cup of hot chocolate. Who is with me on this?

It has been a long time since I have been on skates, but it is coming back to me. I think the sparkly clearing has helped me with my balance and ability to see what is ahead faster. I just missed falling in that hole in the ice. The point is, I did not fall in. Had I not been able to see beyond that stump and shadow, I would have fallen into the freezing pond. I am really thankful that my senses are coming on line clearer and with a faster response.

This is a great way to spend an afternoon. When you are ready, give your map to your Avatar and it will get you back to the Center. I am going to skate a while longer. I love the feel of gliding.

See you tomorrow!

MONTH TWELVE – DAY FIVE

Aside from some sore muscles, I feel great and ready for a new adventure. We are now in the long nights and short days of the year, which are normally considered the Holidays in most parts of the world. Where I live it is nearing the Christmas Holiday. There are traditions of decorations for the various celebrations. We are going to go on a learning journey where we will be given the opportunity to gather what we need to create our own variety of decorations to honor our wants, needs, and belief system.

Our Avatars can come with us if you want them to, but we are mostly going to be walking with the villagers from around here, with a cart and many tools. We are venturing down the path on the ground so we can be closer to the items we need. Our cart is filled with a variety of tools, like a saw, trimmers, wire, gloves, a shovel and a smaller digging tool. We get to help gather the items needed for decorating the Center we are staying in.

Our first lesson is to be thankful for all that is provided for us here. There is more than we need, but we will only take what we require for this project. We are being told that, as we prepare to clip, dig, or remove any part of plant, it would be best if we gave a form of respect and thankfulness for it. It is like a class I took on harvesting herbs. It is the spirit of the plant we are thanking to start with. We are also thanking the Earth that it grew in, the water that gave it life, the air that it shared life with us, and spiritual fire within that gives and shares with us.

Let's take our time in thoughtfully gathering the items we need. Some are digging instead of cutting down a tree to be decorated. It was in an area that needed to be thinned in order to be planted in a better place later. It had outgrown its space and it will be looked upon with great honor in the hall in our Center. Its branches are firm, ready to hold the lights and decorations with pride while assisting in creating beauty in our world.

Some are in an area where more thinning is needed. They are being shown how to cut the branches to be used for wreaths and wired together in long streamers for lining the stairs and hallways. Others are gathering pine cones that have already fallen, ready for us to just pick them up. Pods have exploded with an abundance of seeds for us to use.

The dried berries will give another color and texture. Feathers! There is a pile of feathers just waiting for us to pick them up. So many different kinds! I think some are peacock, hawk, bluebird, woodpecker, and some I am not sure of, but they are all beautiful. I think we have enough items to get started with. Let's head back to the Center.

The doors have been opened for us to enter a giant room filled with tables of other decorations we may need to help pull all of it together. There is a table of so many different types and colors of ribbons, many sizes and shapes of ornaments, and so much more. There are tables around the room and rows of tables in the middle. It is like walking into a holiday factory of creation. I think there is a table for each of us to create anything we can imagine.

We get to decorate this entire building and, of course, create items we want to take home or send to others for gifts. There are so many resources at our disposal right here in this room. There is a table full of tools to use for these creations. I think I will need some wire and clippers to start with. There is also a table of various adhesives. I am familiar with some of these, like a hot glue gun and a fast-drying, clear glue, but some of these I will have to ask what they are used for. Each of these tables has people to assist us with creating in this medium. We just have to give them an idea of what it is we are trying to do, and they are right there to help.

I just heard that the key to learning with these projects is to utilize each item and not be wasteful. Just like White Buffalo Calf Woman taught the people how to use each piece of the antelope or buffalo. The hide, the bones, the hooves, even the intestines all have a purpose in how we can better our lives. The same goes for the plants. The roots, the stems, leaves, and the flower in each of its stages all have a specific quality they can bring into our lives.

As we go from table to table, we are given the items needed with an explanation of how they represent a part of our lives. Most of this information I have never heard of. One is how the ribbons tie up the threads of our families and bring them closer. The greenery is about the Everlasting Life we can live and how we can brighten each person's world with our life-giving energy. The seeds and stems are from a life-sustaining aspect, like the Circle of Life that happens each year. Then there are the feathers for a very special touch. Feathers represent so many different things. Sometimes they carry messages to the heavens or they are a representation of those that have passed over. Or they can be a sign that your Angel is near.

I really hadn't given much thought about each of these steps of why we have certain decorations, and how they represent how our lives evolve and revolve around each creation on this Planet. Our ancestors that started these traditions knew so much more about this part of life than we tend to recognize now. In fact, many of these traditions are not discussed in our daily lives with our families. Maybe it is time to make some changes in that area. I am going to see what I can do about that in my world.

See you tomorrow!

MONTH TWELVE – DAY SIX

Oh, the traditions of winter or the dark months. Sometimes they are wonderful and sometimes I am ready to let a few of them go back in time to where they came from. After all, many things have changed over the years. Let me tell you a real-life story that helped me move out of old traditions.

Every year, when my children were young, we would have a so called live or real tree that had been cut down. Then there was that one year when my husband was working out of town. We had one of the worst winters in a very long time. I was out one evening after work with our three children, the youngest less than a year old, scouring the tree lots for the perfect tree that would fit into our house. It was freezing cold for all of us.

I was at the last stop as we were freezing, and the kids were getting fussy. This final tree lot was in a plant nursery. I had to take the kids inside to warm up. In there, I saw the most beautiful fake trees ever. There were lots of branches that were made out of wire, & would hold any or as many ornaments the kids wanted to put on them. Of course, I can't leave out the fact it was perfect. No bare areas, not crooked, only one top … You know, all of the main things you look for when picking out a special Christmas tree. And just the right size.

At that point I made an executive decision that we would no longer have a tree cut out of the forest or from a tree lot. I would buy a beautiful fake tree to save other trees. Plus, it would last years, as I just had to fold it up and put it back into the box for the next year. No more standing in the freezing cold with little ones. We could decorate that tree as soon as we were ready to take it out of the box! It made holiday time much easier.

I know that sounds a little strange, but I was being a practical, very busy Mom as well as saving the forest. Actually, I was ready to give up the old tradition of having a tree in my house that would lose its needles which we were allergic to. But, I didn't make that decision until I had to. Sometimes we are given some pretty big boosts in the rear to get us to move out of the same old programmed patterns.

It is the same with the programs we are working on within these Portals. The programs that have been carried for many generations within our energy fields, our codes, and our DNA that create the patterns we follow about Money. Sometimes, it is reflected in the idea that there is no way you can have what you want, because, if you do, will have to share it with someone else. Then there won't be enough again. Another idea is you are not good enough to get what you want, or you don't deserve it. The only way to get more money is to work harder. You can't have that money, because you didn't work hard enough for it.

Let's see if we can crack some of these codes today and restructure them into an Anything is Possible format. Or, a format of money coming easily to you and more than you can ever imagine. Or, a pattern of "I deserve it. I will share if I want to after I pay my own bills. I have more than enough, and there is a lot more where that came from. I am ready to clear these old programs and rebuild my money codes"

Ready to ride that Avatar you manifested? Who else could have manifested such an amazing beast except you! The sky is clear, and if we leave at the six o'clock angle from the north door we will have a good opportunity to miss any storms. Let's just ride until we are given the direction of what we need to do next.

Well, that didn't take long. We have a whole neighborhood of Fairies with their Pegasus flying along with us. They are asking for our help in their village. That is what we are best at. Helping when those in need ask! Their village is just a little further. They say that we will need our Avatars to help too.

I can now see what has happened. The flow of ice in the river wiped out a bridge that is in the middle of the town, and they can't get from one side to another. Of course, we can help with this. I think we have some bridge-building engineers in our group that know exactly how to fix this structure back in a way that the ice won't hurt it anymore.

It looks like we are needed to help remove debris that is causing the water to back up before it floods some of the homes. We are right on it while the engineers consult with the villagers to get the okay for what we need to do. Our Avatars can easily move the broken wood and large stones. Some do this with their strong claws, and others help lift as we put ropes around some of the wreckage. We are being very careful to get the river flowing without flooding anything. The whole village is also helping.

We can also dig out the damaged area and create a better support system as we are instructed to help. This is moving along at record speed. I see the Fairies above us sprinkling their Time Management Dust around. Amazing how that works. It is like we are getting weeks' worth of work done in just a matter of hours.

Wow! It is completed, and it is better than ever. Everyone is so excited. Now they can have the celebration they had been planning for months. We are being invited to join them in their celebration tonight. I think that would be great fun for all of us.

Of course, there is plenty of food and games, but there is one booth that is very important we take time to visit. It is run by the Fairies. I don't know why we need to, but when I get this strange feeling it's a need not a want, I know I must follow that nudge.

From the outside, their booth looks to be like the rest of those that are here. As we enter the back door, there is a teleportation spot. It looks like an old-time telephone booth. I don't know where it leads to, but it is important to do this.

I can feel myself right in the village, then, all at once, I feel myself in a healing chamber. It looks like it can find some of the codes in my field that have been damaged. I can see them as they show them to me. Some are very complicated, and others are very simple, like a pyramid shape that has had parts of it dissected away.

This chamber is helping rebuild these codes. I recognize this one has a money code as they showed me the dollar sign right in the middle of it. The dollar sign is also damaged. The lights in the Chamber are repairing it. No wonder I was having a problem on some days. I am really thankful that this machine helps me see what I needed repaired. If it gets a feeling from me to fix it, it just does it. I forgot about the feeling of allowing the repairs to happen. It is one of the Universal Laws. We have to give permission before help can be given to us, and we have to receive it.

I am ready to say yes. Fix these codes, please! There are many of these telephone booth-looking chambers in this room. Plenty for everyone. Time is not a problem the way these Fairies play with energy. Each of us can stay in the healing chamber as long as is necessary. As much clearing as I have done throughout this year, I had no idea that I still had a few codes that were damaged.

I feel much better and ready to ride my Dragon back to the Center. I feel, that in a short time, I will be in a recalibration process, and it would be best if I were laying down.

See you tomorrow!

MONTH TWELVE – DAY SEVEN

This is wild adventure day. Our Avatars are waiting for us right outside the door. The maps have been handed out to the Avatars, and we are heading right down the center of this whirling mass of a Portal. I get the feeling it may be one of those hang on days, as I have no idea what is going on. Of course, it will be an amazing journey no matter what happens.

We are headed to the waterfalls. This is what happens when you give a Dragon a map! I can see there are many sizes and shapes of them. They are getting louder the closer we get. The mist and steam are boiling up and creating a lot of foggy moisture that is hard to see through. It's interesting there are rainbows here, even though there isn't any rain, just lots of mist. It is beautiful here. Yet, it still stirs a little intimidation in me. I think I am going to have to take swimming lessons again, maybe this summer, so that I am not so nervous around water events.

I am glad I hung on tight with my legs, because, suddenly, we are diving straight down the edge of the waterfall's ledge. There is a lot of spray and noise. I really hope that you didn't hear me scream as we started the dive. I wasn't scared, just very surprised.

We are nearly at the bottom of one of the rainbows. The mist isn't so thick here. At the bottom of this canyon the grass is still green. Some of our Avatars are loving the fresh greens, and I am still catching my breath from that exciting dive. I see we have a place to relax and enjoy a few games and refreshments.

One of the games is a new form of blowing bubbles. Yes, it looks like the regular bottle of soapy bubbles that kids love to play with, but we are going to do this somewhat differently. It is for shifting our consciousness and our Money Codes some more.

First, hold onto the bottle, close your eyes, and feel yourself being in your Heart Space. Now think about all the things you can do to create money. Think about it down to the smallest detail. How many clients do you want? How many hours a week do you want to work? Take a moment and do the math to see if it will work for what your needs are. Now, does it add up for what you want and how to get it to add up? If it doesn't, put the amount that you really do need and want deep into your heart, then transfer that focus into the bottle of bubbles.

Take another look at your plans on how you want to get the money you need. Is it possible to do it the way you want? Now add on another thousand dollars for the month. Does that feel like it is possible? Did you feel a little bit of "That can't happen" in your heart or mind?

Do the focus on the amount you need plus an extra thousand dollars a month. Hold that feeling in your heart. Let the Universe know this thought. That could be via a specific prayer or whatever works into your belief system. Once you have taken these steps. Start blowing those bubbles. See how big you can make them. How many little ones can be blown at the same time? Or, how many can you string together? Maybe make doughnut-shaped ones. Blow them at each other. Chase each other with them. Try blowing bubbles while you ride on your Avatar. Keep doing this until the bottle is empty.

Wow, that was fun. How do you feel about those extra thousand dollars you put out there to the Universe? I bet you forgot all about it for a few minutes, right? That is how you create and bring in more money. Focus on the details, know what you want and need, and just give it to the Universe to figure out how to get it to you. Stay focused on what you can do for fun and also what you know you can do to bring in what you need. Stick to your business work ethic.

Now, look in your backpack! I found a check for $1,000 dollars in mine! Unbelievable! This is how the Universe can answer prayers for you. It is all right there. Just ask and let go. It will come back to you. If it doesn't happen today, be careful not to go into thoughts like "I knew it wouldn't work," or, "That is too easy, it can't happen that way." Stay focused on the outcome, and let go of the Oh-Poor-Me Victim energy. That is not who you are anymore.

You can do this. It will work. Now, let's get back to the Center before the light is gone from this day. Hang on, it is a steep climb getting out of here.

See you tomorrow!

MONTH TWELVE – DAY EIGHT

I am amazed how fast this Divine Portal journey has been. We are over halfway through, and there is so much more to complete. While we are in here, have you noticed the movement of the Portal today with the whirling of the outer layer being very much like a tornado whipping in and out of the energy as it spins faster, and slower, then faster again? When looked at on that level it can be a little like being on a roller coaster. We are lucky that, while being in the center of it, we get to experience a more stable aspect of it.

This Portal is a little different from some of the others in that the Center we are staying in is being moved along daily as the Portal moves. This building is on a type of medium that is being transported right along with us. This really helps me to understand why the weather patterns and the things we see change so rapidly. We are actually in a different area of the Portal each day.

Today's adventure is to ride our Avatars to a new lake that is much deeper than the others we have seen here. It's beautiful, cold, and frozen. The frosty trees and bushes here are a little different than at the ones from yesterday's canyon trip. There are stable-like buildings for our Avatars to stay comfortable in while we go into that cabin to get warm.

Oh, my goodness. Now I know why I wasn't briefed about our journey. I probably would have said "Absolutely not!" We are being outfitted with diving gear to go under the ice on that lake. By now, all of you know how I feel about swimming in normal water, but this is beyond my comfort level. Yet, I'm here to clear a lot of my codes around Abundance and Money. If this is related to how I Manifest and Receive or push away money, then I am all for today's excursion.

I won't be leading it. We do have a specialist in this underwater world to guide us. He looks sort of like a Merman. I am told he knows these waters better than anyone else. I guess that sort of helps me trust him. He doesn't need all the gear that we do.

We have choices in the gear we use. Some of it is basic diving gear. Another choice for those of us that are not fans of being in water or under ice is a huge bubble to be in that can float underwater, has plenty of oxygen, and a way to reach in and out of it without breaking the seal. I don't know how it is propelled, but I am assured that it works just fine. Oh, it works with what I think it to do, another way of using the Consciousness Technologies I incorporate in so many other parts of my life.

Let's go. I am now ready to see what this underwater journey is all about. We are also being given a bag to collect things.

This is really a strange feeling going underwater while in this bubble. It is actually amazing to be able to look out and see what is around me without worrying about breathing or feeling claustrophobic. We each have an earpiece to help us listen to what our guide is telling us about the area. This is much more enjoyable and relaxing than I thought it would be. Wow there are really some huge fish in here. I didn't think they got that big in lakes. Glad I am in a protected bubble.

We are entering an area where there are some shiny, precious objects on the lake floor and on the sides of underwater canyon we are going through. We have been told that we are to only pick the ones we feel will be of use to us. Use your inner gut feelings to notice what you are being drawn toward or what is being drawn to you. Put what you need in your bag. Remember, there is plenty for you and everyone else. At first, the feelings of only taking a few to not be greedy crossed my mind. That must be one of those codes I still need cleared. I am reminded that, if I need it and take it, I am not being greedy.

I wasn't sure how I was going to get something through this protective bubble, but, as soon as I recognized I still needed help clearing that feeling of Enough or Not Enough, a purplish, fluorescent stone popped off the wall of the canyon right into the bubble for me. As soon as I touched it, I felt a change happening. That is amazing. I also felt White Buffalo Calf Woman reminding me that there is always enough for everyone.

As my heart opened to receive even more, another stone that was white with pink flecks popped through the wall right into my lap. It really felt like a nice, peaceful energy. This is an amazing way to choose what I need. It is like the waters and stones are interacting with my emotional system.

This time, I just closed my eyes and felt the emotion as I stated, "I am ready to receive all that I am ready to receive." Oh, My goodness! A whole pile of stones landed in my lap. I am not sure what they all are, but they feel really pleasant and like they truly are exactly what I need right now. I am putting them into my bag as I notice we are back at the cabin ready to exit the lake.

I hope you had as good of an experience as I did. I feel much better about the water and being under the ice. Now, with this bag of new stones to investigate, I have a lot to keep me busy once we get back to the Center.

Our Avatars are ready for us to ride back. It will be an easy pace as the Center has now moved closer to us. Not so far, this time.

See you tomorrow.

MONTH TWELVE – DAY NINE

After yesterday's experience, I still feel the effects of the various stones I was given. It is hard to explain how different I feel. It is as if the stones we just picked up in this last journey are creating a harmonization with a lot of the other changes we have experienced throughout the twelve months. It is like things are coming together.

One very strange shift that I experienced throughout the sessions is how much I despised diamonds, and, with the experiences last month, I am actually looking at advertisements with diamonds in them. That has not happened with me since I had watched *Blood Diamonds* many years ago. At that point, I swore I would never wear a diamond again due to the horrible treatment of the workers.

One of the experiences I had was a clearing by the Diamond Stone and a realization that it isn't the stone that carried that vibration; it was the people that ran the mining operation. Since that has been cleared, I even feel like I deserve wearing diamonds and would accept one if someone gave it to me. These code clearings are amazing. I wonder what will happen today.

We are to get on our Avatars and fly to the top of the Portal. I am not sure how to get there, but our Avatars do. I am trusting them to take us on this journey of what I am told can be beyond our wildest dreams. Each Avatar has been given a flight pattern, and we are to just hang on.

The pattern is sort of like climbing a trail up a spiral. As we move upward we also go around in a spiraling vortex in the Portal. As we go down, we are also spiraling around the vortex and are directly opposite of the up vortex. We are crossing at various points. It sort of looks like a DNA spiral. As we cross the points of intersection it feels like a spark happens. Sometimes it is a sharp spark, like getting shocked by someone that has static electricity built up within them. Other times it is just a little spark.

Each time a shocking spark happens it feels like a new code is activated into its correctness. Then, I feel a shift in my vibrational field. Each shock creates a new or corrected sacred geometry within our DNA. At times, it also feels like it is starting to add in a third strand. I am not exactly sure what this entails. It's just what I heard.

Once the spiral actively creates a continuing up-and-down movement, we are shown there will be a new activation of some sort. A catalyst creates an activation. A catalyst is usually fire or something to create a bigger movement or activation. The sparking was just a little activating catalyst, I feel like something bigger is going to happen.

We are at the bottom, ready to move up this spiral, when my Dragon suddenly decides to breathe a huge burst of fire right up the middle. This creates the catalyst for each of us to burst into the world we want to be in. Well, not literally, but to put ourselves into the space we need to be to create our new world once we are finished with this last journey through the Portals.

The fire from my Dragon is not a burning heat, but an icy-hot feeling. The flames going directly up the center of this spiral activate as much of our DNA as we are ready for and prepare the rest to turn on for us automatically when we are home.

The DNA helps activate the new codes we healed and have received within each of the Portals. It is up to us as to what we do with this new information.

White Buffalo Calf Woman is also standing at the bottom of the spiral with her sacred pipe blowing blessed smoke up through the center. It circles each of us with a sacred cleansing as we are being activated within the Light of our Purpose here on this Planet.

Thank you for this activation and cleansing of direction of purpose. I know that this is a sacred experience within this Divine Portal. I am really feeling many of my energy lines and centers coming alive with a purpose on this big blue orb flying through the Universe.

I am ready to go back to the Center and journal about it to not forget about this inspirational journey.

See you tomorrow.

MONTH TWELVE – DAY TEN

In my dreams, I was reminded of the many, many reasons we are here right now participating in this Divine Abundance Portal. We began this journey to clear ourselves of money blocks and make corrections within ourselves on the physical, emotional, and spiritual levels of how and where we were storing these blocks. What we found was that, as we went on journeys, our entire being became engaged in the process, and we could feel the changes or shifting happening on various levels within us. I can tell for myself, and many of the testimonials that have been sent to me, that these unusual, miraculous changes that are happening in our lives.

What are you noticing? The biggest way to notice a change is to just ask within what is different. Am I walking different, or talking different? Perhaps I am not falling apart over things that were very traumatic a few months ago. Am I being paid the same? If you are a person that gets tips, is the amount changing? How are you feeling about how you communicate with people and how they communicate with you? Has that changed?

I would suggest that, as you are preparing to complete this last Divine Portal journey, begin thinking about how to prepare a new resume. Notice how you word things this time, and notice what is different. It also may be different as to what or who is showing up for you. Their pay scale may be beyond your expectations. Remember to not put a limit on your worth or the value of your work, especially within your own mind. This is to allow unlimited possibilities in your earnings.

As we venture out into our journey today, let your mind do a little multitasking on what is new that you may be putting on your resume. Too bad they wouldn't understand your skills in working with your Avatar. Wait, who am I to say that they would not? Being able to ride the wings of change is a great asset.

Let's ride for some fun today. As we are getting closer to the exit point, the Portal is getting smaller and spinning faster. We can see the layers of the walls easier as we fly close to them.

This Portal is amazingly beautiful. Notice how clean it is. The colors are layered with iridescent stones that sparkle as they move within the vortex. As we fly near the wall close to the top, reach out and pick a stone that will fit into your pocket. It will contain the reminder of how much you have allowed yourself to change and the work you have done to create the new You. It will also remind you that you can go back to any of the journeys and revisit them for even more change when you feel you need a little boost.

As you now have a stone that fits into your pocket, take a close look at it. Notice how it feels. Is it smooth, rough, or maybe mostly smooth with a sharp area, or something entirely different?

Now, how do you feel when you hold it? You may or may not notice anything. If you don't, imagine what you think it might help you feel like in a certain way. Just pay attention to where your imagination takes you. It may just feel nice, or it may remind you that you need to read the Month Six again for an example.

This is an area in the Portal where there tends to be a lot of rainbows. Look over there. It is a double! Let's see if we can find that Pot of Gold this time. Remember how we experienced that in one of the other journeys? Let's see if we can hold onto some of that gold since we have had so many codes cleared. Okay! Nearly there. Yes, that one down there. Not too far. It ends in that outcropping of trees. Yes, there are two Pots of Gold. Which one is yours?

I notice how all of you are working together to achieve this. Your telepathic skills have improved immensely! The idea of circling the area before we land is a great idea. As we get closer, I see a Pegasus guarding the pots. We don't want to hurt her. She is just doing her job. She is letting us in close enough to negotiate. She is telling us that, since we have come so far on these journeys, she will share with us. She will keep one Pot of Gold for the rainbow world, and we can share the other one There are no tricks, as this Portal is about "There is always enough for everyone."

Let's land and see what it is we are sharing. We can spread a blanket on the ground and sit in a circle to divide it up. It carries such a wonderful feeling. A frequency of Having All That is Ever Needed is radiating from it.

As we each start picking one as we go around the circle, notice what happens to the gold coins. It was quite a jolt within me the first time I picked a coin. How did it affect you? I felt that, as soon as I picked up my coin, it went into my whole being and activated a feeling of Standing in Strength, and aligned having exactly what I need and want. There wasn't the Needy & Greedy separation, as what I wanted was now being aligned with what I truly needed.

There wasn't the wanting due to just wanting or not having. I was being aligned more and more each time it was my turn to pick a coin. I began noticing there is no greed when a person is aligned with this level of already Having. There is no Victim energy involved. There is no lack of Having, as this frequency is aligned with the Divine. That is wonderful, exactly nine coins for each of us.

Let's just sit with it a moment. Take a few really deep breaths and allow ourselves to recognize how far we have come and how much we have changed. We can now get back to the Center and have time to journal about this experience before we take on the last one.

See you tomorrow for our last ride in the Portal!

MONTH TWELVE – DAY ELEVEN

Today is a bittersweet ending to this amazing journey with you. We have had the opportunity to move ourselves into a level of consciousness creation that supports our ability to have a new outlook about Abundance. We have gone through so many different time warping experiences. It is amazing we are still in these bodies. Since you have participated in these amazing journeys with me, I firmly believe that you are now ready to take what you have learned out into the real world on Earth. You are now ready to receive and hang on to your Abundance in a totally different way than you did when these journeys began.

We still have time for a little adventure before this Portal turns us out to the real world and closes in upon itself. You will get to decide what to do with your Avatar. You can turn him loose to be a part of the collective consciousness where you can call upon him when you need to make a little journey of your own. You can also keep him around as one of your guides to be with you on a daily basis. My Dragon is with me at a moment of thought. He shows up before I even think I need his amazing energy. We have participated in our Dimensional worlds of work and play for so long; I think our communication has gone beyond telepathy.

Yes, let's get back to a one last adventure! Let's ride to that sacred medicine wheel area near the exit. There is plenty of room for us there, including our Avatars. The seating is in a circle around the edge. It has a ledge that is a good height to sit on, so we don't have to be directly on the ground unless you want to.

If you have never participated with a medicine wheel before, we will be directed in how to enter and the direction to walk to follow the sacred path.

Before we can enter, we will be cleansed with the smoke from sage and the sweet grass. I don't know why both today, but I am certain that there is some reason. I am not educated as much as I would like to be in this form of sacred. I just trust that there will be people available to assist in the direction of it.

Stand facing the person with the sacred smoke and feathers and follow what they ask you to do, such as hold your arms out as they fan the smoke over each area of you. Lift your feet, one foot at a time, after you turn around, so they can clear your back, and then clear yourself with the smoke as you take it into your hands and pull it over your head and into your heart. It is okay to inhale. I have been told that the reason this smoke seems to not ever affect my allergies is due to the sacred use of it in this manner. I always feel so renewed after this experience.

White Buffalo Calf Woman is now coming over to participate with us. She will speak to us first and then give each of us a special blessing. Notice her energy as she moves within the sacredness of this Divine Abundance Portal. She is reminding us that money is sacred and abundant. It is a gift to be used as a tool to navigate through this Planet. As you have noticed throughout the journeys you have cleared a lot of the old patterns that held money away from you. Now you are ready to participate with money on a level of equality. You are ready to receive as you ask and participate in your journey of life.

Remember that life is to be lived. Each moment is a gift to not be wasted. Acknowledge your life. Yes, acknowledge your work and acknowledge your resting time. Both are to be in balance. You are ready to move out into the world in this level of balance. Now, the blessings from White Buffalo Calf Woman will begin. If closing your eyes helps you listen, it is ok to do so.

Be patient while you wait your turn. It is nice if you can enter a prayerful, meditative state while you wait your turn and again after. Or, you may want to write the information down that she gives you, as it is meant for you specifically. Take a moment to tune in and listen to your message. If you have your journal with you, go ahead at this time and write down your message so that it doesn't lose its value and you don't forget the meaning of what is said.

Mine was very special in how I am to now go out into the world and do my work on a level I have never done before. I will be safe as I travel to where I am called to serve, and to teach those that are ready. She told me a lot more than this, but this is what I can share with you at this time. I am certain that the doors will be opened for what I am to do, as they will also open for you as you are ready.

As we are now preparing to leave, I want to remind you that, in alignment with why you are here, you have released many of your money blocks and changed your vibration with money. It is time to go out into the world and create ways to utilize this spiritual work and turn it into increased income. You might have already started the process of looking for new opportunities, perhaps an advancement in your job. You may have started to create new resume ideas for another direction with more money opportunities, extra sales, investments, or perhaps ways to decrease spending. New ways to hold onto what you bring in instead of spending more also increases your income. You have learned and processed into a new You.

I want to remind you that, once you have leveled out and you need to have more clearing and another boost, just start all over and do the journeys again. You will be surprised how these journeys are timeless.

It is now time to walk to the exit point, step across the doorway, and be transported back to your world.

Thank you for being with me on this life changing Journey. Remember you can always visit me on Facebook or at my website www.alchemyuniversaltherapies.com.

See you soon with Truth, Love, and Gratitude

Pat, The Cosmic Cowgirl

Track the Changes Made with the White Buffalo Calf Woman and Winter Introspection

ACKNOWLEDGMENTS

So much gratitude to my family who stood by me as I've worked with the beings of the Universe; The Galactic Federation of Light, Angels and Guides participating within my healing practice and in the creation of these Shamanic Journeys. They may not have understood everything I've been doing, but they have always allowed me the space to do it.

I love my Purple Dragon Avatar, which Chelsea Glanz brought to life with her magical brushes. She beautifully illustrated my wonderful companion, noted throughout this book, making it even more real for me and those that come to my office where the original is displayed.

My great appreciation to many of my teachers including Dr. Richard Bartlett, D.C.,N.D. and the many Matrix Energetics conferences I have attended to help me unleash the unlimited possibilities in this world and beyond; Ken Graydon from AU, who introduced me to the Regeneration Technologies from Russia, and literally pushed me to step out of my comfort zone and teach this advanced unlimited healing technology; Dr. Bradley Nelson, author and creator of the Emotion Code and the Body Code; Rosemary The Celtic Lady, creator of the AMAHT, and founder of the Global Psychics and Healers, who has been a friend, co-worker and teacher for many, many years. Thanks to all of you for all that you have taught me.

Finally, Richard Keller, a man that did not give up on me getting this book published. Thank you!

ABOUT THE AUTHOR

Patricia Vance Forbes is a member of the Galactic Federation of Light Hybrid program. She has decades of extensive Earth and Universe training. Her unique gifts and healing power is a result of her combined training here on Earth and healing modalities and information from her ET healing guides. She has taken on the role of knowing Earth Shamanic realms combined with Universal Shamanic realms, bringing the eternal workings of both together to assist us in moving to the next level of who we are to be. This would include our physical health, our consciousness abilities, and working with our Soul in a Benevolent manner.

Pat offers a variety of Consciousness Technology workshops with certifications. She lives in Fort Collins, Colorado with her husband and has several children and grandchildren close by. Find her at www.alchemyuniversaltherapies.com or pat4bs@gmail.com